9/25

Easy Pieces

EASY PIECES

GEOFFREY H. HARTMAN

New York
COLUMBIA UNIVERSITY PRESS
1985

Library of Congress Cataloging in Publication Data
Hartman, Geoffrey H.
Easy pieces.

Includes index.
1. Moving-picture plays—History and criticism—
Addresses, essays, lectures.   2. Literature—Addresses,
essays, lectures.   3. Humanities—Addresses, essays,
lectures.   4. Social sciences—Addresses, essays,
lectures.   I. Title.
PN1995.H384   1985   001.3   84-23772
ISBN 0-231-06018-1

Columbia University Press
New York   Guildford, Surrey

Printed in the United States of America

*Clothbound editions of Columbia University Press books are
Smyth-sewn and printed on permanent and durable acid-free paper*

For
Henri Peyre

Geoffrey H. Hartman is Karl Young Professor of English and Comparative Literature at Yale University.

Books

The Unmediated Vision. An Interpretation of Wordsworth, Hopkins, Rilke and Valéry   1954

André Malraux   1960

Wordsworth's Poetry 1787–1814   1964

Beyond Formalism: Literary Essays 1958–1970   1970

The Fate of Reading and Other Essays   1975

Akiba's Children   1978

Criticism in the Wilderness: The Study of Literature Today   1980

Saving the Text: Literature/Derrida/Philosophy   1981

Editions

Hopkins: A Selection of Critical Essays   1966

Wordsworth: Selected Poetry and Prose   1970

New Perspectives on Coleridge and Wordsworth. English Institute Essays   1972

Romanticism: Vistas, Instances, Continuities. With D. Thorburn   1973

Psychoanalysis and the Question of the Text. English Institute Essays   1978

CONTENTS

Contents

PREFACE

T HESE FUGITIVE ESSAYS were written in response to specific
occasions and often for non-university audiences. They have
for their subject modern authors or trends, and sometimes new
ways of looking at older writers (I found nothing very satisfying concerning William Blake as illustrator and tried my own approach). They
are more journalistic, in brief, than academic; and that was, to me,
their value and challenge: how to reply decisively yet undogmatically
to a new film or book or something that seemed to represent a larger
wave in the ever-moving, unsettled weather map of intellectual affairs.

I must admit that collecting them is not a disinterested act. The polemics, often silly and obtuse, that surround the Yale School have projected the image of an obscurantist conspiracy emanating from an
"elitist" institution. Because I voiced doubts about the hegemony of
the conversational style in criticism, or about the reduction of literary
studies to pedagogical norms, and because my own way of writing
could be difficult, or at least experimental, the idea got around that
teaching was not an important issue, and that my (our) head remained
in the clouds of theory. In fact, those associated for good or bad with
the Yale School have spent most of their time practicing criticism not
theory; the latter imposed itself as an outgrowth of reflections on the
act of reading, and reading broadly: in philosophy, in religious and
social thought, in psychoanalysis, as well as in "literature."

My understanding of literature is like David Hume's, who wrote in
an autobiographical sketch that he "was seized very early with a passion for literature" and felt "an insurmountable aversion to everything
but the pursuits of philosophy and general learning." While his family

[ix]

thought he was poring over legal and theological treatises of Voet and Vinnius, "Cicero and Vergil were the authors which I was secretly devouring." Literature, that is to say, encompassed for Hume much more than fiction or creative writing: today's use of "creative," in fact, seems much too restrictive. So there is a mildly apologetic element in bringing these essays together. In an atmosphere which is ideologically heavy, and where some zealots even keep tabs on the number of women compared to men cited in books of criticism (watch next for affirmative action bibliographies), and where accusations are made about the elitist and abstruse character of advanced literary studies, it is useful to recall the engagements that have in fact taken place.

Hume, already mentioned, thought there were different species of philosophy, and so there may also be different species of criticism. His main distinction was between "the easy and obvious" mode, which "enters more into common life, molds the heart and affections, and, by touching those principles which actuate men, reforms their conduct and brings them nearer to that model of perfection which it describes," and its contrary, the "abstruse" or "abstract" mode, which seeks to examine and regulate the human understanding rather than to cultivate manners. The latter labors under the charge of contributing "nothing either to the advantage or pleasure of society, while [its practitioner] lives remote from communication with mankind and is wrapped up in principles and notions equally remote from their comprehension." Nature itself, adds Hume, seems to favor the easy style. He puts the following words into Nature's mouth: "Abstruse thought and profound researches I prohibit and will severely punish by the pensive melancholy which they introduce, by the endless uncertainty in which they involve you, and by the cold reception your pretended discoveries shall meet with." Certainly Hume's own ambitious *Treatise of Human Nature* was much less successful than his "easier" moral and political essays.

The best to be hoped for, then, is a mixed style; and that is what I would like to think these "easy pieces" occasionally achieve. It seems remarkable that literary studies still maintain a sort of place in contemporary life, given the pressures of exact science or strict philosophy on the one hand, and the technology of entertainment on the other. That technology, helping to popularize the fundamentalist strain in religion or the tangible successes of science, also stages elaborate spectacles of its own. Add to these pressures utilitarian or utopian politics, that devour the consciousness and sometimes the conscience of thinking people, and it is surprising that reading has not suffered more. But perhaps it benefits from the very encroachment of these public and consuming activities. Reading, especially when it becomes indissociable from a desire to talk back to the page or to correspond with minds that have cherished their own thoughts, is relatively unencumbered by the stimulus-flooding characteristic of the media, the business of news and announcements, and the burden of extreme self-differentiation. The cultural overhead of reading, in short, may have increased, but it is preferable to the compulsions of a publicitarian life. To read and then write about a book—to do this by oneself though not for oneself—may still be among the freest imaginative endeavors.

There is limited room for optimism, however. What John Dewey observed in "The American Intellectual Frontier" (*The New Republic,* May 10, 1922) remains appropriate. The occasion was William Jennings Bryan's campaign against the theory of evolution. The frontier mentality, Dewey averred, had ceased to be a menace to orderly life, but symptoms of anxiety persisted in America's illiberal attitude toward new ideas, evinced in revivalist and sometimes xenophobic outbursts. "Attachment to stability and homogeneity" Dewey wrote, "seems essential in the midst of practical heterogeneity, rush and unsettlement. . . . The depressing effect upon the free life of inquiry and criticism is the greater because of the element of soundness in frontier fear, and because of the impulses of good will and social aspiration which have become entangled with its creeds. The forces which are embodied in the present crusade would not be so dangerous were they not bound up with so much that is necessary and good."

It is not different today. Intellectuals have to come to grips not only with their own quest for certainty but also with the quest for security exhibited by others—who may be less playful or speculative, and for whom the political frontier must be kept relatively stable. I regret, however, that the traditions of journalism have, if anything, deteriorated; that, especially with regard to literary matters, the *canard* continues to circulate that most academic critics are divorced from what goes on in "the real world." This charge could have a healthy effect on the academician, who will never grow fat on tenure but does become flaccid. In the long run, however, such a charge undermines all investigative criticism and every style of discourse that refuses to give up inventive terms. It is strange to find a "frontier fear" still prevalent, and journalists, however liberal in politics or art, exploiting the idea that literary criticism is decadent and self-serving.

Faith in literary studies is hard to maintain because faith in words is hard to maintain. We are always running up against words as personal objects of hope, anxiety, or frustration, and turn for enlightenment to the systematic study of language and literature. Yet what we learn at that "impersonal" level is not particularly comforting. Literature repeats, in a more elaborate manner, or more reflectively extended, the difficulty of relying on words. Nothing can lift us out of language into a surer medium. Some turn to linguistics or philosophy for canons and rules of interpretation. Some try to save literature at the expense of literary criticism, overestimating primary works of art and subordinating criticism as a purely ancillary, even parasitic, activity. Others want to escape reading altogether, by studying what makes literature possible: the social determinants or psychological conditions. They all fall back into words, however, and our dependency on texts. To change the world is also to change the words of the world.

ACKNOWLEDGMENTS

"The Aesthetics of Complicity" and "Between the Acts: Jeanne Moreau's Lumière" were first published in *Georgia Review* (1974), 28:384–88 and (1977), 31:237–42.

"Barthes' *Vita Nuova*," "Coleridge and the Counterfeit," and "The Minor Art of Borges" were first published in the *New York Times Book Review*, February 4, 1979, March 12, 1972, and December 13, 1970.

"Reflections on French Romanticism" first appeared in *Romanticism: Vistas, Instances, Continuities*, David Thornburn and Geoffrey Hartman, eds. (Ithaca: Cornell University Press, 1973), copyright © 1973 by Cornell University.

"The Malraux Mystery" and "The Weight of What Happened" were first published in *The New Republic*, January 29, 1977, and January 9 and 16, 1983.

"Symbolism Versus Character in Lawrence's First Play" first appeared in the *Bulletin of the Midwest Modern Language Association* (1977), 10:38–43.

"Plenty of Nothing: Hitchcock's *North by Northwest*" was first published in the *Yale Review* (1981), 71:13–27.

A portion of "Six Women Poets" was first published in the *Kenyon Review* (1960), 22:691–700. The remaining material, on Marianne Moore, first appeared as jacket notes for the recording "Marianne Moore Reads from Her Own Works" in the Yale Series of Recorded Poets, DL-9135.

"Representation Now" was first published in *Annals of Scholarship* (1981), 2:4–15.

"The Interpreter's Freud" first appeared in *Raritan: A Quarterly Review* (1984), no. 4.

Acknowledgments

"Social Science and the Humanities" first appeared in *College English* (1976), 38:219–23.

"The Humanities, Literacy, and Communication" was first published in the *ADE Bulletin* (1981), 70:10–16.

"Wild, Fierce Yale" was first published in *The London Review of Books*, October 21–November 3, 1982, pp. 9–10.

"Reconnoitering Chaos: A Statement on Contemporary Criticism" first appeared in *Innovation/Renovation: New Perspectives on the Humanities*, Ihab Hassan and Sally Hassan, eds. (Madison: University of Wisconsin Press, 1983), copyright © 1983 by the Board of Regents of the University of Wisconsin System.

"The Dubious Charm of M. Truffaut" was first published in the 50th Anniversary issue of *Partisan Review* (1984, vol. 51).

Easy Pieces

I

The Aesthetics of Complicity

THERE IS an important difference between recent French and Anglo-American fiction. The purism and programmatic self-certainty of the French novel, particularly the *nouveau roman*, have no genuine counterpart over here. For us the novel remains what Northrop Frye, and Friedrich Schlegel before him, call a modern encyclopedic form: it can absorb anything. It is still that loose and baggy monster Henry James wished to reform. Even when strongly experimental it does not aim at refinement or purification, but rather to extend borders and break taboos.

The French novel, however, at least since the Second World War, has followed a negative way and inspected its premises with rigor. Natalie Sarraute, for instance, wants to do without psychology. "The word 'psychology' is one of those no contemporary novelist can hear without lowering the eyes and blushing," she says. By "psychology" she means Freudian or depth psychology, but the purist intention is remarkable apart from the thing purged. The contemporary French novel has become Cartesian with a vengeance and turned on itself the philosopher's "methodical doubt." Where the insufficiency of a particular mode of realism (such as psychology) merely spurs the American novel to new and starker realisms, the French novel attacks its own form, its apparent autonomy, the very features that make it "novelistic." Yet it does so in the space of fiction itself, remaining engaged with its own project by doubling a *réflexion complice* with a *réflexion purifiante* (Sartre).

To show that this purifying reflection aims at more than Freudian premises, let me turn to Natalie Sarraute once more. In *L'Ere de Soup-çon* she quotes André Gide's remark that Dostoyevsky's characters are always motivated either by pride or humility. Sarraute disagrees with Gide. According to her, there is instead a basic overriding motive which she describes in Katherine Mansfield's words as "the terrible desire to establish contact." This, I would agree, is the one most banal theme not only of Dostoyevsky's fiction but also of the modern novel generally.

What is interesting, however, is Sarraute's attitude toward this banal desire. She views it with ambivalence, with fear, even with disgust. For the Age of Suspicion is especially suspicious of complicity, particularly those small, sly, rodent kinds which result from any strong desire for intimacy and contact. Such complicities, or self-deceptions, are our daily bread, as well as the subject matter of Sarraute's novels. Her purifying reflection discovers them everywhere; her novels tend to be a pleasing pastiche of fallen *topoi*. Yet we are always aware that the novelist's eye is on the novelist: it is her own engagement which is being clarified. She knows that spying is complicity raised to an art, and that the novelist is a socially tolerated spy in league with many of our cruder instincts. A licensed trespasser, as George Eliot remarked. It is quite understandable, therefore, that Robbe-Grillet should have started his career with a detective novel, putting the detective, and through him the novelist, in question. Let me be specific and compare (too briefly) a novel of the 1930s with one of the 1950s.

Malraux's characters are not exempt from "the terrible desire to establish contact." The temptations described by him, though political as well as private, are sparked by a thirst for solidarity or communion at any price. In *Man's Fate,* Koenig, Chiang Kai-shek's chief of police, stages a neat little communion ceremony to win over a prisoner he wants to seduce as a man even more than as a communist: he invites him therefore to an intimate yet sparse table for two, with coffee, milk, slices of bread, a brotherly cigarette . . . An extra place setting, a communion cup, reappears formulaically in Robbe-Grillet's *Jealousy.* Whenever we see Franck and the woman A together, there is a third unoccupied setting. I will not try to prove that it does not belong to A's husband, if indeed she has one. For whom is it intended, then? For reader or narrator—the only other person present: secretly sipping

[4]

that cup and eating from that plate. That the presence of reader or narrator is natural to the novel does not absolve the author. The implicit here—the convention itself—is the complicit; and if it cannot be helped, it must be recognized as fundamental to the *situation* of the writer.

The "new novel" engages reader and writer in a new relation. The reader is as much a partner as the personages *en chair et os* with which fiction conventionally deals. *Of course,* we mutter wearily, so much in contemporary criticism has tried to define exactly this: the reader's share. But the point is ideological rather than technical. It revives a worry Rousseau had expressed powerfully about the novel, theater, perhaps about fiction as a whole, and which is later echoed by Baudelaire. Fiction now confronts the reader ("Hypocrite lecteur, mon semblable, mon frère") with its seductive power, with the consciousness that "reading" is allowing oneself to be seduced. Robbe-Grillet's novels, one might say, are a modern version of Rousseau's *Lettre sur les spectacles.* They reveal, especially when filmed, that the conventions of the bourgeois novel from Richardson through Proust are licensed trangressions of privacy: a genteel voyeurism feeding the erotic impulse. Or, to use a fashionable term, Robbe-Grillet "deconstructs" those conventions, showing them to be quite properly a *limitation* of that "terrible desire" for intimacy which the novel cannot but nourish—*limitation* in the sense of Justice Holmes, when he speculates that law arose to limit the desire for revenge.

We see how, in the era that spans Malraux and Robbe-Grillet, the theme of complicity is extended. The Age of Suspicion, with its interest in the complicities of the writer—we can also recall Sartre's critique of Mauriac and Faulkner—is clearly not the Age of the American Novel. True, it may not have dawned without the American novel of a previous generation. That technique is ethos; that it has direct substantive or moral implications is realized nowhere so strongly as in Henry James, who knows well what may arise between a writer and his work. Literary history often regresses in order to move forward, and the contemporary French novel goes back to the concerns of Henry James via the rejected yet slyly prevailing influence of Gide. Even so, it was less to James than to the *roman d'aventure*, predicted by Rivière, that French writers turned in the era between the wars, finding a new direction in Dostoyevsky and the American novelists during the thirties: Faulkner, Hemingway, Dos Passos, Steinbeck, Caldwell. To these we should add Conrad (his influence on Malraux is demonstrable), especially his sophisticated use of the adventurer-narrator.

Yet the novel of adventure and violence, once *had*, and naturalized in France, does not speak strongly to the generation of the *nouveau roman*, which worships not the old and wrathful gods but the cool and cunning ones. Only Hemingway partially survives this *Götterdämmerung*. Roquentin, at the end of *La Nausée* (1937), dreams of a novel "beautiful and hard as steel and making people ashamed of their life." It is not surprising, then, that Camus' *L'Etranger*, with its ascetic virtues, should have gained such influence. Robbe-Grillet, asked about his literary ancestry, replies: "The first fifty pages of *L'Etranger* and the works of Raymond Roussel."

Few writers are candid about their literary debts, but the spirit of that answer matters as much as the facts. Whatever genealogy of influences we establish for the new novel, it is clear that American fiction is only indirectly among them. For America has not yet emerged out of *l'âge du roman américain:* most novels by Mailer, Bellow, or Pynchon remain a grotesquely limbed Hercules when compared to the Dior silhouette of a *nouveau roman.* And the difference between the two traditions is all the more clear and demonstrable because that banal theme, "the terrible desire to establish contact," is central in both. "Herzog," says a French critic, commenting on Bellow's novel, "is not a Hemingway gentleman, his moral value is primarily that of pity." It is this "pity" Mailer attacks (because he cannot escape it) with Nietzschean vigor, and which Malamud still accepts so wryly. To show the unity of the Anglo-American tradition in a demonic light we can say that Forster's "Only connect" is strangely satisfied by Gelber's *The Connection* (not a novel, but that hardly matters). No English or American writer, however, would openly admit with Maurice Blanchot that "novels are a work of *mauvaise foi.*"

Perhaps this *mauvaise foi* is simply bourgeois "pity" demystified. It is no accident that Blanchot's remark comes in an essay on Sartre's novels. The question remains whether American fiction, despite its frontier virtues, does not oversentimentalize family or community relations. Take Faulkner's *Absalom, Absalom!*, the very granddaddy or *locus classicus* of the American writer's concern with the technique of story-telling. Does not Faulkner's technique serve to hide rather than expose the sentimental core of the story? It also, of course, helps to keep readers as outsiders: they are not allowed the pleasure of easy or superior access to the heartland of the "family" tale. Faulkner is aristocratic enough to resist that kind of intimacy. But his intricate novel-machine turns, for all its sophisticated technique, on a brutal if moving failure to say "thou," to establish contact. The novel's terror and pity flow from the opposite of a recognition scene: from a moment in which a father refuses to cry, like David, "My son, my son!"

The American novel honors technique and takes pleasure in craft. Yet the relation of craft to craftiness, of technique to a fictional infighting which pits the artist against art, is rarely felt. Technique is relatively neutral: a technology. It opens new vistas, challenges habits, and increases production. "Technique as discovery": Mark Schorer's essay of 1948 is justly famous. But in France technique is no longer innocent. The cinema-novel *Last Year at Marienbad*, for example, dissociates (by a genial extension of the principle of montage) screen image and narrative voice, refusing to grant them the harmony we desire in this as in other realms, so that the very structure of the art medium is implicated. It needed the Old World once more—James' experienced, corrupt, historical Europe—to remove a last assumption of innocence: that fictional techniques are clean, impersonal, and beyond the contamination of ideology.

Between the Acts: Jeanne Moreau's *Lumière*

THE MOVIES ARE our epics; and the formulaic or quotational nature of artistic transmission can be studied there to effect. This is because of the voracious demands of the medium (it must be fed, if necessary, by recycled plots and images), its wide dissemination (one can hardly not undergo the influence of particular movies), and the closed character of the international community created in the process of filming.

Jeanne Moreau's *Lumière* is yet another story about the actor's life. Its special twist is that Jeanne Moreau herself has written and directed it—but such a twist or trope is not my concern. I am interested in the fact that a film as derivative or quotational as *Lumière*— so full of what might be called movie diction—can be a powerful statement.

To examine the resemblance between Moreau and Bergman is not sufficient, though it may be one beginning for appreciation. *Lumière* is a film that catches the imposed or self-willed discontinuities in the actor's life: the "cuts" (Moreau, who plays the actress Sarah Dedieu, collects knives) which are the essence of cinematic composition. In a typical Bergman film, and most brutally perhaps in *Face to Face*, habitual life is suddenly invaded by a radical uncertainty. This sudden arrest of the natural rhythm is not motivated any more than a heart attack might be, and Bergman uses psychoanalytic inserts for their imagistic rather than explanatory power. Existence is cut, formally, by something known only through its effects: even clock-time cannot be trusted; persons must talk themselves, as a mother does with her child, into trusting the next step; the simplest words have to be recovered; no

[8]

relation holds. We classify what happens in *Face to Face* as a "psychotic episode," but it resembles very closely what actors provoke in themselves as they switch back and forth between a daily self and the framed self-image which they assume in front of the camera.

Correlative with the tyranny of "Cut!" is the imperative "Lights!" and Moreau's film has chosen to develop the resonances of that figure. Her film is luminous: more subdued and tender than Bergman's usual mode (his camera can caress, but when his characters caress it tends to draw blood), and indebted to Truffaut's conception of the romantic thriller. Yet Moreau's touch, however womanly, does not disguise the hard glare of the action. We learn how the person in the actor responds to an exposure demanded by those "lights," an exposure outrageously justified by an ethos of total submission to auteur or director or the wish to transcend all shame.

It is a world, then, where identity is created out of nakedness. Careers may begin with pornography and rise into loftier blues. *And they knew that they were naked:* that trauma is repeated in various ways by the actors' willingness to live within a circle of fire created by the searchlights of camera and set.

Lumière depicts this intensification of the human condition. After an awkward expository scene introducing us to Sarah Dedieu and three other women, we are switched to Paris and the "fatal week," whose focus is to time what spotlight is to character. The awarding of the "Prix Diamant" to Sarah is to climax that week, and it reunites her with three women friends: two of them young actresses at different stages of their careers, and Laura, an older Italian friend of fifteen years' standing. Scenes from Sarah's life of scattered intimacies are shown as they converge on the award ceremony, which also brings together the men in her orbit. The awarding of the prize is made to coincide with Sarah's attempt to commit herself to marriage, or a steady relationship; but in the aftermath, which includes the death of one of the men she relies on, Sarah returns to her cinematic role of "femme fatale"—that is, to the next "shooting." Despite the film's stereotyped plot and its reliance on Jeanne Moreau as the only developed character, it sets up a moving contrast between the dehumanizing demands of the cine-

[9]

matic medium and the residual womanliness brought by Sarah to each relation (with women even more than with men).

I come now to a crucial moment of formal quotation in the film. The play on names (consider Heinrich Grun, Saint-Loup, Sarah Dedieu) prepares us for it, as does the affecting scene where Grun, a German novelist who wants to live with Sarah, hands her a torn page with scribbled lines of faulty French which Sarah proceeds to read to him. His love letter speaks for him through her voice: his muteness allows or demands (auteur-like) her complicity. It is the test or trial for a "shooting" which may not take place. Writing, in short, precedes the complicity of the individual in its utterance, approximately as a given or proper name defines the person who bears it.

The crucial moment I refer to comes as the action verges on a death. By certain devices Jeanne Moreau makes us feel that death is imminent—there is too much insomnia around, and the act of love seems to have lost its dream-like power to entice or extend sleep. The need for rest becomes absolute, although we are unable to say who must die in order to achieve rest for us. We anticipate a suicide, a *Liebestod* of some kind, motivated by a despairing or frustrated imagination.

Just before death chooses Grégoire (a fatherly friend of Sarah's, associated with a detached attitude toward death because of his clinical study of tumors), an apparently unmotivated scene occurs. We accept it because it fits in with the atmosphere of an actor's life. Someone plays a recorded voice reciting in French: "La Trobe leant against the tree, paralyzed. Her power had left her. Beads of perspiration broke on her forehead. Illusion had failed. 'This is death,' she murmured, 'death.' "

The intrusion of this voice is ghostly, gratuitous, premonitory. We sense, if only casually, an *It Is Written*. The action that is going on, and is about to reach a climax, has gone on before, is going on elsewhere too: we are dealing with a universal drama. The recorder's uncanny expansion of the frame of reference could be compared to that of the chorus in Greek tragedy. What *there* is stylized and apodictic—a voice powerless to intervene yet movingly banal—is *here* a technical input, and recognized at first only as something cut out of another frame (and cut off). In short, a quotation.

Yet it is an allusion as well as a quotation; and to recognize that precipitates discovery. The voice is reciting a passage from Virginia Woolf's *Between the Acts*, a novel she had almost completed at the time of her suicide. One of the young directors in Moreau's film is called Saint-Loup. Moreau is herself directing this film: so she is "Sainte Loup"—that is, "Virginia Woolf." As in *Between the Acts* there is a question whether the director has the power or inspiration to bring the play to its end. The "Hour of the Wolf" has come, that indeterminate moment which Sarah actually talks about and which Bergman has used effectively in a film of that title. The action falters, it needs a death, and perhaps it falters because of that realization.

Hearing of Grégoire's death on waking up after a night of love—at last she has slept well—Sarah complains of the light for the first time: of the "lumière" of the sun entering her bedroom. She understands how her life between the acts is infected by acting, which is a light to prevent the real light from coming in. We rarely see Sarah in sunlight: she is a screened figure, moving about in the movie world's artificial day and night. Now the sunlight punishes her or makes her as guilty as Racine's Phèdre. It reveals the devouring character of a theatrical and usurping light that is far more exposing, that leaves an actor no hope of cherishing a secret, whether "Grégoire" or a child in the womb. An actress is by definition without child—a sterile Sarah.

Finally, of course, the quotation from Virginia Woolf stands for "Virginia Woolf." It is a charged symbol for the career or life of the woman writer aspiring to room, child, a creation: this film of her own. *Lumière* takes leave of Jeanne Moreau, alias Sarah Dedieu, as she submits to the next act, to the hysteria of makeup, lights, directors; as she handles the gun that symbolizes the *crime passionelle* which, in this film, we never get to see—perhaps because it is really a crime against herself already committed, perhaps because it is the trivial implicate of all those shooting lights.

Indeed, the metaphor of "shooting," which transfers a property from gun to camera, suggests that art starts beyond that crime or invests it in the formalistic power of the medium. Moreau's "spectacle sur les spectacles" contains, therefore, an unavailing scruple. To be seen is to be sinned against: the drive toward visibility or exposure is almost a religious passion, a suffering that must be undergone. Why? To break the images, to see "Nothing that is not there and the nothing that is" (Wallace Stevens), or to transcend the self-images called roles and again achieve a kind of invisibility. Perhaps invulnerability, for to be seen is also to die—of shame; but only so that shame may die. In the Moreau of this film there is a tender coldness, as if she had become clairvoyant. The subdued darkness of this Snow Woman is especially remarkable in her voice, which moves deliberately fast and glitters like a gun you see, then don't see.

The end of all this shooting is that a new self is born, free as a "star." Yet the star must be a woman again, and the reverse metamorphosis is not completed in *Lumière,* though aspired to. A star and yet a woman too—Moreau has tried to create a work of art in which the character of actress is "half-hidden from the eye," and nurturance, shelter, motherhood, are not excluded. The pathos of the film resides in that hope which Laura (pregnant, monogamous, family-centered) represents.

The generalizing power of quotation and allusion mediates raw visual desire: the imago-centered or pornographic wish that films struggle with. In terms of an extension of Aristotle's *Poetics* to film dramaturgy, this wish coincides with what is there called the "scene of pathos" or "the suffering," and it may parallel Freud's "primal scene." The poetic—that is, artistic—cinema works against the grain of its power to represent graphically—as flesh-writing—scenes of this kind. Films are, like surgery, so crude yet sophisticated an intervention that their potential to expose the psyche to phantasms of every kind calls for a Rousseauistic scruple; and it is interesting that Jeanne Moreau has drawn this out of a reflection on the woman writer and woman actor.

Her film, in its deliberate cosmopolitanism, wanted to make contact with Virginia Woolf, but what it represents is a New Eloise, a woman who realizes like Rousseau's Julie "the nothingness of human affairs." She differs from her, of course, in agreeing to marry the cinema, as nuns marry the Church. Jeanne Moreau, in her film, embodies a fatality closer to the spirit of Rousseau's novel than to Laclos' *Liaisons Dangereuses,* or other fictions inspiring her previous roles.

The Dubious Charm of
M. Truffaut

HOW DIFFICULT it is for the French to come to grips with the Occupation, even so long after the event! That is the first impression one receives from the aesthetic distance, the glassy, antiseptic touch, with which sensitive matters of collaboration and anti-Semitism are treated in Truffaut's *The Last Metro*. Though set in occupied Paris, and focusing on the plight of Jews trapped there by Vichy sympathizers and the Gestapo, the film remains curiously unthreatening and apolitical. One is tempted to raise the question of Truffaut's aestheticization of politics.

But as the film takes hold, one is obliged to modify that question. Truffaut's gift for lyric clarity seems almost a byproduct of the impermeable presence of Catherine Deneuve, who, as Marion Steiner, plays the role of the wife of a Jewish theater-owner in danger of being deported. As the star of the film, Deneuve is a register separating by perceptible yet fine modulations a series of closely adjacent and vibrant emotions. There is, always, sexual attraction; there is fierce and loyal dedication to the Jewish husband whom she hides and looks after; there is the cold calculation that enables her to continue his Theatre de Montmartre under the nose of the Jew-hating Daxiat; there is, finally, her training as an actress which enables her to remain formal, even haughty, whatever she actually feels. Truffaut communicates a temperament at once passionate and inviolable. The entire movie participates in Deneuve's makeup; it is *porcelaine de Paris;* and the medium of film gives merely an extra gloss to the sense that everything in Paris is an extension of Deneuve and her kind of theater, despite the trivial

[13]

"Norwegian" (i.e. Nordic, non-Jewish) or pseudo-Ibsenian play being rehearsed during the film.

As if by a magic wave of the wand, there are no victims. We know they exist, and a couple of scenes remind us of their suffering; yet the action is *determined* by people who are, or feel they are, on stage. Truffaut takes sides, of course, but he does not judge. The collaborationist villains not only do not occupy center stage, they are overstylized. Yet the good people too are reduced by a silhouette effect that either aestheticizes or eroticizes the action. It is as if the Homeric gods, who do look down occasionally, were still disposing of humanity's fate through the imperturbable sway of Eros. As viewers seeking to understand, we come to an impasse, or to its comic equivalent. It coincides with the film's ending, when Catherine Deneuve as Marion Steiner acknowledges the applause of the audience, linking hands with her husband, Lucas, who now comes out of the shadows as her director, not lover, *and* with the leading actor, who has replaced Lucas as her lover. It is a deliciously amoral moment in which the eternal triangle is deprived of emotional agony.

It is a bypass, then, rather than an impasse. This bypass exemplifies the seductive strength and danger of theater: Deneuve is all theater, spectacle personified. Her very stylishness, the cool resonating touch, the feeling that even in highly rhetorical speeches more is implied than said, harmonizes with Truffaut's own visual stenography. An example of that is the sequence in which Bernard Granger, the leading man, and a member of the Resistance, converts a record player into an explosive device by a series of maneuvers whose meaning viewers cannot infer until the radio blares out the news of its successful detonation in an *attentat* against a Nazi admiral. Truffaut, of course, lets out the stops when he wishes: the same Bernard provokes and then assaults Daxiat in a posh Paris restaurant. But Bernard's fate, like that of the other men, rests in the hands of Deneuve. Truffaut appends the men to her, because they are clumsy and intemperate, because they cannot really bear to stay undercover (they must disclose the truth or lay bare the life-lie in Ibsenian fashion), and so would perish without a woman's dissemblance to protect them.

[14]

The Dubious Charm of M. Truffaut

Perhaps that is enough of a message. Truffaut's link to Ibsen is real, after all; yet the women remain so undemystified that one suspects Truffaut of protecting *them*. This *amour courtois* of the cineast is a weakness, the indulgent flourish of his signature as filmmaker. Truffaut pays tribute to the power women have, who declare themselves when in love, and never in politics.

Truffaut's own power lies elsewhere, beyond the male/female split, even beyond the ability to create believable characters. He engages in an anarchic, nihilistic, and by no means unjoyful exploration of the interchangeability or substitutability of destinies. *Jules and Jim* was a pure instance of this. And, in the present film, every attractive woman is like every other for Bernard, who himself transits with ease from Grand Guignol to Ibsenian theater. One actor or person can be replaced by another; and whether this or that Jew is betrayed, or this or that Resistance fighter is caught, or one is Daxiat or Granger, or homosexual or heterosexual—it all seems equally a card dealt by fate.

The human condition, in Truffaut's films, is shown to be absolutely duplicitous without becoming, at all, ambiguous. As Bernard is fond of repeating to the women he desires: there are two women in every woman. But the proposition of *The Last Metro* goes beyond duality to a more basic duplicity. As Marion ascends the circular staircase to see Dr. Dietrich in the Nazi *Kommandatur*, she sees her lower-class double descend the other side on the arm of a German officer. She is, or could be, that other, and no judgment is involved. The ultimate duplicity, however, is more subversive still. It is that between theater and life, and leads to the question "Which imitates which?"

Is Steiner really a Jew? Or is he an actor, who, by playing the part of a Jew, must undermine the part he so cunningly embodies? Is Daxiat really an anti-Semite Fascist? Steiner, at one point, puts on a nose to imitate the Nazi caricature of what a Jew looks like; another episode shows him reading Marion anti-Semitic propaganda that claims the Jews take over everything, including beautiful non-Jewish women— as he begins to make love to her. Daxiat talks so earnestly to Marion about his esteem for Steiner's "Israelite" theater that one senses his envy, or a rhetoric that could entrap him rather than his prey (Marion). Daxiat's influence through the notorious newspaper *Je Suis Partout* is, moreover, symmetrical with Steiner's covert presence as the souffleur-director of his theater. Steiner too is "everywhere." And so on.

No wonder an atmosphere of comedy prevails. The villain Daxiat is allowed to escape and die of an unspecified cancer, and Marion can hold hands with her lover and with her husband—her love having saved a husband who has led her into a great stage career and the arms of the leading actor. The cool passion or strange duplicity of human nature, that *paradoxe du comédien* Diderot observed, saves a theater, as well as a Jew. And perhaps Truffaut intends it to save theater itself, by suggesting a fairy tale marriage between Hellenic beauty, with its gentile sang-froid, and that intense Hebrew or Puritan moral fervor which has always resisted the idolatrous charm of spectacle.

Reflections on French Romanticism

THERE IS general agreement that the first important Romantic is Rousseau; and although no agreement exists as to what makes him a Romantic, it is fair to assume the following reason might often be given: for Rousseau nothing is more important than breaking through to individuality, unless it is breaking through individuality. Not that he is free of shiftiness, obliquity, and bogus. They show that to know or reveal oneself is not a simple matter; the transparent turns back into the opaque. But there is greatness in the trenchancy of Rousseau's theoretical formulations. He knew what was needed, he knew that it must be based on the individual, and he uncompromisingly stated the fact: "Trouver une forme d'association . . . par laquelle chacun s'unissant à tous, n'obéisse pourtant qu'à lui-même, et reste aussi libre qu'auparavant" ("To find a form of association . . . through which each person, uniting with all, nevertheless obeys only himself and remains as free as before"; *Du Contrat social*, Book I, ch. 6).

If there is a first Romantic, is there a last? It would be difficult to find him. The reaction, for example, of T. E. Hulme, T. S. Eliot, and the New Humanists appears to us more and more as one within Romanticism. When Eliot declares, in his new poetics, thinking to modify the confessional style, "Poetry . . . is not the expression of personality but an escape from personality," and adds, "But, of course, only those who have personality and emotion know what it means to want to escape from these things," he is a knowing witness to the irreversible self-centeredness of modern writers. The theory of personal and expressive poetry, attributed to the Romantics, and that of impersonality, professed in reaction by a line of poets from Rimbaud through Eliot, responds to the same problem. Such poets value art for its power to re-create ideas into feelings or self-consciousness into organic and communal vision. This is an intrinsic, an ontological task intending to modify man's nature; but also a public effort, aiming at more than a small educated group, so that there is always the danger that visionariness becomes rhetoric—the Romantic megaphone.

Romanticism, in any case, is neither essentially irrational nor unreflective. We recall it was John Stuart Mill who named Wordsworth the poet of unpoetical natures because of the reflective pressure exhibited by his verse. We also remember Keats' judgment, that Wordsworth thought more deeply than Milton, at least more into the heart. These formulas, of course, are deceptive: did not Dante, for instance, think into the heart? Can we nominate him as our first Romantic? And what of Saint Augustine?

It remains true that the Romantics are strangely self-involved. They spell "Art" with a capital "I," to adapt Oscar Wilde on Whistler. Byron's comment on Keats, that in *Endymion* he "viciously solicited his own imagination," is partly just. Such behavior is the penalty for thinking about one's imagination, about one's relation to it, and having sometimes to prompt the relation. But Byron was wrong in believing that the relation was a private, quasi-incestuous affair. The theme engaged by the great Romantics is that of a general (Keats called it "gregarious") progress of imagination, of which the artist is a mediator. Artists reveal in what relation they stand to their own mind—which presupposes for mind (or imagination) an existence apart from ego. Authentic self-consciousness includes a strongly objective attitude toward the self: the mind is seen as a *daimon,* not invariably right, perhaps beyond simple categories of right and wrong, but a respondent and secret sharer. Self-consciousness is the feeling of being on the spot, but it is also consciousness of one's consciousness in its various relations.

Poetic and analytic attitudes can keep company, therefore. Yet, as Keats said, the creative must create itself: it is not a matter of listening to the radio of one's mind or leading genius about like a lobster on a string. What Byron observed disdainfully of Keats, that he teased his own imagination, became methodical, even programmatic, in the antithetical poetics of Hugo and the synaesthetic experiments of Rimbaud. To keep in touch with imagination is an increasingly heroic task.

Perhaps this desire, so characteristic of the present era, though not unknown in previous ones, to achieve a direct or unmediated relation to oneself, is an illusion. If so, the illusion remains to be explained. It may be an illusion as vital to life as dreaming. At least to life in contemporary society: the dream of a direct communion reacts against the multiplication of secondary objects. Even art feels itself to be *écriture*, signs of signs. As Matthew Arnold wrote in 1863,

> Modern times find themselves with an immense system of institutions, established facts, accredited dogmas, customs, rules, which have come to them from times not modern. In this system their life has to be carried forward; yet they have a sense that this system is not of their own creation, that it by no means correponds exactly with the wants of their actual life, that, for them, it is customary, not rational. The awakening of this sense is the awakening of the modern spirit. ("Heinrich Heine")

The advance of civilization seems to foster a diversification of knowledge, a pluralism of values, fragmentation, and a sometimes fruitful indifference to the one necessary thing. In these conditions does not emphasis on the self play a functional role? To echo Emerson, who is the modern hero if not the immovably centered man? There is a nostalgia for commitment, and honest commitment goes via one's self, one's body, one's conscience. In some sense, of course, this surfeit of options, of multiplication of properties, frees individuals by diminishing the expectation put on them. They are never in one place and so can never be "on the spot." We have too wide a stake in the world to be messianic: paraphernalia, material or spiritual, are a mode of anti-self-consciousness. Yet it was always the accumulation of relationships, with property or family or history, which sparked an at once explosive and ascetic passion to return to the naked, human source. Affluence fosters the dream of spiritual poverty; and crime, we have learned, is the result of affluence as well as deprivation, a way of forging one's identity. Two men like myself, says Schiller's Robber Captain, could destroy the whole moral order.

The contemporary situation differs from that of the Romantics only in its apparent irreversibility and uncompromising nature. A hundred and fifty years ago, the sequence of revolutions and restorations seemed to argue that history had a definite structure, yet one which allowed some scope to the individual. Many thought it probable that history alternated according to the Saint-Simonian scheme of "organic" (religious, strongly uplifting) and "critical" (skeptical, full of reasoning and unbelief) ages. They felt they were living in a "critical" age, in a time of unbelief or at its turning. "De quel nom te nommer, heure trouble où nous sommes?" ("Prélude," *Chants du crépuscule,* 1835). Hugo does not know whether this twilight, the "époque en travail" through which he is passing, heralds night or a new dawn. In England it is the early Victorians who share with the French Romantics this concept of an Age of Transition, and the historical self-consciousness it fostered. The crucial question was whether to be of one's time or whether to hasten the turn into the coming (organic-religious) phase. To be of one's time might mean standing against the historical "stream of tendency."

Where are we today? In the West, the critical spirit has absolutized itself except for our belief·in the individual. In a technological society, which seduces the individual into what may appear as false modes of participation, into complicities, the individual has an even greater responsibility to I-Thou relations. At the same time, however, as if there were no contradiction, we insist on the importance of community, on larger than individual or family purposes. Have we advanced significantly beyond Rousseau? Have we not simply discovered more obstacles to the realization of his magic formula? Our dream is still to generate the communal from the individual, or to regenerate it from within self-consciousness. I wish to review some aspects of that problem in the following general sketch of French Romanticism.

In 1818, P. S. Ballanche, one of the most interesting social philosophers of the Romantic period, published his *Essay on Social Institutions.*

[20]

The chapter discussing the influence of the French Revolution on the arts flirts momentarily with the ambition of "une poétique appliquée à l'âge actuel de l'esprit humain"—a poetics in tune with the present era. Accepting the French Revolution as an irreversible event, even as a providential shock to consciousness, Ballanche is disturbed by a paradox strangely similar to Rousseau's "Man is born free, and everywhere he is in chains." The French Revolution emancipated human thought, yet there are no or few institutions reflecting the fact in 1818. Our thoughts are free, and everywhere they are in chains. The arts are institutions too: is it not time to renew our poetics?

A decade later Hugo would launch his famous slogan, "A peuple nouveau, art nouveau." It comes as no surprise to those who have heard of the Battle of *Hernani* that the French Romantics considered the reform of the arts a political matter, as combat against the "hommes géométriques" (Lamartine's phrase) or the "arid heritage" and "proud sterility" of the *siècle des lumières* which immortalized the masterpieces produced under Louis XIV as if his monarchy were equally absolute in the realm of spirit. Ballanche, an enlightened Catholic, and hardly a Jacobin, went so far as to assert that the literature of the period of Louis XIV was beginning to be ancient literature, "de l'archéologie." If the social institutions are outmoded, then the period's literature must be outmoded. His grim consistency has the same reason as Hugo's flamboyance: years after the French Revolution, with so many ideas burgeoning, no new forms and few social reforms seemed forthcoming.

The close association of literary with social reform typical of Romantic statements in the exploding 1820s is due to this disproportion between ideas and realities. The great literary event of 1819, for example, was publication of the poetry of André Chénier, who had died in the Revolution. And in 1820, which at least saw Lamartine's *Premières Méditations,* Hugo writes sadly: "No important book yet this year, no strong pronouncement *(parole forte);* nothing that could teach, nothing that could arouse. Is it not time someone appeared out of the crowd, saying, Here I am?" Hugo's emphasis on the *parole forte,* on poet as advocate, is strongly colored by these years of national sterility.

[21]

It is uncertain what caused the lateness of French Romanticism as a *movement*—Rousseau, Chateaubriand, and Mme de Staël were great but single waves.[1] Perhaps the turmoil and proscriptions of twenty-five years. Or something endemic to French civilization, which Guizot noticed: whereas English history, he thought, showed the simultaneous development of different forces, so that no older principle was totally discarded, and no special interest prevailed absolutely, in France each political or intellectual principle developed separately and completely.[2] When Matthew Arnold remarked that most of the English Romantics, compared to the French or German, were not men of *ideas,* he may have been interpreting the same phenomenon.

The lateness of Romanticism in France had, in any case, important consequences for the kind of art produced. A reservoir of forces had built up: energies to be ignited, voices to be heard, ideas to be fully expounded. Ballanche points to the explosive character of the moment when he apologizes for his "incoherence," which is really a tendency to say everything at once: to give a public, even publicistic, form to post-Revolutionary thought about social institutions and the historical destiny of France. "We are at a point in history where all ideas must be expressed, and all important human problems set forth at one and the same time."

French Romanticism, however, is delayed not only with respect to 1789 but also with respect to other Romanticisms—to the cultural upheavals in England and Germany. If the death of Byron in 1824 marks the end of two major phases of English Romanticism, it but signals the beginning of an accelerating tempo of events in France. That country had to catch up with surrounding nations as well as with its own past. The 1820s were a highpoint of the influx of ideas from Germany begun earlier with Mme de Staël, while Italy and England also make

1. It would be more exact to say that Mme de Staël and Chateaubriand created a *circle* rather than a *movement*. Romanticism in France is chronologically remarkable in being both very early (Rousseau) and very late.

2. See F. Guizot, *Histoire de la civilisation en Europe* (Paris: Didier, 1840), "Première leçon." The lectures were originally given 1828 to 1830.

their presence felt. Michelet's *Journal des idées* has the following entry for May 1825:

> Our interest in Socrates' death comes not from the fact of his innocence but because his death expresses the struggle of two moral powers, the subjective (or individual) and the objective (or State). The subjective principle, not having achieved self-consciousness, was then merely something dissident and corrosive which the objective principle, the State, had to purge.[3]

Clearly, Hegel is in the wings. But so, as we read on, are Shakespeare, Milton, Byron, and Kant, examined by Michelet for their understanding of history as the story of liberty, of humanity "condemned" to self-development.

Foreign influences revive, in turn, neglected native resources: ballads, popular themes, literature before the age of Louis XIV. The dozen years from about 1823 to 1835 are a cultural apocalypse. For once a simple listing tells a great deal. During this period Hugo publishes *Han d'Islande* and collections of poetry ranging from the *Odes et Ballades* and *Orientales* to the *Chants du crépuscule;* Fauriel, *Chants populaires de la Grèce moderne;* Loev-Weimar, translations of English and Scotch popular ballads; Lamartine, *Le dernier chant de Childe Harold;* Berlioz, *Harold in Italy* and the *Symphonie fantastique;* Stendhal, *Racine et Shakespeare;* Sainte-Beuve, writings on Ronsard and sixteenth-century literature. Guigniaut begins to issue his adaptation of Creuzer's *Symbolik,* which Renan characterized as a "panthéon scientifique de tous les dieux de l'humanité." Furthermore, Delacroix exhibits the *Death of Sardanapalus;* Shakespeare is successfully brought to the French stage by Kemble's troupe; Beethoven is discovered; Nerval translates *Faust* (part I). Again, Delacroix makes his *Faust* lithographs; Berlioz composes music for *Huit scènes de Faust;* there is a translation of Hoffmann's stories and of De Quincey's *Opium Eater* (the latter by Musset). Musset and Vigny enter onto the literary scene; Daumier starts work for the

3. Michelet's journal is reprinted in *Écrits de jeunesse,* P. Viallaneix, ed. (Paris: Gallimard, 1959).

Caricature; Hugo's *Cromwell* is followed by *Hernani* and Dumas' *Henri III;* Guizot, Ampère, and Michelet publish their first historical works; Ballanche brings out *Orphée* and the *Palingénésie sociale.* Scott's historical novels are translated as they appear. Delacroix sketches his Moroccan journey, Berlioz writes the *Return to Life* in Italy; Stendhal publishes his first great novel; George Sand's *Lélia* comes out. The Saint-Simonians take over the *Globe;* Lamennais founds the community at La Chenaie as well as the short-lived *L'Avenir;* the *Paroles d'un Croyant* is published; and Balzac is inspired with the idea of linking his novels into a *Comédie humaine.* "La Boutique/Romantique," as Musset calls it catchily, is open.

To complete this picture of an *école,* add Paris. It centered these events and gave them their milieu. Berlin and Vienna never became this kind of center; and it happened that most of the great English Romantics lived away from London, in the countryside or exile. As for Rome, it was no longer in Rome, as Du Bellay had lamented three centuries before, and a powerful letter by Lamennais confirms. In Paris, theater, dinner parties, salons, everything acted as a cynosure. Lamennais was acquainted with Liszt, Liszt with Berlioz, all with Victor Hugo or Nodier; and at a salon like that of Marie d'Agoult, one might meet Sainte-Beuve, Heine, Mickiewicz, Baron Eckstein, Balzac, Lamennais, George Sand. Paris was more than a milieu: it was a microcosm and the heart of a nation.[4]

An art conspicuous, preachy, panoramic, national, was inevitable. It is the art, quite distinctly, of a movement: artists felt they contained multitudes. We understand Berlioz's *Lélio,* conceived around 1830, which condenses into the figure of the artist the emotional and literary syncretism of its time. Lélio leads us from Goethe's ballad *Der Fischer* through reminiscences of *Hamlet* and *The Tempest* to the song of Neapolitan bri-

4. There are, in Ludwig Boerne's *Briefe aus Paris, 1830–31,* amusing descriptions of various salons and festivities. See his letter entries for November 5, 1830 (on Gérard's salon, which included Delphine Gay, Humboldt, Mayer-Beer, David, Vitet, and Stendhal); December 3, 1830 (a romantic evening devoted to listening to a translation of *Macbeth*); and December 8, 1830 (his reaction to Berlioz's *Symphonie fantastique*). See also, for the salons, Daniel Stern (Mme d'Agoult), *Mes Souvenirs, 1806–1833* (Paris: Calmann Lévy, 1877), pp. 301–2.

gands which marks the high point of the artist's return to life. "Yes!"
(I quote from Lélio's unifying monologue), "Yes! poetical superstitions,
a guardian madonna, gorgeous loot heaped up in caves, dishevelled
women panting with fright, a concert of cries of horror accompanied
by an orchestra of guns, sabres and daggers, blood and lachryma Christi,
a bed of lava rocked by earthquakes . . . voilà la vie!"

Romantic agony, you say, *l'esthétique du mal*. True, from Chateaubriand's *Génie du Christianisme* to Baudelaire's *Fleurs du Mal* and Hugo's
Fin de Satan, the beautiful embraces the blues. It is drawn from passion
in its basic sense of love suffering: amour-passion, heavenly or earthly.
"Je viens gémir, luire, éclairer," says the Angel called Liberty to the
Satan of Hugo's epic medley. It could be the *devise* of the French Romantics. Victor Cousin, in an elegant commonplace, called the beautiful "la splendeur du bien," but when sacred and profane themes
commingle in Hugo and Berlioz it is the radiance of passion.

There is, obviously, as much *feu d'artifice* as fire in all this, and the
uneasy combination of make-believe and sincerity raises difficult questions. Theatricality, role-playing, infects everything. "Suis-je Amour ou
Phébus? Lusignan ou Biron?" The tragic note of Nerval's identity crisis
blends precariously with this trill from some gallant aria. Where now
is Rousseau's distrust of theater or his critical distinction between
"l'homme de l'homme" and "l'homme de la nature"? Where is anything resembling Wordsworth's insight, after being disappointed in political action, that nature had infinitely more ways of forming or re-
forming the individual than society could muster? There is little real
nature poetry in French Romanticism; it had to await a later generation, composed of painters. The point is that French Romanticism is
social through and through, and subjective through and through: it
shifts from subjective to social with *sprezzatura*. For Hugo an artist is
always Man Representative, with "le peuple" as his constituency; and
exile, the isolation of Guernsey, only intensifies this sentiment. His
Contemplations (1856) contain, according to the preface, "all the
impressions and reflections, all the realities and vague fantastic thoughts,
bright or dark, that conscience recalls and examines, ray by ray, sigh
after sigh. . . ." Each day is a day of destiny for Hugo, and the critic

who objects to such egotism is put down with "Fool! who think I am not you!"

We are in the midst of the crucial question of Romantic "subjectivity." Is it, in France, despite the scruples of Rousseau, as unproblematic as it appears? Where are its depths? When Musset calls his Muse "seul être pudique et chaste" after the stormy affair with George Sand, do we not groan without being enlightened? Does not Stendhal have our sympathy for wishing to fight a duel with a friend who defended Chateaubriand's "la cîme indéterminée des forêts"? There are, it is clear, naïve and self-deceptive moments. Michelet, as a very young man, writes his *Memorial* because, he says, "Rousseau ne sera pas le seul homme que l'on ait connu." This sense of mission, of historical vocation, of being the bearers of an enlightenment that will flood the earth like the knowledge of God, is both exhilarating and absurd.

But our sensibility, of course, has been affected by the post-Romantic reaction: faith in art as spiritual politics only increased the tension between politics and letters and brought on movements which renounced "destiny" and "depth," mythic décor and grandiloquence, the bourgeois-imperial complex and the whole "mensonge romantique." While in a poet like Vigny artistic vocation and the idea of destiny are central if problematic subjects, with Rimbaud the very word "destiny" seems outmoded. What he calls "la lumière *nature*" replaces the heaven of aims. Rimbaud's life, similarly, in contrast to that of Nerval, refuses to become allegory: Rimbaud rejects all *mythes de profondeur* including that belief in historical destiny which the Romantics kept from the time of Louix XIV but extended to include the masses. The early Rimbaud enjoys (though with a difference) the "opéra fabuleux" of the Romantics, but he soon becomes the Cézanne of French verse, stripping away affluent color and exotic decor, while substituting terse preachment for the *emphase* of Romantic predication:

> Jamais l'espérance
> Pas d'orietur
> Science et patience
> Le supplice est sûr.

Let us return to Hugo's aggressive I-Thou relation, so uncatty compared to Baudelaire's "Hypocrite lecteur, mon semblable, mon frère." His spirited dismissal of the idiot questioner ("Fool! who think I am not you!") makes the artist into an idiot creator, which he isn't. Hugo can be stupid at times, as Leconte de Lisle acknowledged, yet his stupidity functions as a force of consciousness that leaps directly from the I to the you, from subjective to social, from self to all. This reflects, too often, a lust for certainty eliminating transitional states—perhaps because Hugo, between 1830 and the *coup d'état* of 1851, had tried to suffer the "clair-obscur" of an Age of Transition. It is remarkable how he returns in the 1850s to the primitivity of white and black, to the apocalyptic distinction between night and redemptive light, or its reversal. The antithetical poetics announced in the preface to *Cromwell* return with a vengeance.

Hugo's problem is that of French Romanticism generally. The way from selfhood to a purified self, or from isolation to a larger, imaginative or communal life, seems more uncertain than in Rousseau. Or, like history itself in the period from Rousseau to Hugo, it is subject to greater vacillation. That pure "feeling of existence" which weighs so lightly on Rousseau ("Entirely inside the present, I remembered nothing; I had no distinct notion of my individuality") and which disperses as if they were mist all factitious mediations ("I perceived the sky, a few stars, and a little verdure. This first sensation was a delicious moment; only through it could I feel myself. In that instant I was born to life")[5] is usually a pregnant and burdensome feeling in Hugo, a "nuée sombre" rather than a luminous darkness. "La grande plongeuse" of the imagination dives into this cloud, as the promenade becomes a

5. *Les Rêveries du promeneur solitaire.* Deuxième Promenade. Available in English as *Reveries of the Solitary Walker,* translated by Peter France (Harmondsworth: Penguin, 1979). Cf. Hazlitt "On the Character of Rousseau" (1817), which delineates the shadow side of this passage from *Les Rêveries:* "The only quality which he possesses in an eminent degree, which alone raised him above ordinary men, and which gave his writings and opinions an influence greater, perhaps, than has been exerted by an individual in modern times was extreme sensibility, or an acute and even morbid feeling of all that related to his own impressions, to the objects and events of his life. He had the most intense consciousness of his own existence."

fantastic journey, and revery turns into brooding. Sky and water, memory and vision, God and people converge on the poet as if he were the only thing betwixt and between, the one mediator. He is always on the spot.

Perhaps Hugo did not have enough of what Keats called "negative capability"; perhaps he was too irritable in reaching after truth, and taking his objective by emotional or rhetorical storm. But the situation of the artist seemed to demand clairvoyance and social prophecy. The Keatsian way—or impasse—was not possible in so public a time. This burden of leadership is the theme even of a man like Vigny, who accepted, disdainfully, his lot. In terms of Romantic aesthetics, what is essential is more than the disappearance of trustworthy mediations between self and world, contigency and destiny, natural man and social man, the masses and humanity. It is that while existing or "legitimate" forms are felt to be inauthentic, the idea of exemplary social action and of manifest national destiny is magnified rather than doubted.

No other national literature raised the "social question" more insistently than the French. Saint-Simon, Ballanche, De Maistre, Bonald, Fourier, Lamennais, Michelet, and Comte are as essential to an understanding of the period as Berlioz, Hugo, and Delacroix. Whatever their political differences, they connect the renovation of society and that of the arts. Whereas Sénancour (and it is his truth) can never emerge from "le vide de l'autri" and "le néant de l'ordre sociale," from 1820 on art is predominantly "aesthetic education": it strives to occupy its providential place in the making of men and the development of true social forms.

For most, the new image of man had to arise from the depth of subjective spirit. The Romantic artist is haunted by scenes of solitariness: Prometheus on the rock, Christ on the Mount of Olives, or as in Jean Paul's influential *songe,* standing in cosmic silence amid the ruins of the world. What return to life there is comes from a solitude expressive of this abandonment or decay of social supports. The nakedness is not absolute, however: to revive such ancient symbols of loneliness is not to be alone. In these scenes of desolation, we are still accompanied by images which assimilate man's fate as of old. Man is alone, yet alone with thought, with a great conception he has un-knowingly, fatefully repeated. I live my life like a novel, Nerval writes in *Aurélia*. His life becomes an allegory: it is greater, more fraternal than he knew. However deep the solitude depicted, art continues to provide a nursery of forms, that reserve of living types that Hugo calls *Adams*.

This reserve, in 1820, contained a very small number of works, mainly from the time of Louis XIV. They had to sustain thoughts of French greatness when that was increasingly in doubt. To deflate these works would impoverish the reserve even more. Obviously new role models, new spiritual and imaginative possibilities, had to be created: the "mal du siècle" showed that, while many of the young felt a *career* was still possible (the Napoleonic code provided, after all, for "une carrière ouverte aux talents"), a *vocation* was not in sight.[6] Villemain, en-lightened apologist for the glories of tradition, can do no better in 1824 than to echo the Napoleonic code and insist that "La carrière est en-core ouverte" in the arena of political and religious oratory. But pre-cisely: a career is not—or no longer—a calling. The distinction was sometimes illusory: Julien Sorel is a careerist in a time when being such is a vocation. As Vigny remarked bitterly: "No young head could think, because made giddy day-in, day-out by the canons and bells of the Te Deums" (which marked Napoleon's victories). Only art, how-ever, could now renew the image of a vocation that was more than careerist, or of a heroism tied to inward or social reform rather than political ambition.

Villemain again did not help with his suggestion that the young might develop their imagination by reconstructing the "immortal epoch" of

6. According to Chateaubriand, in the *Génie du Christianisme*, "Il y a eu dans nôtre age, à quelques exceptions prés, une sorte d'avortement général des talents." In our century Van Wyck Brooks has made the pertinent observation that "Obermann . . . reduced himself to pure virtuality. . . . He demands independence of society and refuses to rec-ognize any middle ground between the strictly individual and the strictly universal. It follows that he cannot accept as his vocation any of those ready-made professions that spring from and support the social order." See *The Malady of the Ideal* (London: A. C. Fifield, 1913). Sénancourt's *Obermann* was published in 1804, republished with an in-troduction by Sainte-Beuve in 1833, and again, with an introduction by George Sand, in 1840.

[29]

Louis XIV, "the atmosphere of glory and enthusiasm which emanated from a conquering, enlightened and magnanimous king, whose courtiers even were often great men." No wonder Hugo fulminated in his *Jacobin Journal of Ideas* (1819–1820) against this sector of thought, which "does not want the earth to turn or talent to be creative, and which orders the eagles to fly with wax wings." Even Hugo, however, did not degrade the seventeenth century, since no other art was present, and its immense influence revealed the artist's role in shaping the national consciousness. His attack is centered on eighteenth-century negations. He wished to replenish the reserve, to generate or recover forms allowing the I to be Other and raise itself to a more comprehensive vision of national destiny. "La tragédie court les rues," Ducis had said during the Revolution; but it is not till Hugo and Balzac that the giant forms of art frequent the streets again, and street-forms the world of art.

The reserve of which we have spoken is composed of acknowledged works of art which guarantee, even when they do not directly influence, the paper in circulation. Many draw on that reserve without knowing it, but in times of crisis it is a conscious and challenged possession. Something like a museum, something like a pantheon, it gathers together those structured spiritual forces that have guided men in the past. To young artists it may be a burden or else a bait: an angel they must wrestle, a double or secret sharer that haunts them.

The French Romantics augmented this reserve by bringing from the basement neglected works—of "impure" taste, religious or popular character or foreign extraction. But the crisis, the felt spiritual need, was too deep for representative measures. The gap between canonical and noncanonical art had become so great that only a new idea of their interrelation could suffice. While the notion of living "without reserve" did not catch on because of the quest for role models (Romanticism conceiving itself, on the whole, as a modern or more broadly based Classicism), we do find the beginnings of the anthropological view that art comprises more than canonized masterpieces. An unstructured or semistructured reserve—customs, ceremonies, oral traditions, artifacts of all sorts—receives consideration. Realia of this kind are Balzac's gold: he gloats over them like another Grandet.

How radically, on this point, Voltaire differs from the Romantics! For Voltaire, the philosopher of history interested in ancient customs is a man in danger of methodizing madness ("mettre de la raison dans la folie"). Reason is reason and folly is folly; and history, on the whole, is a ship of fools rather than an ark of salvation. But the Romantics view formal history on a large scale as an epic in prose, while historical fiction triumphs in all the genres. Ballanche, who creates a new myth of redemption drawing on Vico's analysis of Roman law, writes his *Orphée* as "l'histoire condensée de quinze siècles du genre humain," and remarks of Bossuet's *Discours sur l'histoire universelle* that it is "a magnificent literary conception, a kind of epic embracing all times and places." A "légende des siècles," in effect, two centuries before Hugo.

To oversee history is an old ambition. But now history includes so much more. More races, cultures, lifestyles. The perspective has widened, both horizontally and in depth. History is no longer sublime in the old sense—restricted to a progress, triumphal or tragic, of semidivine persons. Herder's influence grows in the 1820s and brings with it an existential query. How is the acculturated person, standing genuinely within his time, to sight all this and gather it into a synoptic frame? The situation is, once more, mythogenetic: the comprehensive forms or guiding myths must come from the depth of the individual mind. Wanted: a hero of consciousness.

Even if history exhibits a divine plot (as most continued to believe, following in this Bossuet or Vico), the gods themselves have departed. Heroes must fathom alone their way through history. Actually, Ballanche remarked, there were two divine departures. With the advent of Christianity, "the gods departed but their images stayed. Now another voice is heard in the literary world: the *images* of the gods are departing." We approach the last act in a divine striptease of the imagination. As the historical consciousness grows, a multitude of fallen gods comes to light. Surrounded by ancient images of the divine, the Romantic is more alone than ever.

[31]

The hero of consciousness, therefore, is a solitary haunted by vast conceptions in which he cannot participate. This is the dilemma, basically, of Faust and Ahasuerus, two figures that come to the fore in the Romantic period. There are many others, of course. As heroes they are often more pursued than pursuing—by gods they defy or disbelieve. They must be redeemed in various ways: some by "negative capability," some by a more positive power of assimilation. The latter way is stressed in French Romanticism. So Ballanche flirts suggestively with a feminine figure, the sibyl. He asserts that France had its sibyl once in Joan of Arc: a woman of the people, almost anonymous, through whom the whole nation found its expression. "A people feels the need for territorial unity, for unity of language and unity in its traditions. This feeling focuses on a person who has great assimilative powers; it identifies with her; it becomes her very self. Repressed by acts of violence, that need flees from spirit to spirit until it finds shelter in une *organisation de sibylle.*"

I am unable to translate this final phrase, which points to something less crude than Hugo's Adams and archetypes. It may express that subtler, more diffused power of shaping or unifying which art exhibits intrinsically. Finally, of course, the hero of consciousness is the mythogenetic artist rather than any one of his creations. History's host, he must live among "departing images." Their burden is better than sheer self. What is he without them except a porous mind? And how could the new myth, the new order, come from nothing?

Let me, to conclude, give one example of the sibylline or assimilative labor of the French Romantics. In November of 1825 Michelet settled on the project of writing "un discours étincelant sur l'unité du genre humain." This project took him, in a sense, all his life, although the first fruits were his essay on universal history published in 1831. He was not thinking, however, of an essay in the months immediately preceding November 1825. A different form was struggling for expression:

> Dialogues des morts intitulés: Les Amours. J'étais enterré depuis peu, et je commençais à reconnaître avec effroi mon nouveau gîte. C'était au mois de février. . . . La nuit venue, je m'étais assis sur la balus-

trade dont on a entouré mon monument, lorsque j'entends une voix, si basse et douce qu'une ombre seule pouvait l'entendre: *Ami, tu n'es pas seul*. . . . La description des amours et des assemblées des morts au printemps, leur attente du jugement, etc. (*Journal des idées)*

(Dialogues of the dead entitled: Love Stories. Recently buried, I was beginning to recognize with fright my new lodgings. It was the month of February. . . . Night had fallen, and I was sitting on the railing that circled my tombstone when I heard a voice, so low and soft that only a shade could have heard it: Friend, you are not alone. . . . A description of the love-making and assemblies of the dead in springtime, their waiting for judgment, etc.)

This is June 1825, and by September the conception has developed:

une histoire dramatique du dogme de la fatalité. . . . Ce serait un ouvrage tout dramatique dans le style. On parlerait successivement de la croyance de chaque époque, comme d'une croyance vraie. On emploierait quelquefois les idées de Lucien, mais sérieusement. Voici les chapitres ou époques: Le Destin, Jupiter grec, Jupiter Capitolin, Jéhova, Jésus-Christ, Jésus et les saints. . . . L'ouvrage serait présenté comme celui d'un rêveur du Moyen Age qui regarderait comme vrai tout ce qu'a jamais cru la majorité du monde civilisé.

(A dramatization of the dogma of fatalism. . . . It would be a work thoroughly dramatic in its style. The idea would be to talk successively of the belief of each epoch as if it were a true belief. The ideas of Lucian would occasionally be used, but seriously. Here are the chapters or epochs: Destiny, Greek Jupiter, Capitoline Jupiter, Jehovah, Jesus Christ, Jesus and the Saints. . . . The work would be presented as emanating from a Medieval Dreamer who accepted as true everything the majority of civilized people in the world had ever believed.)

Michelet's first problem is that of intellectual perspective. He thinks of history as the story of liberty, not of fatality, yet he knows how extensive and real the reign of the "dead" has been. What point of view can convey this twofold consciousness? There is, further, the formal problem of what convention might best express a modern, synchronic perspective. The choice seems to lie between something over-

[33]

credible, like the medieval dream vision, and something overskeptical, like Lucian's *Dialogues of the Dead*. Beyond all this, however, lies a perplexity of the heart, a hint of the deep, emotional side of Michelet's undertaking. *Ami, tu n'es pas seul.* This history seeks to embrace all humankind. The consolation is unmistakable even though the imaginary situation could have taken a demonic turn: into history as nightmare, *Walpurgisnacht*, or dance of death. The universal historian risks this danger rather than yielding to solipsism.

Like Ballanche, Michelet was unable to discover an up-to-date poetics. His vast prose effort walks among the dead—the ancient credibilities—with too confident a step. Another abortive, if highly expressive, attempt at a synoptic rendering of departing myths is made by Edgar Quinet. Also deeply influenced by Herder, Quinet clarifies the horror of unbelief which drove Nerval to the delusions of *Aurélia*. (I was mad, Blake has Cowper say, as a refuge from unbelief, and you are as mad as any of us.) In Quinet's *Ahasvérus* (1833), the splendid machinery of romance, the historical tableaux, the cosmological dream visions are illuminations set off in a ruin. The author summons pageant after pageant to delay the fatal sentence spoken by Eternity: "Ni être ni néant, je ne veux plus que moi." With that the visionary clock runs down and leaves nothing but ego behind. Quinet's tired theological insight hides a ruinous solipsism: "I don't want being, I don't want nothingness; I want myself." If we strip the mind of myth and metaphysics—those historical errors—what remains but the naked self?

Why continue the story? Each artist faces the problem anew. From 1830 to the 1850s there is intensification rather than advance. In the *Légende des siècles*, which remains a sequence of diachronic highpoints, Hugo does not progress beyond the poetics of the preface to *Cromwell:* "Croiser dans le même tableau le drame de la vie et le drame de la conscience." It is clearly not the "épopée idéale, à la fois successive et spontanée" which Ballanche programmed in the *Vision d'Hébal* (1831). The *Fin de Satan* is perhaps more remarkable, but Hugo's conception of Satan, peculiar and powerful as it is, is also embarrassingly intimate. Satan's desire is so vast that it feeds the fear of isolation. The implacable solitary becomes a love-monster:

c'est là l'inoui, l'horrible, le divin
De se dresser, d'ouvrir des ailes insensées,
De s'attacher, sanglant, à toutes les pensées
Qu'on peut saisir, avec des cris, avec des pleurs,
De sonder les terreurs, de sonder les douleurs.

Desire may be infinite, but art is limited. Later writers, especially the symbolists, resist Romantic pressures to convert the palace of art into a brothel of forms. A pantheon is not a pandemonium, and poetry is not opera. Art cannot long subsist on the energy of nostalgia, on the remembrance of obsolete myths and lapsed fidelities. It seemed more honest to render consciousness as such: believing less the more it knows, the fuller the emptier, and basically unconsummated. Is not soul as soul always immersed in departing images? "Ces nymphes, je les veux perpétuer." Here is the constant to which historical periods, faith or roles are the variables.

Nerval is an important transitional figure because he creates a new poetry by incorporating rather than rejecting Romantic assumptions. For Nerval, all art, but especially theater, remains linked to vast presuppositions of a magical or metaphysical nature. So Goethe's mythopoeia in the *Second Faust* is analysed in terms of a metaphysics of the imagination. Nerval will not allow Goethe the wide whimsy of art, or a more radical autonomy. Blending, as in ancient systems, ideas on the abode of the dead with cosmological speculation, he imagines that the world we live in, the "monde matériel," is shadowed about by concentric circles of centuries which have shed their materiality and are pure "intelligences." The phantoms Faust draws into his world come from that planetary sphere, where all things exist in a state of "divine synchronism":

Elles co-existent toutes, comme les personnages divers d'un drame qui ne s'est pas encore dénoué, et qui pourtant est accompli dans la pensée de son auteur; ce sont les coulisses de la vie où Goethe nous transporte ainsi. Hélène et Paris, les ombres que cherche Faust, sont quelque part errant dans le *spectre* immense que leur siècle a laissé dans l'espace; elles marchent sous les portiques splendides et sous les

[35]

ombrages frais qu'elles rêvent encore, et se meuvent gravement, en *ruminant* leur vie passée. C'est ainsi que Faust les recontre et, par l'aspiration immense de son âme à demi dégagée de la terre, il parvient à les attirer hors de leur cercle d'existence et à les amener dans le sien.[7]

(All coexist, like various characters in a play that hasn't reached its resolution yet is already complete in its author's mind; Goethe transports us thus into the wings of life. Helen and Paris, the phantoms sought by Faust, are wandering somewhere in the immense *shadow* their era has left in space; they stroll under the fine arcades and among the fresh, shady walks of which they still dream; they move about gravely, ruminating their past life. Faust encounters them thus; and, by the immense aspiration of his half-unearthly soul, succeeds in drawing them away from their circle of life and bringing them into his.)

The intellectual detritus carried along is part of the problem. But we recognize the need of the Romantics for an airy Hades of this kind, for a reserve of ideal or imaginative forms. The status of these forms is what we find difficult. What being do they have? They are not ideas merely, not even Platonic ideas, and to say they have the being of art forms begs the question. Nerval thinks of them as existing in the "coulisses de la vie"—in the wings, between acts, waiting to go on stage. Mythology would call them daemons: inhabitants of the middle air, neither all divine nor all human, and desirous of a more individuated existence.

When Nerval's prince recites, "Je suis le ténébreux, le veuf, l'inconsolé," we do not think of daemons or middle beings or the limbo of art. We do not even think, necessarily, of an actor stepping from the wings. Suggestive as it is, this poetry carries its burden lightly. Its metaphysics are held, so to say, in reserve. Yet is not the "ténébreux" one of those "ombres . . . quelque part errant dans le *spectre* immense que leur siècle a laissé dans l'espace"? The artist, another Faust, draws him out of the shadows into life, *his* life. Behind the *Chimères* is that "histoire universelle . . . synchronisme divin" which haunted so many

7. See Nerval's introduction to his translation of Goethe, *Les Deux Faust de Goethe*, F. Baldensperger, ed. (Paris: Librarie ancienne Honoré Champion, 1932), p. 233.

Romantics. Nerval's phantoms rarely console, however. An ontological uncertainty remains which is of the essence of art and its paradigms. The "ténébreux" may be an archetype drawn by the artist into his life, but he could also be the LaBrunie who has remained a mere dream of himself, powerless to leave the limbo of his "musée imaginaire." The shadow is all there is. Nerval's "ombre" remains inconsolable and his message is the obverse of that heard by Michelet—*Ami, tu es seul.*

Barthes' *Vita Nuova*

THESE ARE still the Banquet Years in France, though not everyone will savor the feast of books and essays produced there since 1945. One might have thought that Jean-Paul Sartre, Claude Lévi-Strauss, and Maurice Merleau-Ponty had exhausted a certain vein. Philosophy and literature invaded each other's realm; science mingled with cultural criticism. Yet Jacques Derrida, Michel Foucault, Roland Barthes, and others are still taking on linguistics, semiotics, structuralism, sociology, and psychoanalysis. New and fantastic words appear on the scene to express this mixture of disciplines: "economimesis," "anasematics," "mimology." It is a heady period of scribbledihobble.

There is a danger to literature in this Parisian plenty, for it loses part of its privilege. Literature is seen as one kind of "inscription" or sign system among others. Semiology, the study of signs, nourishes this tendency; and Roland Barthes, its most protean and engaging prophet, is as interested in the culture industry, fashion, and popular art as in such classic writers as Racine and Balzac. He is himself rapidly becoming an institution, having received the accolade of the Modern Language Association and of Susan Sontag. Sixty thousand copies of the French version of *A Lover's Discourse* are said to have been sold in a little over a year. Ten of his books are now available in English, and he's beginning to have a guru-like influence.

What lies behind his success? Quite simply, he's a fine pedagogical

A review of *Image/Music/Text: Essays,* by Roland Barthes; selected and translated by Stephen Heath (New York: Hill and Wang, 1977). And of Barthes' *A Lover's Discourse: Fragments;* translated by Richard Howard (New York: Hill and Wang, 1978).

[38]

writer in whom toughness of intellect and a remarkable erudition have not killed readability and charm. He actually enjoys doing criticism. It does not seem to him a secondary or subordinated sort of work. We are allowed to see his mind thinking, tussling with metaphors, throwing off aphorisms, constructing and deconstructing systems. More of a scout than a pioneer, he brings essential news from the frontier; but his real importance, I think, might be in doubt were it not for his love of literature, constantly threatened but never overcome by ideological and scientific modes of thought. His passion for science stops short of wishing to substitute a more positive knowledge for what he has labeled "the pleasure of the text."

The dominant perspective of the thirteen essays collected in *Image/Music/Text* is semiology. Barthes extends the "empire of signs" over film and photography, music criticism, biblical narrative, the Bunraku puppet theater, and writing and reading as historically situated activities. Several essays, like the early "The Photographic Image" and the famous "Introduction to the Structural Analysis of Narrative," are frankly didactic. They review and expand the domain of a certain terminology: interpretive codes, narrational systems, functions and indices, denotation and connotation. Yet those impatient with special terms will not mind too much, for where else do they get, under the same cover, Beethoven and *Goldfinger,* the Bible and *Double Bang à Bangkok?* Besides, as the insights come fast, the terminology has to show athletic prowess in ordering them.

Barthes is perhaps most interesting when he focusses on the fate of reading in a modern technological culture. What makes a reader active rather than passive, a producer rather than a consumer? We see that semiology can be a weapon as well as a science, for it helps Barthes to demystify the realism of media that penetrate life more deeply than we have time to observe. Any medium that, like photography, pretends to give a direct image of reality hides its encoded and manipulative character. Nowhere else, Barthes remarks, "does connotation assume so completely the 'objective' mask of denotation." His careful analysis, revealing the coded structure, builds a resistance to those who fabricate "reality."

[39]

If Barthes' interest in mental hygiene seems familiar, it is because of our acquaintance with the New Criticism, which attempted to preserve culture in the 1930s by stressing the intellectual probity of artifacts as compared to political messages. It overemphasized, however, the independence of literature from what Saussure, the founder of semiology, named "the life of signs within society." Barthes shares with Kenneth Burke a refusal to exalt art at the expense of other cultural activities, while still rejecting vulgar sociology. There is an oblique or even gratuitous element in all sign systems, which the thinker can extend but not purge. Barthes writes of "a kind of voluptuous pleasure in inserting, like a perfumed dream, into a sociological analysis, 'wild cherries, cinnamon, vanilla and sherry, Canadian tea, lavender, bananas.' "

"Unfortunately," Barthes adds, "I am condemned to assertion"; and he attributes the fault to the lack, in French, perhaps in all languages, of "a grammatical mode which would speak *lightly*" of important matters. Must every philosopher be high-serious in style? Is there not a teacherly frivolity? The scruple does Barthes honor, and of all recent French thinkers he has the least German philosophy in him, no Hegel or Heidegger to perplex the mind, no Teutonic straining. He is technical without being heavy, and a professional without ceasing to be an amateur. His precise yet fluent prose treats personal insight and systematic concepts with equal courtesy: as different vocabularies to be matched rather than as dialectical contradictions. This makes him hard to type intellectually. He is a man of roles rather than of allegiances (some affinity with Gide in this); what he is producing is not so much an *oeuvre* as a series of texts or at best a *Roman de Roland.*

Yet when he does enter the realm of theory, he is indeed assertive. "Writing is the destruction of every voice, of every point of origin," he proclaims in "The Death of the Author," published close to the revolutionary turmoil of May 1968, and included in *Image/Music/Text.* This concept of writing, which he opposes to the idea of original genius, is elaborated into a theory—better, a vision—of literary history. Genius implies individuality. It is related to our image of the author as one who has a real and potent self that is the source of his creative talent. According to Barthes, however, writing always works against stability of self or any fixed meaning. As he puts it, literature "disseminates" (a fertility metaphor) rather than establishes truth. He introduces the word "scriptor" to make his point that, at least in the modern period, literature does not create something original and stable but rather a "multidimensional space in which a variety of writings, none of them original, blend and clash."

To some extent this re-envisioning of author as scriptor returns us to a medieval notion of the anonymous scribal artist. To locate the scriptor only in the modern period is obviously a myth; but the important thing for Barthes is that through this notion of scriptor we come to reinterpret all art, not only modern works. He wants to purge from criticism the Romantic idea of a personal genius writing a personal book that only he was capable of producing. Barthes proposes a belated and desperate theory of impersonality.

Already a century ago, Matthew Arnold denounced the "French mania" for translating ideas into a revolutionary program. The Anglo-Saxon reserve in matters of theory has something to do with the assertiveness of theory. (Compare Barthes' propaganda for a radical change in our perception of past works of art with T. S. Eliot's laconic statement of 1919 that a new work of art changes the "order" of all existing works.) Where we confine ourselves to "practical criticism," Barthes summons us toward an "unknown *praxis*," a form of reading that could match the blending and clashing energy of what he calls the disseminative text.

Like most French intellectuals, of course, Barthes is under constant ideological pressure, and especially that of responding to Marxism and allied forms of social critique. By his sponsorship of structuralism, and more recently of semiotics, as well as his special theory of impersonality, he seeks to reconstruct poetics in the midst of politics—a very broad poetics that includes narrative and symbol formation of all kinds. Gide could flaunt the gratuitousness by which art escapes social constraints; Barthes must justify it. He accepts the analogy of art to work or to a mode of production; also of writers to workers that produce meaning. But the obliquity of signs and the impersonal energy of literature show that art is productive precisely because it is plural and

[41]

escapes ownership by any one person (even the author) or social group. If ownership is anywhere, it is with readers.

All art aspires to the condition of music, as Walter Pater said; and rarely has a translation caught, like Richard Howard's, the musical genius of its original. *A Lover's Discourse* is a Passion narrative or recitative broken curiously into dictionary headings: from *"s'abymer/*to be engulfed" to *"vouloir-saisir/*will-to-possess."

The dictionary form, a cool and unrhetorical mode of presentation, lets us know at once that there is nothing private or confessional here. More important, it suggests that the lover, too, is not an original genius but rather an exploiter of received ideas and stock phrases. The lover acts the part of the lover. Convention prescribes his role; the arts supply his feelings and words. His anguish is nonattainment, but in the sense that he cannot bypass convention to realize his desire by more direct means. He is forced to magnify sign or fetish, token or trace, the loved one's "absence," which is the only "presence." In short, his desire—even when realized—remains unreal. Barthes associates this pattern, enacted so many times since Petrarch, with semiotic process. The ego on love's stage is a passionate machine: a restless producer and consumer of signs.

No distinction is made between a man's and a woman's discourse. Barthes remains a structuralist who will not give up his search for universals, even if they prove to be as arbitrary as linguistic forms. Language rather than anatomy is fate. How much evasion is there in this slighting of sexual difference? The "dazzling" of love, as Stendhal calls it with a nice lapse into English, is diminished in my mind by Barthes' indifference to sexual difference.

Yet Barthes is profound in showing that while the unstable and voluble sign is love's very element, it achieves exceptional permanence in the structures we call texts. The writings of Plato, Proust, Balzac, Boehme, Winnicott, Lacan, Schubert, Goethe—and more!—feed a meditation that also embraces conventional exchanges ("I-love-you/So-do-I") and anonymous fragments of inner colloquy. All these orders of discourse blend into a single musical mélange. And though the word "discourse" (as in the title) seems odd—it suggests a highly analytic writing purged of figure and fable—Barthes is clearly seeking to invest analysis with a music of its own. The beast of "discourse" is to be made beautiful.

Hence only the pleasure of the text is felt in this text about pleasure. Here is how Barthes describes what goes on between lovers: "Nothing but signs, a frenzied activity of language: to institute, on each furtive occasion, the system (the paradigm) of demand and response." Is this how a lover would perceive or speak his passion? Surely Barthes's language is a stylized, uncolloquial product, made up of technical expressions and exegetical *pensées*. His erotics of semiotics approaches at times the diction of the *précieuses* ridiculed by Molière.

Yet Barthes persists in his folly, and succeeds. Not only does the influence of the fortuitous and the trivial emerge hauntingly in love, but by refusing the novelist's way of dealing with the power of trifles—the way, essentially, of "Romantic irony"—Barthes rethinks Racine, Valéry, and the Neo-Classical tradition. The discretion and minimalism of signs is a "Classic" virtue, and what is signified recedes, as in periphrasis, until it approaches a second muteness. "With my language I can do everything," we read in *A Lover's Discourse*, "even and especially *say nothing.*"

Barthes, like Flaubert, writes that "nothing." Whether our language is veiled, as in the Classic manner, or exhibitionistic as in the modern, we confront, says Barthes, "the *muck* of language: that region of hysteria where language is both *too much* and *too little.*" So Barthes' own style shuttles between too much and too little, between operatic and Classic.

In this book, then, the "discourse of an Amateur," as Richard Blackmur called criticism, seeks to become "amorous discourse." Barthes as critic, semiotician, master of metalanguage, constructs an elegant confection out of his struggle with both fictional and systematic forms of learning. From these, by a recycling that literature is always meditating, he draws a new "primary" language. Jacques Derrida in *Glas* (1974) and Norman O. Brown in *Love's Body* (1966) accomplish, in very dif-

[43]

ferent ways, a similar feat. Is criticism finding its own style at last? Or recovering a formal possibility that is, in truth, very old? To make criticism creative, to reconcile learning with the language of love, inspired one of the first essays of the vernacular muse in the Renaissance, appropriately entitled by Dante *La Vita Nuova*.

The Malraux Mystery

EVERY LIFE poses a question. It consecrates an issue, sometimes by mere persistence, sometimes by a dedicated will that does not stop short of sacrifice and tragic outcome. We feel such a will or persistence in André Malraux, who died in November 1976 after reaching seventy-five years of age. His life was marked by an intensity which recalls Emerson's definition of the hero: he who is immovably centered. Can we begin to understand Malraux's interesting if perplexing career in the light of a central purpose?

Perhaps his denial of the kind of search here proposed gives us the clue we are looking for. "There are no more secrets," he said. There was about him a relentless and driven instinct for self-exposure. Not the kind that animated romantic confession or the darker prose of Dostoyevsky's heroes, but the kind we all suffer from in an age of speed and of the split second. Depth is explored, in such an age, only to be exploded—hence the penetration of the mystery story into so many fields, a mystery story that cannot be resolved. For as it is worked through it merely generates further mystery, or endlessly elaborated photographic surfaces. Think of the film *Blow-Up* or of Robbe-Grillet's novels and scenarios. Instead of a *whodunit*, I once surmised, we get the *whodonut*: the story with a hole in it.

It is amazing with what speed of action and notation Malraux's *The Conquerors* (1928) and *Man's Fate* (1933) move: we are clearly in an era where continuity is filmic, superficial in a deep sense. "His Majesty the Ego" is in danger of being elided by the tempo of events, by news-

The present essay was first published in January 1977.

[45]

mongering, stimulus flooding, political upheavals, mass movements. "Poisoned by speed" was Valéry's epitaph for our age. Against this self-alienation Malraux invoked a counterforce. "The greatest mystery," he wrote in *The Walnut Trees of Altenburg* (1943), "is not that we have been hurled by chance between the profusion of matter and the profusion of the stars; it is, rather, that in this prison of ours, we are able to draw from within ourselves *images* that have the power to deny our nothingness."

Where Pascal found only a religious defense against the terror of this nothingness, Tchen, one of the revolutionaries in *Man's Fate*, politicizes the terror he feels, then embodies it by hurling himself with a bomb against Chiang Kai-shek's car. As he determines to do that, "the only thing that his present state of mind did not transform into nothingness was the idea of creating those doomed Executioners, that race of avengers." Tchen's vision of a race of terrorists is the only thing that survives an all-consuming nihilism. It consecrates him after all, gives him an image, or what the author of *The Psychology of Art* will call an "anti-fate."

Malraux turned to art because the images that deny our nothingness are encountered there in a fraternal and more permanent context. But the world of art now includes the film, where speed factors itself into imagistic frames, or where the technical input is so great that we once again lose sight of the individual maker. And when we turn to modern painting or sculpture—there too speed meets us in the changeable style, the immense fertility of a Picasso, or in the very concept of metamorphosis itself. Central to Malraux's theory of art, it is said to have changed even the gods into pictures. It teaches us that no cultural values are absolute except as they are transformed by time. The work of the most solitary genius becomes fraternal despite itself. "We cannot separate," Malraux writes, "an important work from its metamorphosis, a 'Night-Watch' from what the centuries that followed believed they were seeing. It only exists within the framework of a dialogue, and it cannot be for us what it was for Rembrandt."

Malraux does not use "dialogue" lightly here. The epic history of art which he began to compose in the late 1930s animates all those silent pictures and statues made more available by photography—the "printing press" of the arts. Malraux was haunted by the life of images in time, their survival and change. A man like that should have been an iconoclast, someone so disturbed by the proliferation of images that he would have to destroy them. Yet the opposite happened. He became our greatest animator of paintings, sculptures, and masks.

We feel the tension, however; his animating fury seems at times quasi-erotic. It is as if he could not tolerate the mute or masked nature of all those still-life photos. He emphasizes the distorted features of a certain kind of art and opposes it to the sealed expression of Classical or Renaissance masterpieces. Under his reanimating gaze the art image is restored to its character of colored effigy: something that has died, like love, into transcendence, or "the desolation of reality."

Fable, says Malraux somewhere, is the nude of the narrative mode. It is to his credit that he does not use the enticement of fable—some "legend of the centuries"—to interest us in his epic survey. But he does allow himself the metaphor that gives his most popular book its title: *The Voices of Silence.* We all know the definition of a poem as "a speaking picture"; and for Malraux artifacts from anywhere on earth are poems that speak to each other and to us. (The world of art too was intended to end as a fine book.) In Malraux's novels, of course, or such memoirs as *Felled Oaks* (on de Gaulle), there is a similar gift of stylized conversation that hovers midway between the charged exchanges of Classical tragedy and Lucian's imaginary dialogues. The books on art are, in fact, a dialogue of the dead. Their author is a necromancer who knows that history writing is the nearest we will get to resurrection.

To "voice" his images, Malraux employs the principle of movie montage: a series of daring analogies supported by wonderfully glossy juxtapositions. Magic masks, nail-studded fetishes, and grotesque gods mingle in his books with the suave portraits of Leonardo or Titian, or contorted Western modes of sculpture, from Romanesque churches to the period of Brancusi and Picasso. But the most important "dialogue" remains that between the West (even after it has assimilated African and Polynesian artifacts) and the "undying East."

[47]

Malraux founded that dialogue in 1926, with his first mature work, *The Temptation of the West*. It preceded *The Conquerers* and was clearly an outgrowth of his Indochina adventure, when he rescued—or stole—Khmer Buddhas from the Cambodian jungle. *The Temptation of the West* purports to be an exchange of letters between a Chinese student in Europe and a Frenchman in China. It diagnoses our Western sickness unto action: a compelling game of self-alienation and self-isolation, totally different from the Oriental's careful extinction of the ego passions. This accelerating and strangely clairvoyant madness is what Western art reveals in its galleries, movies, and novels. According to Malraux, it all began in Greece, where man was first singled out as an individual by the gods he invented to put him in question.

But today the gods have died, or entered the museum. So it is the museum that now questions us. In the book translated as *Picasso's Mask* (1976) Malraux returns at moments to his obsession with the east. Takanobu's portait of the statesman Shigemori is called "the most imperative cross-examination of Western art." Malraux's animating force rivals that of Pater as he describes the Japanese masterpiece:

> Taira no Shigemori was a great minister around 1200. His life-size portrait—with legs crossed under an angular kimono that allows us a glimpse of the tiny and irreplaceable ornaments on the pale-blue, garnet, and salmon-pink accessories–is a form of absolute geometry, as eternal as a triangle, as sovereign as a *Guernica* attuned to the cosmos: an ideogram of the word "hero". . . . The materials of the portrait seemed as fragile as butterfly wings, just on the point of crumbling into dust, and held together solely by the architecture of the work. As rigorous as a Braque collage, black gashes against a dead background. The character himself has as little importance as the real women Italy transformed into Venuses. Had it not been for a kind of intoning from the beyond, one would have tended to think in terms of Cubist construction or of the folded papers children make—birds, arrows, little boats. Actually, that ancestral portrait is a ship of death, topped by the face of the dead man being borne away. It was difficult not to think of the way other civilizations have signified man—of what Picasso called "the Mask." In this case, the Mask was the painting itself. (*Picasso's Mask*, translated and annotated by June Guicharnaud with Jacques Guicharnaud)

[48]

Malraux views art through the art we know, which has influenced us, given us our present eyes—Picasso, Braque, cubism, and so forth. These modern mediations are not used, however, to jazz up a foreign work but rather to convey its fundamental austerity. What is intimated is that our museum must accommodate a style even more severe than was created in the period from Goya to Picasso. Malraux evokes an image that almost destroys itself as an image, a painting that denudes itself of its subject—here, one of the powerful men of Japan. *Shigemori* is more of a mask, more of a "mere painting" than the West has achieved. Haunted by the analogy between prehistoric art and the increasingly abstract and even ascetic mode of European painting after Cézanne, Malraux finds that Takanobu's "mask" has taken over the whole space of the painting, not only face but body as well.

Art is our sphinx, and Malraux has solved its riddle. There are no more secrets, he claims, now that we have recognized the convergence of East and West in the ascetic impulse that marks their greatest creations. But while in the East asceticism means peace, inaction, nirvana, in the West it denotes activism and possessiveness: erotic, religious, political furor. Consequently, the "art of Takanobu transforms ours into an art of antagonism. With the exception of subtle and private inclination restricted to Vermeer, Chardin, and Braque, something in our works of art is always fighting something else. Compared to the great art of Asia, our painting . . . indeed, all of western art, from the first Christian figures to Van Gogh, seems clearly to be an art of devastation."

E. H. Gombrich objects slyly that Malraux wants mankind to be a super-Picasso. This is true in the sense that "Picasso" includes Goya, El Greco, and a peculiarly Spanish art of devastation. But Malraux's real ideological debt was to Nietzsche and his view of the energizing and agonistic nature of Christian asceticism.

Nietzsche considered the death of God a logical outcome of the tortured image of Christ. That death must be proclaimed so as to confront Western humanism with its real aim and temptation: self-transcendence through any means, including nihilism. Had Nietzsche lived to see the invention of film, that too might have been valued for its ascetic potential. Walter Benjamin, quoting Pirandello, noted in 1936 the alienation effect of moving pictures. They separate a person from his "aura" and deliver only his "shadow" to the public. The actor, whether movie star or public figure, is divested of real presence. He too becomes a mask.

I shall return to this view of technology as an advanced instrument of self-torture. Malraux's view of human history takes us by way of Pascal and Nietzsche very close to Freud's "the goal of life is death." That certainly is the goal of many of Malraux's heroes, terrorists, adventurers—mortals too conscious of mortality. Freud enunciated his *pensée* in *Beyond the Pleasure Principle* (1920), a clear-sighted tract with a title that fits Malraux's career.

Yet in the novels that follow *Man's Fate*, Malraux modifies the Western, or activist, hero's descent into hell, his willful torturing and testing of the self. The later heroes as they move toward their fate also move toward a more redemptive theme, increasingly associated with the world of art. It is the theme of the living rescued from the dead. When Vincent Berger remarks at the end of *The Walnut Trees of Altenburg*, "I know now what those ancient myths mean which tell of people snatched from the dead," he expresses Malraux's belief that the idea of man's survival on earth is more dependent on the evidence of art than on the evidence of history.

But what sort of *evidence* is art? And what evidence, in particular, is provided by modern art? Oswald Spengler's *The Decline of the West* (1918) provoked the young Malraux to a refutation that became an independent philosophy of art. Spengler charged the modernist movement with decadence. He asserted that all cultures were subject to a law of birth and death, to a life cycle that went from barbarism to barbarism through a period of overcivilization. When a culture had reached the technocratic, or overrefined, stage, it would have to rebarbarize itself. What caught Malraux's attention was, in addition to the general theory, Spengler's use of art as evidence. Modern art was for Spengler an obvious reflection of the decline of the West, because of its interest in primitive forms and rejection of the picture space of the Renaissance—

that magical third dimension which endowed the canvas with something of nature's own power of representation.

Spengler's book has faded, though Northrop Frye recently paid tribute to it. Its ambition to sketch the outlines of a "Morphology of World History" is only a little more grandiose than Malraux's *The Metamorphosis of the Gods,* a secular epic in three volumes completed only a year before his death. It was Spengler's opinion, and Malraux had to face it, that there was more intelligence, know-how, and character in a good banking or engineering firm than in all of contemporary European art and music. "What are we offered today by that which calls itself 'Art'? A counterfeit music full of contrived noise produced by masses of instruments, a counterfeit painting full of idiotic, exotic, and poster-like effects, a counterfeit architecture which every 10 years 'founds' a new style on forms out of the treasury of past centuries (and justifies in this way whatever it wants to do), a counterfeit sculpture which plagiarizes Assyria, Egypt, and Mexico."

Malraux saw the hidden truth in that prejudice. What Spengler interpreted as overrefinement turning into barbarism was in fact a second and more broadly based Renaissance. The revival of the gods by modern art showed that our culture differed from all others in not rejecting their pantheon or museum, but tolerating and even resuscitating it. Picasso, for example, through his understanding of African masks and fetishes, was preparing us for a worldwide resurrection of art forms. So Malraux retrieves Khmer statues from the Cambodian jungle and is almost killed trying to discover from the air the city of the Queen of Sheba.

Malraux's apology for modern art magnifies the cubist program, already enlarged by Picasso, into a new myth of the harrowing of hell. His novels converge similarly on the theme of the living snatched from a realm of death. There is a legend that Christ will someday descend into hell, to save the virtuous non-Christians. What Malraux called the "Museum Without Walls" incorporates and extends the myth. Artists like Picasso, and technological developments like photography and film, are now rescuing the world's hidden treasures. Once in the museum, however, gods or fetishes metamorphose into pictures and statues; and many modern works too are estranged from their original function. "What do we care," Malraux wrote in *The Voices of Silence*, "who 'The Man with the Helmet' or 'The Man with the Glove' may have been in real life? For us their names are Rembrandt and Titian. The men who sat for these portraits have lapsed into nonentity. The effect of the museum was to suppress the model in almost every portrait."

Thus the Museum Without Walls changes our entire conception of art. We realize that what other cultures considered as the transcendent or the "really real" is simply the power of man anywhere to break through the world of appearances. This breaking of nature's images, a form of iconoclasm, produces new images—abstract, distorted, stylized—to which we give the name of art, and these today express simply the artist's exorcism of a strange, insidious, or overpowering world. It is our own creative strength we recognize, a violence from within pressing against a violence from without, as Wallace Stevens said of imagination.

One problem with Malraux's theory of art is the style which transmits it: his prose, like a chain of barely smoked cigarettes, extinguishes one insight in favor of the next. Contradictions are not explored but become part of a rhetorical surface that is intellectually hectic yet indulgently reminiscent. So concentrated, moreover, was Malraux on his own experience of art that he rarely acknowledged the thought of others: T. S. Eliot's concept of tradition, Valéry's and Walter Benjamin's observations on the way technology has penetrated our lives, and Lévi-Strauss' refusal (he is a true son of Picasso in this) to archeologize primitive thought.

That Malraux's theory may be based on the "negative Classicism" of post-Impressionist painting may also be problematic; but perhaps all theories of art have a parochial base and prove to be apologies for their time. Malraux has shown powerfully, in the light of the modern movement, how art is linked to a questioning of nature, to a "lucid horror of seduction" which allows man to survive the jungle of history and the internal jungle of his psychic combats. Even technology is part of that conception of art as an "anti-fate." Exorcism through the fetish or god figure was the technology of art in the religious ages; now that the artist knows he is not portraying a sacred realm, he must still break with nature either by the austere style of a Cézanne or by technological devices.

This anti-mimesis, or break with nature, is also seen, according to Malraux, in the life of the individual artist. He frees himself from nature by pastiching a great precursor's style. Giotto's sheep do not compete with real sheep but with those of Cimabue; but the young artist must then break with the seduction of the precursor, or the very style that helped him to question the "reality" imposed on him. It is always, then, the child that has to be overcome in the man; and perhaps, as the opening of *Anti-Memoirs* suggests, real manhood, real maturity, is out of reach. If there is a Malraux mystery after all, it masks itself here, in this repeated quest for virility and self-transcendence. But whatever his relation to his own childhood—a relation certainly as negative as Sartre's, or as that of Delacroix, who said children didn't interest him because they were "episodic beings"—Malraux's psychology of art contains a remarkable theory of anti-mimesis, and all future aesthetics will have to deal with it.

II

Illustration 1. "The Ancient of Days." Frontispiece, *Europe: A Prophecy* (1794).
cr.: Yale Center for British Art, Paul Mellon Collection.

Blake's Designs; Or, Conversing with the Man

And did those feet in ancient times
Walk upon England's mountains green.

CONCERNING BLAKE'S PICTURES, even the novice can make certain claims. Their polemic against the classics is as vigorous as that of his poetry or broadsides:

> The Classics, it is the Classics! and not Goths nor Monks, that Desolate Europe with Wars. ("On Homer's Poetry")

> A Warlike State never can produce Art. It will Rob and Plunder and accumulate into one place, and Translate and Copy and Buy and Sell and Criticise, but not Make. Grecian is Mathematic Form. Gothic is Living Form. ("On Virgil")

"Gothic Form," in Blake's illuminated printing, breaks the circle, like the pointed a Roman arch; the sphere or globe or "mighty circle" of heaven becomes a malevolent container of the energy within it; orb therefore turns into Orc, sphere into spear, or round forms into flaming spirals that peak, though not like a pyramid. In the frontispiece to *Europe* (illus. 1), the "Ancient of Days" crouches within such a Grecian circle, which the outstretched compasses will duplicate. But the compasses, though rigid, reflect the lumbar strength of a mailed or

Lecture delivered at the William Blake Symposium, British Art Center, Yale University, 1982.

scaled arm that alone breaks from the circle; while the apex of the geometrical instrument is evocative of the deferred vertical closure of Gothic archings that counterpoint Urizenic and self-enclosing types of boundary. The hunched relation between arm, trunk, and legs, more fetal and massive in other depictions of Urizen (illus. 2), is modified by the elongated shoulder that terminates in a hand mocking, by such mathematical extension, the parted fingers of a priestly blessing. The perfect inverted **V** of the compasses complements the **V** of their rough, rocky, anthropomorphic source; that inverted **V** shape, moreover, could be a parody of **V** for Vision, or a Roman **U,** Urizen's initial.

My last thought obviously goes too far; it discloses not something demonstrable but the impotence of interpreters who search for iconic meaning in pictures that resemble, at one and the same time, crude cosmographic emblems and heroic frescoes. We are offered a form of hieroglyphics that owes a debt to emblem books inspired by the very technique of printing: a technique that "expansed" or "opened" ancient esoteric wisdom, the book of nature and the book of God, to the eyes of all. The compasses, in this light, circumscribe the very benefits they bring; their spearlike tip is not a thyrsus or lingering finger (illus. 3) through which a vital influence still communicates itself. We move away from the hand, like mechanically printed page away from manuscript.

In illustration 1, however, there is still an unusual coexistence of Greek and Gothic form. The illustration seems an apt representation of a famous dictum in *The Marriage of Heaven and Hell.* "Energy is the only life and is from the Body and Reason is the bound or outward circumference of Energy." The Gothic element in Blake's pictures is often more extravagant or militant. Consider a Fuessli print from Boydell's *Shakespeare Gallery* (illus. 4). Giants mingle with such fairies as the "small Sir" who dictates to the poet both in the "Introduction" to the *Songs of Innocence* and in *Europe.* These forms, tall or tiny, cosmic or comic, are always, despite clear outlines and stylized proportions, of a most peculiar texture. Are they animal, mineral, or vegetable? The fluid sculptural bulk of the *larger* figures (illus. 5) gives the appearance

[58]

of an articulated skeleton or anatomized body clothed with recycled flesh, with a postnatural garment. As elastic forms they are certainly more Gothic than Grecian, yet their face, unless bearded or coiffed, is relatively insignificant compared to their body, which by this disproportion becomes a torso and sends us back to Michelangelo's own source of inspiration in, for example, the *Belvedere Apollo*. In Blake's pictures, whatever the motto or iconic intent, haunches are all, just as for the interpreter of Blake, I fear, hunches are all. It is the *déhanchement* or strong stationing of Blake's figures I will now try to understand by quick excursions in and out of his poetry.

"Mighty was the draught of Voidness to draw Existence in." This sentiment from the *Four Zoas* embraces fear of death, fear of losing the natural world (or the body image associated with self-identity): above all, fear of formlessness. Blake is more Greek than he knows. Yet fear mingles with desire, and Blake names that desire, tautologically, "the indefinite lust"—that is, lust for the indefinite. And here we come upon a central paradox. Is not vision itself necessarily in the sphere of the indefinite: the "draught of Voidness" that literally "draws" its own picture of existence, and so draws it in, to fill, impossibly, a void? There is a wind that blows through Blake's pictures, and it is as hard to stride that blast (illus. 6) as for the mother to bring back her child in Spielberg's *Poltergeist*. "Night the Ninth," for example, like so many Blake visions, takes it start from this sense of absolute loss or separation, which causes a panic reaction, as if a vacuum were being created that would suck everything in; and this spooky hole—whether in the mind or in the body of the world—has the ironic effect of making Blake's shapely figures hold on so tenaciously to nature that it begins to tremble and crack and cycle into apocalypse:

> Terrified at Non Existence
> For such they deemd the death of the body. Los his vegetable
> hands
> Outstretchd his right hand branching out in fibrous Strength
> Seizd the Sun. His left hand like dark roots coverd the Moon
> And tore them down cracking the heavens across. . . .

[59]

We understand why Blake's poems detail one creation story after another, why there are endless theogonies, and worlds hammered, crafted, woven, compelled into form. "The hard dentant hammers are lull'd by the flutes' lula, lula." We behold with wonder Enitharmon's looms and Los' forges, the Spindles of Tirza and Rahab and the Mills of Satan. Everybody is fabricating new bodies for old; afraid, and justly so, that the natural body may not suffice. We also understand why Blake's illuminations depict such strong tarsal figures, all haunch and hand, balancing their step against the "draught" into which they must go, like Milton into that fiery, cloudy void (illus. 7), or Los stepping, in the frontispiece to *Jerusalem* (illus. 8), over an obvious threshold, into a Gothic doorway that opens inward only. (Near his right hand is an effulgent disc, a picturesque compromise between a Diogenes lantern, a solar symbol, and a discus, and which seems to attract as well as emanate beams pouring into the dark interior.) It may be happenstance that Milton's shape bifurcates his name into parts that read, backwards, *Lim Not;* but according to David Erdman, it is a fact that there are erased graffiti on the wall of the door Los is entering, and they read: the "Void, outside of Existence".

Let me shift my perspective slightly. Despite passages that capture and delight our imagination, to read Blake remains a disorienting experience. The reason, quite simply, is that we lose our footing: we cannot get from the "Visionary forms dramatic" to either a stable system of coordinates or, most of the time, to common forms of life. Who can follow, let alone decipher, all the relations between Blake's theoids, as one resounding name and terrific shape replaces another? It is possible, of course, to make out action and reaction, but not really to plot or unify every metamorphosis. Blake's vortex of formulaic and repetitive events depicts a War in Heaven that is also a Mental Fight, yet to identify actions or agents in historical or psychological terms is. only a rough possibility. The organizing principle seems to be a deceptive specular mimicry, each giant form binding or liberating or giving birth to or dismembering or imitating or mocking the other. Yet here and there the true Voice of Feeling rings out and calls for the one greater man, the one true form, the human body divine:

> O how can I with my gross tongue that cleaveth to the dust,
> Tell of the Four-fold Man, in starry numbers fitly ordered
> Or how can I with my cold hand of clay!
>
> (*Milton:* Book the First)

Consider Plate 76 of *Jerusalem* (illus. 9): which of the two figures in the picture is the true form or archetype, and which the "Spectrous body"? In this scene of religious *imitatio,* a man's outstretched arms respond sympathetically to those of Christ, just as Plate 99 (illus. 10) depicts a flame-like merging of two bodies, one human, one divine. Yet again, which is the archetype here? The image remains divided, with the man's arms forming an open and Christ's a closed triangle. The embrace is incommensurate: not a conversing so much as rapture or sublime rape.

Even at the highpoint, then, of these prophetic books, as a carnal conversation moves toward the joining of divided forms—toward an embosoming that is a reintegration of the body—even at this point a disjunction remains. In Plate 99 the *déhanchement* becomes an uneasy levitation; the feet lift like flames; they cancel the firm terrestrial stance of Man in Plate 76: a stance modifying, even as it mirrors, Christ's nailed limbs, so cruelly elevated against a groundless ground, more like a void or an abyss or something too faintly either rock or tree.

The pictures, then, are no less disorienting than the poems: they also seem to present figures that cry with Urizen:

Where shall we take our stand to view the infinite and unbounded
Or where are human feet for Lo our eyes are in the heavens:

I would like now to return to a familiar though disputed text which is clarified by this question, precisely because the speaker cannot find human feet, and so becomes a frenetic, or, in Blake's own words, a "dizzy inquirer."

The poem is "The Tyger." Critics immediately try to fix the character or identity of its speaker. But the speaker is doing away with himself—

Illustration 2a and 2b. "Bearded Figure, Squatting." From *The First*

Book of Urizen.
cr.: Yale Center for British Art, Paul Mellon Collection. *photos:* Joseph Szaszfai.

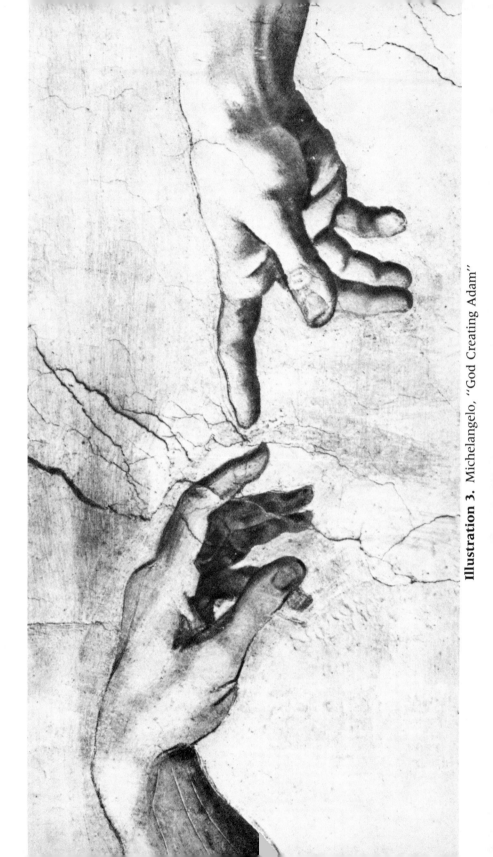

Illustration 3. Michelangelo, "God Creating Adam"

Illustration 4. H. Fuessli, "A Midsummer's Night's Dream" (Act 4, scene 1).

cr.: Boydell's *Shakespeare Gallery*

Illustration 5. "Three Figures." From *The First Book of Urizen.*
cr.: Yale Center for British Art, Paul Mellon Collection. *photo:* Joseph Szaszfai

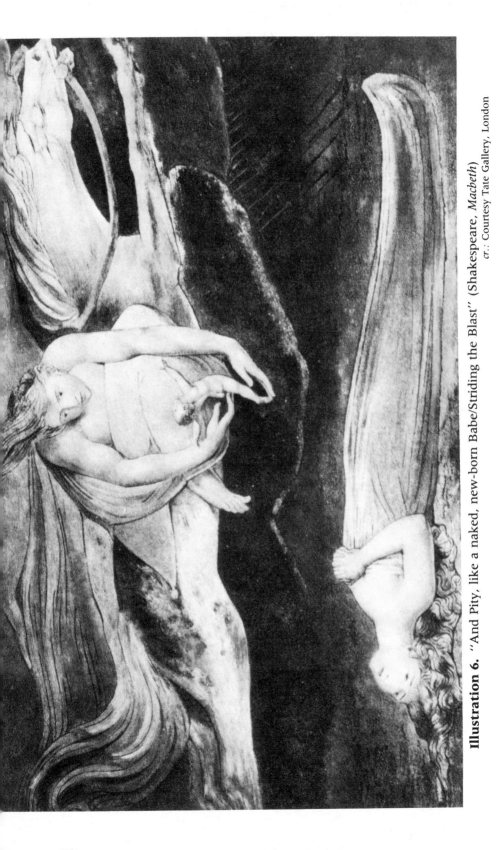

Illustration 6. "And Pity, like a naked, new-born Babe/Striding the Blast" (Shakespeare, *Macbeth*)

cr.: Courtesy Tate Gallery, London

Illustration 7. "Milton"

Illustration 8. "Los Stepping Over Threshold."
Frontispiece to *Jerusalem*.
cr.: Yale Center for British Art, Paul Mellon Collection. *photo:* Joseph Szaszfai.

Illustration 9. "Two Figures." From *Jerusalem.*
cr.: Yale Center for British Art, Paul Mellon Collection. *photo:* Joseph Szaszfai.

Illustration 10. "Two Figures, One Human, One Divine."
From *Jerusalem*.
cr.: Yale Center for British Art, Paul Mellon Collection. *photo:* Joseph Szaszfai.

annihilating his identity in a false way. The subject of this poem is how
to understand imaginatively what exists—that there is something (creation) rather than nothing. The speaker fails to find a human footing,
however, as the eye of his imagination is drawn into its own "draught

[71]

Illustration 11. "Piper and Child."
From "Introduction" to *Songs of Innocence* (1789).
cr.: Yale Center for British Art. Paul Mellon Collection. *photo:* Joseph Szaszfai.

of voidness." Blake turns the Second Commandment of the Bible against itself: you cannot "limn" (or "limb") the void, or a God who is officially conceived of as an unrepresentable presence, a power who has made something out of nothing. If you try to limb the void, you get such dishumanized forms as this tiger, or a distorted conception of what creation is. By the time we reach the hysterical "What dread hand? and what dread feet?" (in one copy, "What dread hand Form'd

Illustration 12. *". . .* like a New born Man issues with songs and Joy." (See p. 75)

cr.: Yale Center for British Art, Paul Mellon Collection. *photo:* Joseph Szaszfai.

thy dread feet"), the "dentant hammer" of the verse is about to dissolve the stubborn structure of English itself. The speaker draws language as well as existence "in" the void, by dint of trying to imagine a creation *ex nihilo*. As Blake writes in his prose notes to "A Vision of the Last Judgment": "Many suppose that before the Creation All was Solitude and Chaos. This is the most pernicious Idea that can enter the Mind . . . and leaves the Man who entertains such an Idea the habitation of Unbelieving Demons. . . ." The stolid cat with the Mona Lisa smile Blake draws for us at least walks on all fours, like a good simile: its surefootedness mocks both Classical imitation, which reduces natural feet to rational proportion, and the religion of nature, which reduces the *imitatio Christi* to vacuous meditations on the creature.

A final remark. "The Tyger" is not a conversation but a fearful if rapturous meditation that fills a void with demons, and jeopardizes not only human eyes, hands, and feet—that kind of symmetry—but also a sense of what it is to converse, to speak humanly. The poem's portentous questions do not expect, do not allow, a reply: they are a howling in the void, similar to that which meets Urizen, when he journeys in "Night the Sixth" through the Abyss. There he beholds "the forms of tygers and of Lions dishumanized men." "His voice to them," Blake continues, "was but an inarticulate thunder . . . nor voice of sweet response could he obtain." Indeed, though Urizen would "stand and question" them, they "were not Vocal as in Climes of happy Eternity / Where the lamb replies to the infant voice and the lion to a man of years." Instead, they attack the Man, "sore / Seizing upon his feet."

In Blake's theriomorphic fantasies, those feet are the alienated feet of man, which like his eyes, hands, and ears have to be converted by verse. But first verse must itself find its true feet or measures again, its own fearless symmetry. Therefore, at the conclusion of "Night the Ninth," Blake discloses a vision similar to that which introduced his entire poetical work. The "Introduction" to *Songs of Innocence* is a conversation—in more than words, in words and responsive acts—between piper and child (illus. 11). There is no riddle here, no sphynx to seize upon our or the verse's feet. So, too, at the end of "Night the Ninth" a *calling* is depicted that brings in not only hands and feet but also Countenance, the turning of the face toward a voice—in short, a calling that can be countenanced.

> And Man walks forth from midst of the fires the evil is all con-
>   sumd
> Each morning like a New born Man issues with songs and Joy
> Calling the Plowman to his Labour and the Shepherd to his rest
> He walks upon the Eternal Mountains raising his heavenly voice
> Conversing with the Animal forms of wisdom night and day. . . .
> In the deep caves beneath his limbs renewed his Lions roar
> Around the Furnaces and in Evening sport upon the plains
> They raise their faces from the Earth conversing with the Man.

Coleridge and the Counterfeit

THE VENERATION that accompanies the posthumous birth-days of great men rose to an ambivalent climax in 1972, bi-centenary of Samuel Taylor Coleridge: poet, literary critic, me-taphysician, political philosopher, psychologist. With the definitive edition of his works in progress, and the first publication of the amaz-ing *Notebooks*, Coleridge scholarship reached high tide. We may soon know almost everything about the thoughts of this "myriad-minded" dreamer, who would wake from his nightmares ("Night is my hell") to record them, hour and date as well. The terrors of the day were often not far from the terrors of the night: he led a miserable, drug-ridden, love-frustrated life. Indeed we know so much even now that we know too much, and seek—as he did himself, in looking always for method—a standpoint from which to master his "being's being" which he once defined simply as "contradiction."

The Coleridge File has more than enough in it to suggest a first-rate mystery. No great change came into the world because of Coleridge, yet extraordinary claims have been made on his behalf. For John Stuart Mill he was, with Bentham, the great seminal mind of his age; for George Saintsbury and Basil Willey, the greatest of our poet-critics; for G. W. Knight his three most popular poems are a miniature *Divine Comedy;* while I. A. Richards has honored him as the Galileo who led us over the threshold of the modern study of language toward powers comparable to those of physics. Yet even as Mill was elevating Coler-idge to the status of philosophic patron, De Quincey, a contemporary opium eater, suggested that his indebtedness to German philosophy approached plagiarism. (De Quincey knew; he had done some poaching himself.) Coleridge's reputation grew; but like a shadow so did the evidence of borrowings from Schelling, Schlegel, and others.

They were not the borrowings of a journalist or literary middleman but massive, unacknowledged adaptations from obscure as well as famous sources. Coleridge praised Kant, but he forgot Steffens, Tennemann, Tetens, Maass, Jean Paul. . . . There are also, of course, his acknowledged sources, often exhibitionistically displayed—erudite quotations from Greek, Patristic, Neo-Platonic, and Latin writers. "Genial coincidence" or not, there is scarcely an idea that is indisputably his own, however finely absorbed. Add to this a poetic talent of the first order dissipating into what, compared to *The Ancient Mariner* and *Kubla Khan,* is an antiquarian and hollow-sounding style, a purely rhetorical sublimity, and the picture darkens beyond relief. Coleridge becomes a kind of ur-Borges who failed to recycle his readings or, more ominous still, an adumbration of the English Mind's incapacity for truly systematic thinking.

Norman Fruman's *Coleridge, the Damaged Archangel* is not so much an explanation as an indictment of the poet, conducted with relentless vigor and humane bitterness. There has rarely been a more arduous attempt at decanonization. Coleridge's genius is acknowledged but only to emphasize the mystery of its ruin. ("Damaged Archangel" is Charles Lamb's vivid phrase describing Coleridge in 1816, and reminds us of Milton's Satan in Hell: "his form had not yet lost / All her Original brightness, nor appeared / Less than Archangel ruined.") The brunt of Fruman's charge against Coleridge is that his literary kleptomania was not an occasional aberration, due to the special stress of a failed marriage, severe doubts about his poetic gift, drug addiction, etc. It was, rather, habitual and basic: inseparable from his literary life, and more deeply enmeshed in it than opium itself.

The habit started as a juvenile technique for writing verse through pastiching ("vamping") other poets. It developed into a transcendent skill with such masterpieces as *Kubla Khan* and *The Ancient Mariner,* where the debts (as J. L. Lowes showed in *The Road to Xanadu*) are enormously complicated and subtle, and it continued compulsively for the rest of his career. Lowes' dignifying hypothesis of a "well of unconscious cerebration" is rejected, or at least challenged; and so is the other "Cambridge defense"—that it is not the borrowings that matter but their interaction with Coleridge's own thinking. Dissecting each reputed achievement of the master, Fruman reveals the hidden debt or the evaded acknowledgment, until the poet's manipulations are just too evident.

That Coleridge should, for example, antedate his own discoveries is an understandable lapse, but that he should use this to accuse others of plagiarism is passing strange. W. J. Bate has speculated that, tormented by his conscience, he left guilty clues all around. The trouble is that he also tried to implicate others. In Chapter Five of the *Biographia Literaria* (which describes his intellectual development), after parading as his own the erudition and insights of a German scholar, he suddenly turns on David Hume and accuses him of stealing important ideas from "St. Thomas Aquinas on the Parva Naturalia of Aristotle"!

There is something sad and ludicrous in this which cries out for interpretation: Why does a man, when originality is in his reach, abdicate it *and* put himself into moral jeopardy? The evidence accumulated in Fruman's 600-page brief certainly proves his point that "Coleridge was by no means so guiltless and disinterested a man of letters as is commonly supposed," and that, to gain an adequate biography, one would have to imagine the possibility that "he was cunning and deceitful, at times treacherous, vain and ambitious of literary reputation, dishonest in his personal relations and an exploiter of those who loved him, a liar."

Written with passion and elegance, Fruman's book is an explosive gift to all Coleridgeans. It will be attacked for its bias (Coleridge is once again made to owe Wordsworth too much), for its interesting if sensational speculations on the poet's homosexual tendencies, and for its method for spotting debts that is so reductive that it would leave no author undamaged. It assigns to private morals or psychic mystery faults that have to do more with the ethics of the literary marketplace of the time—with its party politics, religious polemic, and ruthless journalism. There is also some naïveté: Fruman gives the impression of having

[78]

been an idealist who was shocked to find literature contaminated by the *needs* of the writer.

Yet the book cannot be dismissed. It is a remarkable exercise of the adversary method applied to literary criticism, and a vision of judgment that will haunt Coleridge scholarship a long time. Instead of authority Fruman finds a confidence man, instead of the *Wunderkind,* a vamp of the Western word. The facts he so remorselessly accumulates are, for the most part, well known. But he coheres them, extends rather than extenuates, and draws a consequent if somber portrait.

Then why is his book finally so wrong? Some will say Fruman has gone too far. He has given us mainly one side of the man, however human—the blind side. We must take Coleridge as he is, Southey once declared, "unequalled for moral imbecility and intellectual strength." Fruman's judgment is not so cold or crass, but he too exaggerates the gulf between the self-aware and the self-deceiving Coleridge. Where is the delightful, protean artist, with his perspicacious interest in method, his subtle wording, and, above all, his modern power of introspection? We see instead an intellectual whose eloquence on "double-touch" hides sexual numbness and whose thirst for the unknown, whether German philosophy or native exotica, feeds a blind appetite for literary fame.

Fruman has gone far—yet the truth is he has not gone far enough. He fails to see that Coleridge is not a special case, that his charlatanism is hardly of a perplexing or freaky kind. Is not every claim to fame or authority, especially in the modern period, shadowed by imposture? Fruman's unhistorical isolation of Coleridge takes a poet out of his cultural context. He is best understood in the company of equally strange figures: Collins, Smart, MacPherson, Chatterton, and Blake.

All these eighteenth-century writers labored under what Harold Bloom has characterized as the "anxiety of influence," or a crisis in authorial identity. All are, in one way or another, counterfeiters and plagiarists. Born too late—into an "enlightened age," which had no use for sublime verse; a "retrospective age," which could see only through the eyes of previous generations—they are as much the victims as the inheritors of the past. If the sons are plagiarists, then the fathers are vampires. "Why should not we also enjoy an original relation to the universe?" Emerson asks in *Nature*. Why not, indeed? The odds, nevertheless, are against us. For Coleridge, in addition to the Classics, the Fathers, and the Philosophers, there was the immediate and over-bearing influence of Spenser, Shakespeare, and Milton. In that company he would never be more than mock-sublime—like Neo-Classical poetry in its better moments.

I do not question Fruman's evidence, only the use he makes of it. He confirms, indeed, how deeply disturbed Coleridge was by the precedence of others. Coleridge felt doomed to recover his nature from books, to steal it back from the library. His "abstruse research" is a Promethean ploy. A modern—that is, a *mediated* man—he seeks to be his own man nevertheless. There are strange word chains in the *Note-books* that show, in their very form, his perplexity with influence, causality, derivation, connection—highly technical matters, yet also deeply human: "Spinoso-Kantian, Kanto-Fichtian, Fichto-Schellingeal Revival of Plato-Plotino-Proclian Idealism." Or this mock-definition: " 'Thing': id est, thinking or think'd. Think, Thank, Tank = Reservoir of what has been thinged—Denken, Danken—I forget the German for Tank / The, Them, This, These, Thence, Thick, Think, Thong, Thou. . . ."

There is a complex disgust in Coleridge not only with the Germanico-metaphysical part of his mind but also with the whole enterprise of analytic thinking about origins. Fruman has failed to link the plagiarism issue to the curse of secondariness, of not finding an "original relation," which afflicts us still. He effectively impugns the veracity of Coleridge, but the veracity of his art is another matter. Nerval, also haunted by a loss of identity to the past, writes a poetry of *chimères* ("dream-songs") even more magical and fake than *The Ancient Mariner*. From Melville through Gide, Mann, and Borges, the theme of the con man or falsifier is closely linked to that of the artist, and reflects the troubled relations of authorship to authority. We remain in the age of Coleridge and Emerson. Fruman, I fear, is blinder to Coleridge than Coleridge was to himself.

Symbolism Versus Character in Lawrence's First Play

EVERYTHING LAWRENCE has done is of interest; and his first play, written in 1912 just preceding *Sons and Lovers*, though published after it in 1914, is no exception. It is strange that this play was not produced in America till Arvin Brown staged it at New Haven's Long Wharf Theater in late 1973. *The Widowing of Mrs. Holroyd* is not a difficult play or even an ambitious one; and it is certainly not discontinuous with the Lawrence we know best. But it does pose a problem: how "realistic" is it? On the surface, it is a drama about a coal miner, his wife who aspires to a better life, and a third man, completing the triangle, who offers to take her and the children away from a dismal and seemingly brutalizing existence. The New Haven production centered everything on the coalminer's wife, on Mrs. Holroyd's character buffeted by a choice to be made: whether she should leave her husband. Involved in this choice, and deepening her character, is the developing consciousness that there can be a choice for her, that she dare think in those terms. The other man in the tight little colliery town which is the play's setting is Blackmore, an electrician in a profession "higher" than her husband's and who seems more attuned to her "educated" sensibility. The play ends with Holroyd's death in a pit accident, which stalemates Mrs. Holroyd's decision, and leaves the audience with a *pietà* of two women, the wife and the mother, lamenting over the miner's child-like corpse.

The play may seem at first to support a realistic interpretation. Mrs. Holroyd is certainly the most visible person in the drama: the first two acts end in her agreement to go with Blackmore, while the last act puts everything once more in doubt. (In the New Haven version, Blackmore's exitline, "I shall come tomorrow," is followed by Mrs. Holroyd's slow, repeated negative shake of the head—she will not go with him.) Staging the play this way has the clear advantage of emphasizing its historical and realistic qualities: it would have been a momentous decision for a woman circumstanced like Mrs. Holroyd to run off with Blackmore. It is, nevertheless, a mistake to see Lawrence's drama as a piece of realism and a simple, if powerful, study of a character.

Only the actors' incalculable force of presentation could make it succeed in this light. Though an actress may triumph in the part, Mrs. Holroyd herself—her agony, her passion—cannot, because what motivations the playwright allows us to glimpse are insufficient or trite or unresolved. There is no genuine way of simplifying this drama into a study of character—unless "character" is a muddled composite. Is Mrs. Holroyd frigid, as some in the audience thought; does she have "needs" she is afraid to acknowledge to herself? Is the basic difficulty between her and her husband sexual? Or is it social, attributable to class and education? "A girl who went to Grammar School should not marry a coal miner but rather an electrician"—surely that can't be the moral. And if she is frigid, from whatever cause, why does a sexual electricity surround her from the beginning? Must we reduce her most forceful and pathetic statement about her husband to social attitudes infected by a belief in progress or (Victorian) self-improvement?

> I wanted to be a wife to him. But there's nothing at the bottom of him, if you know what I mean. You can't *get* anywhere with him. There's just his body and nothing else. Nothing that keeps him, no anchor, no roots, nothing satisfying. It's a horrible feeling there is about him, that nothing is safe and permanent—nothing is anything. . . .

The resonances of this cry reach, surely, beyond a woman trapped in a colliery town, as her husband is trapped in the mine itself when "some stuff" falls in. We try hard to deprovincialize her, and to make her a more universal figure, despite her snobbish or squeamish attitudes, merely hinted at in the first two acts, but re-enforced by the playwright in the third: through the naïve device of her children's social mimicry which opens the act (Minnie being the "superior" woman, Jack refusing to play for long the role of inferior or intruder), then through the resilient innuendoes of her mother-in-law. For how cheap it would be to reduce "You can't *get* anywhere with him" to social climbing, or "There's just his body," etc., to resentment of sexual demand. If something clear, pure, and dignified speaks here, it is a woman's fear of false solidity and her desire for a true body or anchor. Mrs. Holroyd does not feel consubstantial with anything—her husband, the setting, her own body or sexuality—even though everything about her seems to glow with a solid material flame. ("It is dark twilight, with the room full of warm fireglow. A woman enters from the outer door. As she leaves the door open behind her, the colliery rail can be seen not far from the threshold, and, away back, the headstocks of a pit. The woman is tall and voluptuously built. She carries a basket full of washing. . . .") What a deceiving image! That room proves to be empty, not full, and no substantial action can fill it. At its fullest it will harbor a corpse being cleansed prior to burial—it is the antechamber to grave-pit as well as to coal-pit.

Yet I seem to have drawn Mrs. Holroyd's character after all. Perhaps the conflict between Arvin Brown's production and my own reading of the play is not as radical as first intimated but turns on what character elements to stress. Perhaps all I am saying is that Lawrence's "realism" of character and setting is deceptive, that this apparent realism is a dream which turns into a nightmare. All solids here are fraudulent, though not the need for roots itself or the material imagination which bathes them in a sensual and poetic light. Perhaps . . . but I would immediately add that the *notion of character* may itself be a false solid, a kind of insurance we take out to make life (or the play) succeed. The later Lawrence, it is well know, talked in terms of will rather than character, and as if vital forces of a quasi-mystical nature, rather than characters, were playing the human drama out.

Where I quoted from the stage directions prefacing the first act, I meant to suggest that the play's action is strongly modified by a *sym-*

[83]

bolic element which cannot be fully subordinated to character analysis. Symbolic action may re-enforce character, but it may also be subversive of it: especially of the claim that everything depends on the choices of realistically motivated persons. How do we interpret the fact that so much takes place on or near the "threshold" from which the colliery rail can be seen, as Mrs. Holroyd enters and leaves the door open? That touch, in this play, is endued with near-sacred emotions? That Mr. Holroyd's three entries are all forcible or difficult, bursting through the door into his own house, or being awkwardly carried in, feet first? Or that, at the end, there is indeed "just his body," transformed into "something else" only if we see those two women laying him out as projecting the emblem of a disturbing secular *pietà?*

The reader, relieved of the presence of real actors, their urgency, their incarnation of "character," develops those images almost too much—they are "negatively" present, since this is a drama and not a poem or a novel. And there is no suggestion on my part that they cannot be integrated with stage production. The question is what the symbolic action means and how it can be respected by a *mise-en-scène*. I have already suggested that to respect it would entail a rethinking of the notion of "character" in the play.

Some symbolism can certainly be developed in terms of character, and some as stage business. In Arvin Brown's version the audience is made to feel the importance of the sense of touch, as in the washing of clothes or of a helpless body; and this is linked to Mrs. Holroyd's half-fearful, half-squeamish "Do you think I could get past him to come inside," when her husband is lying knocked out in the doorway. Similarly, that Mr. Holroyd doesn't cross that doorway by himself, under his own power, can be made to reflect his character. He can't face his wife directly, we think, or else he knows that his wife must be "forced." As the grandmother says, Holroyd lives on suffrance in his own home: psychologically speaking, he is always battering his way in. Moreover, if we enjoy the rowdiness and tumult of Act I, scene 2 so much, is it not because we sense that this battering of Mrs. Holroyd is necessary? Nothing is gained by the husband, but she gains some self-definition, or at least a bit more articulateness. So Blackmore, in a parallel though more tortuous scene, puts her to the question until she cannot but agree to decide between him and Holroyd.

Yet, having paid our respects to character, let us also consider how the symbolic sweep of the play subverts it. Does everything, as the American premiere suggested, turn on the choice Mrs. Holroyd must make? How can it when Blackmore, the serviceable electrician, is not a real choice? Though as a "character" Blackmore is delineated clearly enough, "characterization" here only helps Lawrence to reduce him to a sort of device *(homo ex machina)*, eliminated when its function is over. From the very beginning of the play our sympathy with Holroyd does not make Blackmore's part easy. Both are testing the woman, and one "manages" it more cleverly than the other, but our hearts aren't necessarily on the side of the managers. If we view the play as a whole, in its symbolic sweep, we see that the real troublesome presence is Holroyd himself. Even dead he is troublesome—his corpse in that room so much too small for him. His presence weakens, willy-nilly, Blackmore's, except when the latter becomes a quasi-maternal figure. Blackmore is most there when he is most motherly, when he wipes Holroyd's bloodied face and foreshadows the final laving of that body by the two mothers. He exists less as a man than as an uncle, a motherly father, an ideal whose time has not come. Thus it is not Mrs. Holroyd who says no to Blackmore but the symbolic action of the play itself.

Yet Holroyd, whose presence weakens that of Blackmore, is himself eliminated by the play. *The Widowing of Mrs. Holroyd* might equally well be called *The Casting Out of Holroyd*. Not simply because there is an impossible, puritanical split between the "Angel in the House" and the "Brute in the House." That kind of thing becomes funny, and Lawrence here and there does verge on the comic. But the Casting Out of Holroyd, when comic, is so in an ominous and terrible way. The final scene is unmistakable in its symbolic impact, for, to adopt the grandmother's language, it "lays the child out." A child is what Holroyd becomes; and perhaps he has never had the chance to be more, to be fully a man rather than a child. (The mothers won't let go; it is an obsessive theme from *Sons and Lovers* on.) If Lawrence invents a death that leaves the coalminer's body uninjured, it is because he wants to show, symbolically, that they are washing and laying out a man-child. Does Woman always want a child rather than a Man? Should this idea be present, Lawrence's drama is as much about elemental drives as about character. "Character" in fact would function at best as a device to be eliminated or transcended. Mrs. Holroyd's "superior" aspirations, for instance, would be an extension of her womanly will, of her desire to "bring up" a child, rather than a reflection of the ideas of a social class.

At this point it is easy to fall into that metaphysical murk (blood consciousness v. mental consciousness, biological "will" v. social conditioning, Father-Son v. Mother-Son theology) from which Lawrence constantly struggled into art. Yet can we interpret the symbolic movement of the play without a minimum of metapsychology? Adopting for the moment a Freudian perspective—as the simplest, most consistent metapsychology so far evolved—it is possible to link the Lawrentian or "weak" notion of character to the absence of a real *triangle* in the drama, to the elision, that is, of the father as a mature, realized presence. Whether the visionary Lawrence is struggling to emanate or eliminate that third presence is a matter for scrupulous judgment and cannot be decided here. But the play, if we respect its symbolic action, does touch back to a pre-Oedipal situation, where there is no character conflict and only (for good or bad) the child-mother relation. I said "touch back," and it is indeed true that Touch plays a part in the pre-Oedipal relation which seems to be recovered by its strong and tender role in Lawrence's drama—the symbolic action centers on hands and feet and, of course, on the contrast between educated English and the strange, caressing, semiarticulate vigor of the colliers' dialect, their "mother-tongue."

The first curtain (Act I, scene 1) of *The Widowing of Mrs. Holroyd* falls on an awkward and inconclusive line.

MINNIE *(plaintively):* Can't you stop, Mr. Blackmore?
BLACKMORE: Why, Minnie?
MINNIE: So we're not frightened. Yes, do. Will you?
BLACKMORE: Frightened of what?

MINNIE: 'Cause there's noises, an' rats—an' perhaps dad'll come home and shout.
BLACKMORE: But he'd shout more if I was here.
JACK: He doesn't when my uncle John's here. So you stop, an' perhaps he won't.
BLACKMORE: Don't you like him to shout when you're in bed?
They do not answer, but look seriously at him.

The Long Wharf production tided us over by inventing a bit of stage business that has Blackmore stay and sing a song with the children. The threat of "shouting" fades into song and a promising domestic scene.

What explains the original ending? From a Freudian perspective the shouting that children fear when they are in bed (after the curtain has fallen) evokes the dark, mysterious sounds of a "primal scene." They cannot see what happens; they are dependent on guilty ears; and their fear interprets. They imagine a brutal action which Lawrence's play represents. The importance of this speculation does not lie, for us, in its genetic-explanatory power. Rather, it allows us to understand better the dramaturgic flaws in Lawrence's drama, and to link his "weak" notion of character to this "weak" curtain. Lawrence is always in the dark with respect to the father-husband relationship. He is as uncertain about it as children are, interpreting those shrouded sounds and being compelled to project their own drama in the dark. There is no need to reduce the primal scene to the sexual act, but it is certainly an adult grappling or mating which results now in domination, now in submission. One could go so far as to say that the ability to confront one's own imagining of the primal scene, to see it clearly, neither more nor less mysterious, neither more nor less animalistic than it is, divides the mature (and Oedipal) from the immature (pre-Oedipal) mind. Lawrence's weak curtain makes us uneasy: we want a sharper separation of child and playwright, less rather than more continuity. But he, for a moment, looks through to childhood.

Thus the weak curtain implies that the author is withdrawing as playwright / manager, having become unsure of his own "character." This uncertainty, this half-merging with the dark, is also in his tanta-

[87]

lizing, undeveloped suggestions that Mrs. Holroyd and Blackmore have brought about Holroyd's death by "unconscious" wishing. He would like the Unconscious to be the real playwright, and may not realize that this might be the ultimate triumph of the pre-Oedipal stage—or, specifically, of that childish and fearful illusion Freud called "the omnipotence of thought." By eliding himself as well as casting out the other men, could not Lawrence become as "obscure" as some of Thomas Hardy's protagonists? The weak curtain blots him out.

The Minor Art of Borges

THE REPUTATION of Jorge Luis Borges in the United States is astonishing. *Labyrinths* and *Ficciones*, the first substantial translations of his work, appeared in 1962, one year after he shared the International Publishers' Prize with Beckett; by then he was sixty-three and well known in his native Argentina and elsewhere in Latin America and Europe (though not in Great Britain). These two volumes were followed by *Dreamtigers* (1964) as well as collections of lesser note. Several books have now (1970) been devoted to him; his conversation is avidly taped and printed; he has served as a visiting professor on several American campuses; and the claim is sometimes heard that he ranks with Joyce and Kafka. This despite the fact that Borges has cultivated a methodical modesty and never departed from the minor genres of essay, story, and short poem.

What can this new sampler tells us about the truth of his reputation? It is devoted mainly to the stories, and has a wide chronological range, taking us from 1933 to 1969. But it remains an incomplete gathering, since rights to retranslate some of the most famous pieces (such as "Tlön, Uqbar, Orbis Tertius") could not be obtained. It is irritating to have Borges divided this way by competing anthologies, but it may be a kind of justice since he is, in fact, a scattered Orpheus whose prose parts lament a fading power. The inventor of the "Aleph," a miniaturized replica of all visionary experience, knows that humankind cannot bear much fantasy. The present volume, with its charming "Autobio-

A review of *The Aleph and Other Stories 1933–1969*, Jorge Luis Borges; edited and translated by Norman Thomas di Giovanni in collaboration with the author (New York: Dutton, 1970).

graphical Essay" and its chatty comments on the stories, is well adapted to readers who wish to be reminded of great art rather than to experience it. With Borges they can flee from too vivid an enchantment into a little wilderness.

There is an art which, like the sounds of a clavichord, provides a perfect setting for thought and conversation. The art of Borges is generally like that: cool, well-tempered, with a consciously easy pace. His questers delay, or are delayed; and even in the most dangerous or baffling situation they have time to look off at the trees, at a "sky broken into dark diamonds of red, green and yellow." Lönnrot, the trapped detective in "Death and the Compass," quietly offers his killer a mystico-mathematical reflection before being shot. What is most human—the "irrelevant texture" of ordinary life—escapes from a ruthless plot by running into such asides. Each story, however, continues to demand its victim despite the intricate delay, the charm of detail.

The humanizing asides are felt even more in the stories about the gauchos of Argentina. Here Borges, a reporter of traditions, weaves his thoughts directly into the narrative. In his unusual blend of ballad bloodiness and familiar essay there is sometimes as much reflection as plot: the brutal knife fight in "The Challenge," little more than a paragraph long, is swathed in asides. Its naked brevity is relaxed by the narrator's comment on the courage of the gauchos, their exact way of dueling, an extract from the *Inferno*, *Moby-Dick*, and so on. While time comes to a point which is also a knife's point, the story swerves, a mental picaresque, from the pure moment of encounter.

No Borges story is without this pointed moment, this condensation of time; yet it tends to be undercut by a mock-realistic setting or a whimsical narrator. So the microcosmic Aleph is found in the cluttered cellar of a second-rate poet, the unsavory Carlos Argentino Daneri. The only way that Borges can conduct his narrative is, like so many symbolists before him, by viewing ordinary life as a needful distraction from some symbolic purity. His humorous realism—names, dates, and nature motifs formulaically introduced—is a pseudo-realism. Even the gaucho stories, for all their local color, are fantasies—knives *are* magical in them, and the knife fighter's sense of invulnerability is like the eternity experience recorded in so many of the "fantastic" stories.

The fatality of form, the humanity of the aside—these are the most obvious pleasures given by Borges. There is, in addition, a wealth of small invention, perfect handling of gradual disclosures, and an elegance that makes life appear sloppy. Mixing, with charming ruthlessness, fantasy and fact, Borges reverses that "decay of lying" which Oscar Wilde (one of his favorite authors) had already deplored.

Beyond all this we feel for the narrator, for *his* quest. He is clearly a man trying to get into his own stories—that is, wishing to discover himself rather than an image. Like the fire-priest in "The Circular Ruins" Borges sets out to dream a real man but seems unable to dream of more than an intruder. Thus in a great many stories a stranger or interloper comes onto the scene and is given a predetermined lease on life before being eliminated. This figure, whether person or magical agent, never effects a lasting change: having played out its role, or lived its bit of dream, it is "sacrificed" like the woman in the late story actually called "The Intruder" (1966) or the upstart gaucho in "The Dead Man" (1946).

Surely, Borges himself, as artist, is that intruder. He comes to art belatedly—deeply conscious of traditions that both anticipate him and will survive his bluff. He is their victim, a dreamer who finds he is dreamt by a larger than personal symbolism—the formal world of legend and archetype with which he must merge. He may think he has mastered the magical instruments called symbols, but they have their own will. "I began to wonder," he writes of a strange knife fight in "The Meeting," "whether it was Maneco Uriarte who killed Duncan or whether in some uncanny way it could have been the weapons, not the men, which fought."

This living sacrifice of person to myth, of the individual to magic instrument, haunts Borges and is a source of his peculiar pathos. "I live," he says in "Borges and Myself," "I let myself live so that Borges can weave his tales and poems, and those tales and poems are my justification." We are not far, after all, from Mallarmé's remark that the world was meant to become a book. The symbols that purify us also trap us in the end. Symbolism may be nothing more than the religion of overcultured men; and Borges—curious bibliophile, ardent comparatist—is its perfected priest.

Plenty of Nothing: Hitchcock's North by Northwest

We find certain things about seeing puzzling,
because we do not find the whole business of seeing puzzling enough.
—Wittgenstein

C ABLE TELEVISION occasionally opens a twenty-four-hour movie channel free of charge, to tempt viewers like myself. I confess I succumb; not only because I quite enjoy an hour here, an hour there, of mindless watching, but because I become fascinated with the fact that so many of the movies fall into a formula pattern that can be endlessly varied. A person fights his or her way through, against impossible odds: where the intelligent thing might be to give up or get away, the individual becomes the just one, the involved one, struggling without help against an organized mob, which may include the police itself. Moreover, about these films there often hovers a ballet-like aura; they orchestrate sights and sounds more than sights and words. Fights, chases, and pantomimic scenes of mute eying and sleuthing are relieved only as necessary by expository dialogue. In the Bruce Lee films only the ballet, really, counts—the marvelous gestures, grunts, crashes, sighs, and quasi-verbal phaticisms. We know perfectly well that almost everything is dubbed, that the sound track is superimposed on the action; yet our enjoyment resembles that of seeing dancers on stage and hearing the music to which they move. The difference is that in the realistic cinema, motion and sound seem to come from the same source, which allows us not to think about their relation.

In short, we are transported into a utopian sphere, a secular seventh heaven where what passes for love or justice is winged by pain as by music, and the film is at once a ritual ordeal and a dance of triumph celebrating the ecstatic end of an obsessional quest. From no higher perspective can I view Alfred Hitchcock's *North by Northwest*. Its gaunt luxuries are quasi-oriental; the face of Cary Grant is a vulnerable mask; the face of Eva Marie Saint blandly expressive; together they form a hendiadys, as stylized and slick as the smooth rock face over which they must finally climb to the upper bunk of marital happiness.

Not only, then, do words have to compete with images; they have to compete with a sequence of images that barely need words—with that absence of words; and, additionally, with sound itself in the form of a powerful score. The technique of film composition allows hundreds of shots of a particular scene, "pieces of film" as Hitchcock calls them, that can be spliced as the director wishes; but there are no "pieces of words" unless they become exotic or erotic syllables.

In *North by Northwest* words are generally specious, as in the bad-faith monologue of Cary Grant to his secretary (they don't make secretaries like that anymore!) which opens the film; or they are entrapping lies; or jerky, cool banter, similar to motions in the silent movies; or deliciously inappropriate comments (Saint to Grant, after his harrowing escape from the deadly plane, an encounter which she, of course, had helped engineer: "How did it go today?"). Though there is no counterpoint or deliberate dissociation of image and sound, as in Resnais' *Last Year at Marienbad*, meaning is a sur-face at best. The face of those worded images remains smooth, slippery; they are pictures determined not to be words; they insist on a pictographic as well as semiotic content, a nonsensuous visual stenography. Especially, therefore, do we relish the sequences: long after other details of the film are forgotten, we still recall Cary Grant hunted by the plane with almost no cover, all the redcaps being twirled around, the angular face-off (one of many) of Grant and James Mason at their first meeting, or the final twilit getaway. A choreographic quality dominates image as well as word, effaces everything except surfaces and the precision of the orchestrated sequence.

[94]

Plenty of Nothing: *North by Northwest*

I have some affection, even admiration, for Hitchcock. Yet many European pictures do more for me, however heavy their symbolism. How tediously searing the end of Werner Herzog's *Stroszek*, for instance—those conditioned fledglings performing their stupid dance. I resent that, too; but I am moved by the overt choreographic symbol, as by almost every major French, German, Italian, Polish, Spanish, Czech film that deals with types that remain persons, and where you feel a more creative relation between the actor and the part, or a greater freedom in the actor who assumes the part, in distinction from a relation between actor and director. In Hitchcock everything is on a string, the director's umbilical cord; and the string is cut when and where he wants it.

No wonder mother keeps intruding. She is the watchful presence, mocked at the beginning of *North by Northwest*, and returning alarmingly as the bogus housekeeper at the end. And when I see Cary Grant in that eternal business suit (which he eventually sheds), I think of him as an overgrown dressed-up kid (remember those sailor suits?) or expect him to change at any moment like Clark Kent into . . . *Superman*. Wouldn't mother be surprised if she saw him now! Well, mother is always there, and sometimes she *is* in for a surprise. But no one, of course, could be more watchful than the director, more designing and controlling than Mother Hitchcock.

Hitchcock's precision is legendary. Nothing is left to chance in plots filled with chance encounters. The theme of control or of mastering the uncontrollable is everywhere. At the beginning of *North by Northwest* Grant has everything firmly in hand, yet things immediately get out of hand. The first casual indication concerns his mother; he has asked his secretary to phone her, but then realizes she cannot be reached by phone. Anxious to correct his mistake, Grant, as Roger Thornhill, unwittingly enables the error that precipitates him into the plot: the bellboy pages a Mr. Kaplan, and as Roger gets up to send his mother a telegram, he gives the abductors cause to think he is answering the boy—that *he* is Kaplan. From another angle, of course, this *hasard objectif* hardly matters; it merely motivates an irrational and absurd intrusion that throws the emphasis on how Roger will face a disorienting course of events. He is immediately divested of his identity, one that sits on him as easily as his suit. Only toward the end is he momentarily back in control, when he tricks the Professor and rescues Eve, as played by Saint; but not even then, because the last saving shot—I mean the one before that by which the camera guarantees a happy ending—that shot comes from on high and is an *ex machina* ending keeping the director in charge.

Hitchcock's eye-in-the-sky shots are famous. In *North by Northwest* there is also the glimpse of Roger as fugitive, taken from the top of the United Nations building; a more notorious example comes in *Psycho,* when the camera swoops down, screeching and killing, as the detective reaches the top of the stairs. "This matter is best disposed of from a great height," Mason (Van Damm) says ominously, planning Eve's death. The improbable ending is a high-angle shot that saves as it kills; yet that it saves is not for sure. The penultimate image of Roger and Eve bedding down may be a fantasy flash.

There is generally an oblique angle of this kind within the right angle of the picture frame. For though things coincide—that is, meet at the angle—are not all meetings *trucage?* The angle becomes a slope, a slippery slope: from the strangely tilted credits, turning into the reflecting plane of skyscraper windows, to Roger climbing the steel beams of Van Damm's hideout and the airplane that has to calculate its angle of descent; from Roger in the death car spinning on top of the cliff, to the lovers' hanging onto the edge of Mount Rushmore. Cars and trains, in Hitchcock, are mere vehicles to remove the ground from under you; to put someone else's skids on you; in the scene on Mount Rushmore the rock face becomes treacherous terrain and creates a comic cliffhanger.

If understanding means finding something firm to stand on, then understanding is often removed from both character and audience. We have to take pleasure in the illusion of control *and* in seeing that illusion evaporate. Remember Roger's expression when he thinks he has outwitted another eye-in-the-sky, that plane? Exhilarated cunning, and then a funny abject perplexity. An equally sustained sequence is Roger's roller coaster ride, his drunk bravado in handling the car as he pretends he is in control. In *Strangers on a Train,* where the sinister-angle theme is symbolized by Bruno's psychotic design, his *crisscross,* everything that can does go out of control. Think of the carousel at the climactic finish, with its vertiginous turmoil of hands and feet, of hands against feet; hands and feet, they haunt us throughout this film too.

Where there is the desire for control, there is the fear of things not in control, of going out of control; yet what is the nature of those things? Are they the images themselves as fantasies? Do these images have a "nature," a knowable "substance," or are they surfaces in essence: as smooth or tough as faces that have no certain relation either to privacy of thought or to the words issuing from mouth instead of from eyes?

In literary criticism the question of substance often coincides with that of high seriousness: but "high" in Hitchcock is an angle from which to shoot. The question of substance or seriousness frustrates many viewers: they enjoy Hitchcock's movies, as I do, in an inconclusive and famished way. What is there to understand? There is fascination rather than understanding. The characters have little depth: they are flat, they simply fall for, or toward, each other. They are "blanks," decoys often: persons that need to become real, or be saved from their own role-playing. The heavy psychoanalytic stuff, even in *Psycho,* points to a crypt or a vacuity, like the middle initial in the R. O. T. that appears on Roger Thornhill's monogrammed matchbook, signifying a central blank or zero.

One might argue that in "pure cinema," as it has been called, the framing of every detail replaces questions of substance: that all things empty, as it were, into a cinematic, primarily imagistic, field. The medium itself constitutes a denial of the "myth of depth." Yet is not the world viewed, to echo Stanley Cavell, a world view? Is there something to know or not? To say there is a "language of images" is to substitute metaphor for analysis.

Some progress can be made by returning to our first concern: the relation of images to words in Hitchcock's films. To diminish the space given to words raises the question of the importance of images. Yet it is hard to claim that a Hitchcock movie makes us trust images rather than words. To some extent, in fact, because the words have a screwball charm—especially so in *North by Northwest*—they are lighter on the mind; the images, however, as silent as they are striking, gain their haunting significance mainly by repetition and juxtaposition. They do not have an "inside" more verifiable than the words. Those who claim there is a language of images must mean there is a nonlanguage of images: that the edited sequence has a logic all its own. Things are not helped by the fact that from a certain perspective, that of the written script, the images dub the words—*dumb* them, sometimes. Understanding the editing process, moreover, adds to the problem, since editing involves decisions on what in a potentially infinite series should be shot or selected. It brings back the question of the control exerted by a director, especially one who prefers the authority of the commonplace to iconoclastic experimental techniques, and elides himself into a presence as conspicuously inconspicuous as his fleeting appearances. No other auteurs have Hitchcock's *concept* of style, though they all have a style that singles them out.

Can we define Hitchcock's style in conceptual terms? Might it not be better to talk about his technique or speculate on themes that recur as if they were obsessions? I will argue, however, that we can understand our fascination with him, even if that fascination resists the analysis it provokes.

The principal compositional feature of movies after the silent era is that montage now affects sound as well, so that editing is not only deciding what to shoot, cut, splice, but how to place sound itself, how to accommodate it to the spatial form, or, better, the spatial rhythm, of the images. Moreover, since in the history of the medium the silent image came first, the sounded image—the synchronization of sound and image—is not an automatic gain. It is something to justify, like the third character in Greek tragedy or the third dimension of pictorial perspective. Each new technique, even when intended to be in the service of mimesis, of lifelikeness, alters our consciousness of what life is like. It has a critical as well as an illusionistic dimension: in Hitchcock's case, it makes us aware of the power and impotence of words compared to images. As Stanley Cavell has remarked (in *The World Viewed*): "It is the talkie itself that is now exploring the silence of movies. . . . With talkies we got back the clumsiness of speech, the dumbness and duplicities and concealments of assertion."

Assertion is one thing, art another; they stand in a relationship of opposition. By assertion Cavell means, at this point, the aggressive summing up of a person or a truth in words, a summing up that is meant to impose or deceive. Assertion, in the plot of *North by Northwest*, begins with the bland, imposing stream of Roger's dictation, and continues along a more intense, explicit plane when Roger is denied his own identity, and so is forced to reaffirm it. Like the moving camera, or the network of rails itself, we track from this opening toward a now converging, now diverging, pattern, and never stop being amazed that the "subject" carried down those tracks, as the plot gains momentum, is not derailed, that the switching, splicing, matching, crosscutting, leads to closure instead of an indefinite parallelism or *frayage*.

The problem, then, could be stated as the relation of art to assertion in this vertiginous context. Art finds what can be ranged *against* assertion without being *for* weakness—that is, without allowing the vertigo of indecisiveness or nonidentity to foster by reaction even more dangerous—psychotic or Cold War—assertions. The issue of weakness is central in the detective story. You can't afford to be a sucker. You can't even afford to seem to be one. How can anything except the aspiration to invulnerability and total control survive? In the political sphere this aspiration is coupled with a doctrine of righteousness. Yet art, we know, has always been considered a weak sister, a feminization of culture. It is worse than religion, which, being self-righteous, retains some political clout. Hitchcock takes *the* macho genre, the detective story, and gives it a nonassertive strength, the peculiar strength of art. He creates a music of images, films that could be characterized as urban ballet. Yet they are utterly different from the American musical as it produces *its* form of urban ballet: *West Side Story* and such descendants as *Hair, Fame, All That Jazz*.

[99]

No doubt, as in that other tradition, there is in Hitchcock a movement toward marriage or communion, toward a renewed pastoral oneness with woman, city, or cosmos. In *West Side Story* the mean streets are transformed: gang warfare leads to a larger mythical atonement through the spirit of carnival music. But Hitchcock mocks his mock communions and will not touch massively operatic devices. I don't recall a moment as blatantly communal as the scene in Frank Capra's *It Happened One Night* when the people on the bus are drawn into singing "The Daring Young Man on the Flying Trapeze."

Though Hitchcock too leads us back to a transcended or obsolete form, in particular the silent movie and its rural vestiges, what he wishes to carry over is their economy of means, which is the opposite of a carnivalistic catharsis. His films keep to a *pas de deux*, and are often nearer to ballad than ballet: they are elliptical narratives, as grim as folk tales in their plot. I sense the "Twa Corbies" behind *Psycho;* and many Hitchcock characters could have come out of Hardy or the *Spoon River Anthology* or the "novel turned tale" (Jacques Barzun), as in O. Henry.

It all hinges, in any case, on Hitchcock's sense of economy. In *North by Northwest* we move from city to country, or to a silent milieu, a treacherously empty milieu. In that emptiness the slightest trace becomes charged: you neglect it at your risk. We barely notice that as the bus opens in the cornfield scene it discloses the warning (first glimpsed in the open door of the Chicago train): "Please watch your step." The spectacular develops out of a mere dot on the horizon, as with the crop-dusting-man-hunting plane and the inferno of its crash.

It is with time as with place: every shot counts. Other contemporary thrillers are crowded by comparison. Their suspense is created by multiplying an action, by expense. But Hitchcock is a penny pincher. A particularly thrilling scene occurs in *Strangers on a Train,* when the variable length of a tennis match is juxtaposed with the time it takes the killer to get to the fair and darkness to fall. A similar deadline effect is created when Roger has to catch Eve's attention before she is taken onto the arriving plane and so to her death.

Another kind of reserve also pressures time. Hitchcock's protagonists may be placed in a situation where they cannot know what the stakes are, so that a childlike game of bluff ensues. Roger acts blindly throughout the first two-thirds of *North by Northwest*. The film, it is true, has no word-scene as charged and implicating as the opening conversation between Guy and Bruno in *Strangers on a Train,* or as casual and scary as that between Marion and Bates in *Psycho*. Yet words are not wasted in *North by Northwest*. The banter can turn dangerously precise, payed out like hard cash in the Depression. That clerk at the ticket window, wondering why Roger is wearing dark glasses indoors: "Is something wrong with your eyes?" Roger: "They're sensitive to questions." Roger to Van Damm: "I don't deduce, I observe." Or, my favorite, Van Damm to Roger: "Games—must we?"

This *must* involved in what should be a *game* leads back to the film as art. We go to films to pass the time, to play. We expect a representation, not an assertion; a timed magic that confines us to our seats, that glues eyes and ears to the screen. Yet on that screen we see people who cannot tolerate time except by controlling it. Time is there to scheme with, to lick one's fantasies with, before striking like a clock, or as neatly as Bruno's "Are you Miriam?" "Yes," and the mute strangling that follows at once.

"Games—must we?" From what I have said it is tempting to conclude that an economy of scarcity mingles uneasily, in Hitchcock, not only with Hollywood largesse (its expense of spirit) but with a compensatory game compulsion involving the director as *magister ludi*. His fabled neatness means little if we do not see through it as well as by means of it. As viewers, we are kept off balance between so much and so little; a paunchy Hitchcock pares his medium and disappears from sight. We see as in a very bright glass darkly.

To insist, however: do Hitchcock's images reach some sort of inwardness, at least an "echo of thought in sight"?

Consider Roger's ignorance, which obliges him to use his bare eyes. They repeat the dumb focus of the camera eye. The compulsive viewing by a person who knows next to nothing makes him teeter on the verge of finding out too much. Through Roger's eyes we approach a deferred moment of revelation. That moment becomes inseparable from his quest, because it should deliver him not only from ignorance but also from the necessity of testing and role-playing: it should convert *role* into *identity*, something that is what it is, knowable through and through. "Now I know in part; then I shall understand fully, even as I have been fully understood" (I Corinthians 13:12). Yet this transparency is the predicament rather than the resolution of desire. For against it, against such "exposure" of the self, can there be a cover? The blanket Bates asks for at the end of *Psycho* is as useless as Roger's dark glasses, or the name he chooses, or the starved corn that gives him momentary shelter.

Indeed, the tension I have described has its Gothic culmination in *Psycho* where the eye avenges itself on the eye, because it is so knowing. Bates kills in order not to be watched, not to be seen. Escape is sought from that eye-in-the-sky, or wherever it zooms from at the beginning of the movie as it enters birdlike an anonymous window in— of all towns—Phoenix. The human predicament here is the impossibility of protecting one's inwardness from an intruding, alienating, tricky eye. Bates flees from this eye by washing all ocular proof down a sinkhole (cellar, swamp) as dark as the pupil or the sexual cavity.

Let me recall that sequence from *Psycho*, so brilliant in its obsessional detail that it reflects on Hitchcock himself, and suggests that not words alone but also images are subject to his cinematic hygiene. We are shown Marion in the shower, letting it make love to her with its lustrously spending overhead eye; then, after the stabbing, which we scarcely believe, sinking as though satisfied, not dead; then a still of her still eye and the final lustration, the housewifely care with which Bates's mop and bucket perform the erasure, leaving nothing behind— a no-thing, rather, a place that is cursedly clean, that should have no claim on sight. "Pure cinema"? What is evoked is an *ultimate* purification or "inoculation." To see, oneself unseen, as at the movies, is only less than the ecstasy of an unseeing seeing: of going beyond the non-language of images to the non-language of non-images, or a glance that is not guilty, that is both knowing and pure. "I am nothing. I see all" (Emerson).

Why are we willing to go such lengths to indulge the fantasy of guiltless viewing? In *Dressed to Kill,* for example, Brian de Palma's remake of *Psycho,* the violent plot is but a device to let us enjoy a number of erotic scenes. In order to ogle a woman in a shower (who plays at "being seen without being seen") we are obliged to endure the emetic of several bloodlettings. There is only one fine portrayal that escapes the camera's heavy visual breathing. It takes place in the Metropolitan Museum and shows Angie Dickinson absorbed in art. She gazes with a steady glance, a Mona Lisa kind of smile, at the pictures, and the stray viewers viewing the pictures; and we *almost* recapture the innocence of inwardness or self-effacement, of vanishing into the act of viewing.

What of inwardness in *North by Northwest?* That film is almost too healthy. Roger learns vigilance without being traumatized. The psyche is not involved, or not as a perverse emptiness, always escaping from being watched and therefore ever wary. It is there only potentially, in the ingenious plot idea of the dummy agent who does not exist, who is inferred exactly like the "fingered" psyche by purely external indices (suits, room numbers, etc.). His visibility is a trick function of his invisibility. Roger, however, who barely thinks, who is hardly given time to think—he is portrayed as a silly, yet at best courageous and instinctive, creature—turns up again and again, as apparitional as a ghost. In fact, after disliking him, we become his accomplice, because his heroism does not have the support either of extreme intelligence or any other expensive or ingenious equipment: he throws the enemy off balance by simply reappearing, sporting no weapon other than his own eyes, hands, and feet. *North by Northwest,* glossier than most of Hitchcock's films, uses the overenlarged optics of cinema and the mechanically rousing formulas of detective fiction to honor a purely human economy. Grant is not granite; Eva is no statue. Hitchcock humanizes, even tenderizes, the triumph of the will, exhibiting it in its simple, relentless, unenlarged, unmechanized form.

Despite those huge, unmovable faces of the Presidential range, and despite the fact that every spot within the reach of "camera reality" is either monumental or ominous, we adventure toward a very simple place, that is our own—purged, ideally, of fear and guilt. It should be free of those strange vanishing points that disrupt ordinary life and make the most familiar acts—seeing, talking, eating—overconscious. I have called *North by Northwest* utopian because it cannot give up the fiction that there exists a good place of this kind, and a good marriage in that good place.

A last comment, however, must focus on Hitchcock's own morality as filmmaker. What is his attitude toward the inbuilt giantism of his medium, toward the machine of a camera that penetrates the field of sensibility and creates "panoramic sleights" (Hart Crane) so powerfully illusionistic that even when we remind ourselves of their fictive nature they may enervate our capacity to respond to less massive stimuli? "No one can intensely and wholeheartedly enjoy and enter into experience whose fabric is as crude as that of the average superfilm without a disorganization which has its effects in everyday life. The extent to which second-hand experience of a crass and inchoate type is replacing ordinary life offers a threat which has not yet been realized" (I. A. Richards).

Of course film is not the first medium to raise the problem. It exacerbates the "application of gross and violent stimulants," Wordsworth had noted toward the beginning of the Industrial Revolution. For Wordsworth frantic novels and news-mongering generally expressed a mortal danger inherent in industrialization, as it crowded people into cities and blunted their senses by replacing natural rhythms with a machine-made environment. This intrusion of the machine, or any such artificial enlargement of the senses, into all aspects of ordinary life, has been analyzed by many sociological thinkers aware of Hollywood and Madison Avenue as well as of totalitarian modes of propaganda.

Hitchcock recognizes machination as a problem that existed before the machine gave it an uncanny extension. He tries to bring it under his control by various means; yet to control it may encourage a "mastery" that may have spawned the monster in the first place. As a director Hitchcock alternates between tricking us into a self-conscious, impotent complicity with visual fascination, and parodying his own magical enterprise by the camera's (and the story's) cat-and-mouse game, one that makes viewers realize how endlessly exposed they are to the manipulation of appearances. The viewer is the ultimate "darling decoy" (Eva's fond description, toward the end, of Roger).

"Pure cinema" is moral only in the sense that though the camera is invisibly guided, we cannot throw off our complicity with it. It expresses our own automatism: viewing as an act of baffling and intricate perversity that would like to, yet cannot, come to rest. Through Hitchcock the uncanny eye becomes a canny mechanism, but still a mechanism. Filming is the good use of bad omens.

Epilogue

The spectatorial attitude of moviegoers is that of most persons in our culture as well. Through Hitchcock's manipulation we become Romans at the circus, enjoying the gladiators or Christians facing the lions. By deciding who should live or die—that is, when and for how long we should identify with the characters on stage—he makes us understand the inbuilt callousness, the cultural sangfroid of our situation as visual consumers. Through his films we realize how difficult it is to be moral without taking the camera into our own hands, or initiating a program to educate the eyes—perhaps through the ears, or by becoming aware of a necessary interaction of visual and aural. It is a fact, I think, that the visual arts in this country are not a serious part of the curriculum except in special schools. We rarely use our eyes creatively, and we are certainly not encouraged to *think* about them.

But an educational system that condemns the visual media to marginality is bound to render its students all the more passive and susceptible. This is not to argue that we should replace reading with visual education; on the contrary, reading should be intensified—that is, associated with the study of film, television, and the arts generally. They too are texts. We have not caught up with the fact that, as Henri Le-

[105]

febvre puts it, "the sense of hearing has acquired a greater aptitude for interpreting visual perceptions and the sense of sight for interpreting auditive ones, so that they signify each other reciprocally." The senses, he adds, "are becoming 'theoreticians'; by discarding immediacy they introduce mediation, and abstraction combines with immediacy to become 'concrete.' Thus objects, in practice, become signs, and signs objects; and a 'second nature' takes the place of the first, the initial layer of perceptible reality" *(Everyday Life in the Modern World)*.

Lefebvre tries to account for this development and then to criticize it. His account rests on an attractive yet simplified historical speculation, of the kind introduced by Spengler and continued by McLuhan. He posits a "decline of referentials" and attributes it to technological advances that climaxed around 1910 in the "reign of electricity." However thin his thesis may be, it does connect city life, the media, and detective fiction. We are now faced with a new, quasi-religious duplicity of the quotidian, an authentic inauthenticity that produces "intolerable loneliness" within the very heart of modern society's unceasing stream of communication and information. We have learned, in short, to depersonalize images and words, to merchandise them like any other goods. "Of all the referentials," claims Lefebvre (this was written circa 1968), "only two are still left standing; one, philosophy in the highest sphere of culture; the other, in the most trivial and commonplace sphere, everyday life." But to have everyday life as the sole reference point is unendurable. So, in fact, "we are left with one referential and that the prerogative of higher culture." "One might as well say," he concludes, that "all referentials have vanished and that what remains is the memory and the demand for a system of reference."

The decline of referentials, or the "uncoupling," as Lefebvre also says, of signified and signifier, has lately been *the* preoccupation of both philosophy and theory of art. Today, the energies of everyday life cannot be opposed any more to the idle or mystified energies of the upper classes and their ideologues. Everyday life seems now as uncreative as any other. The detective novel, particularly its cinematic embodiment, suggests at once the desire and the difficulty of giving to daily existence that "seriousness" which Erich Auerbach saw emerging in the great realistic novels of the nineteenth century. For the hopeful and productive aspects of industrialization are being replaced by a purely semiotic and indifferent urbanization. "We are surrounded by emptiness," Lefebvre sighs, "but it is an emptiness filled with signs! Metalanguage replaces the missing city. . . ."

Hence the ghostly sensationalism of detective fiction, in which every detail, however small, is potentially a telltale sign of human purposes, even if it disappoints an imagination it excites into voyeurism. Hence also the new ghostliness that invades our notions of privacy or inwardness, which retreat once more into the nonquotidian, "a make-believe privacy, embellished and sheltered from the outside world, from view, from the sun, by partitions . . . curtains, draperies." Hitchcock conveys to us this lack of authentic privacy or inwardness; he strikes through, like a dagger, those draperies; but the draperies are still those of everyday reality. As Lefebvre sadly insists, "self-realization [now] is a life without history,—total quotidianness, but unseen and evaded as soon as possible."

Can we recover the romance of the quotidian? Or is the very notion of "reality" so technologized, semioticized, mediated, and therefore demystified, that it cannot be disalienated any more? I leave this as a question; a question intensified for me by Hitchcock's movies; but once the senses have become theoreticians, once theory is part of the concrete and environing world, it would be fatal to ignore it and rely on some natural and instinctive balm to restore pristine perception. We can educate the senses, that is all: educate them to resist the media by an active rather than passive understanding, and so take back from the media what is our own.

Six Women Poets

NOWHERE IS THERE more of Nature than in the smallest things," said Pliny; and for Marianne Moore the smallness may be that of woodweasel or word, of prickly leaf clinging to barbed wire or the prickliness of a strange phrase clinging to the mind. Her respect for "hayseed magnitudes" is not, of course, a disclaimer of larger intentions. She knows that basilisk is a "little king," a dragon in disguise. What she admires in creatures and artifacts is really their "compactness compacted," their completely functional yet resolutely aesthetic outsides. How many of her poems deal with plume and wool or other kinds of human and nonhuman armor! It is not that she disdains the insides of things but that, especially in a psychological age, the surface qualities are slighted. There is a peculiarly modern morality in this respect for the surface: content or *fond*, said Valéry, is only form in its impure state. Contemporary painters make everything a function of form; and in poetry too, despite the obvious difference of medium, attempts are made to find a style in which the aesthetic and didactic elements are inseparable. Marianne Moore is so much in this tradition of modern art that one reads her poems less for their message (always suffused) than for the pleasure of seeing how style may become an act of the living—the infinitely inclusive and discriminating—mind.

A review of the following works of poetry: Marianne Moore, *Collected Poems* (New York: Macmillan, 1951); Denise Levertov, *With Eyes at the Back of our Heads* (New York: New Directions, 1959); Ruth Stone, *In an Iridescent Time* (New York: Harcourt Brace, 1959); Jean Garrigue, *A Water Walk by the Villa d'Este* (New York: St. Martin's Press, 1959); Anne Sexton, *To Bedlam and Part Way Back* (Boston: Houghton Mifflin, 1960); and Gwendolyn Brooks, *The Bean Eaters* (New York: Harper, 1960).

This mind, or rather Moore's, is "an enchanting thing": it takes us by its very irrelevancies. Here too everything is surface; she talks, so to say, from the top of her mind and represents herself as a gossip on the baroque scale. But secretly she is a magician, and distracts on purpose. While her message eludes us through understatement, the poem itself remains teasingly alive through the overstatement of its many tactics, till we accept the conventional rabbit, glorified by prestidigitation. Yet the magic of language becomes intensely moral on further acquaintance and her crazy quilt of thoughts, quotations, and sounds resolves into subtler units of meaning and rhythm. The free (but not formless) verse helps break up the automatic emphases of traditional syntax, and respects the more dynamic shifts of the inner, and not merely spoken, voice. It is wrong to excerpt from her poems, because the movement is all, but listen to her describe the mind—her mind—via the motion of a bird ("The Frigate Pelican"):

> the unconfiding frigate-bird hides
> in the height and in the majestic
> display of his art. He glides
> a hundred feet or quivers about
> as charred paper behaves—full
> of feints; and an eagle
>
> of vigilance . . . *Festina lente.* Be gay
> civilly? How so? 'If I do well I am blessed
> whether any bless me or not, and if I do
> ill I am cursed.'

The impetus and Classical one-piece pattern (adjective, noun, verb) of the first sentence is gradually reduced, through the movement of the passage, to a rhythmic trembling and syntactical dispersion, till the quotation (a Hindu saying) turns everything inward, evoking a still more interior and searching mood. This contractile motion is typical of Moore: it shows how "unconfiding" the poet is of her own mind and art, every phrase or mood being an overstatement with respect to her ideal of verbal and moral tact. "Be gay / civilly" is her motto as well as the bird's; though to gain it she significantly changes a rule of prudence ("make haste slowly") into a purely moral and aesthetic precept. It is this same *aesthetic* prudence that often helps her to avoid the vulgarity of straight rhyme, as she counterpoints the syntactical, syllabic, or sound character of the rhyming words ("full" . . . "eagle," both echoing a previous rhyme word, "Handel"). But her technique is not uniform, not abstractly applied; it depends on the movement of the whole poem, and she may therefore unleash rhyme or consonance or heavy abstractions, as in a late and beautiful poem on the sixteenth-century composer Melchior Vulpius. The poem is, I suspect, expressive of her own deepest ambition:

> Almost
>   utmost absolutist
> and fugue-ist, Amen; slowly building
> from miniature thunder,
>   crescendos antidoting death—
> love's signature cementing faith.

Good poetry always teaches and delights in equal measure, but Moore's elusiveness as a teacher forces the critic to be more than usually dogmatic. Is Nature her "argument"? No more, surely, than in the medieval bestiaries. "Oh to be a Dragon," "To a Chameleon," and the poem on St. Jerome and the Lion are as exotic in thought and sometimes in fact as medieval specimens. And when she displays her naturalism, describing jellyfish or hedgehog, it is also merely a way of making creatures *speak* to us. It is their tongue she is after: not nature but nature's idiom. She wants an organic language, an unself-conscious morality. Hence the nature she admires (in Nature or Art) is exclusively *character*, or what Hopkins calls inscape, describing it in his poem on the kingfisher as a natural, bell-like manifestation of the self:

> Each mortal thing does one thing and the same:
> Deals out that being indoors each one dwells;
> Selves—goes itself; *myself* it speaks and spells. . . .

This simple, unself-conscious relation of the inner character of things to their expressive form she has called "propriety" in the poem of that name, where Brahms and Bach are humorously compared to "the unintentional pansy-face / uncursed by self-inspection, blackened; because born that way." La Fontaine, whom she translates, is another hero of propriety. He managed to fable to the most sophisticated society ever formed, and Moore wants to fable to the most self-conscious. His common sense is a flower of Classicism, and the only natural product of that artificial age; her nature sense is a flower in an age preoccupied with selfhood. As antidotes to what she calls "the disease, My Self," the poet commends the old theological virtues of faith, hope, and love—stripped, however, of their dogmatism. In this way they become purely natural virtues, the "household" virtues she celebrates in her poem on Jerome and the lion, "the edgehog miscalled hedgehog," and St. Nicholas. Her final interest goes to the unself-conscious essence of creatures, so that even a jellyfish, emblem of spinelessness, escaping our grasp by its mere being, becomes for her the emblem of everything that resists naturally the voraciousness of man or of his mind.

As in "Bird-Witted" or the poems inspired by World War II, the virtues tend to flow into this quality of *resistance,* whether to an external menace or to oneself. Many poems are really poems of Spiritual Combat, and show in Moore that clear identifying mark of the Puritan: an extreme reverence for created things coupled with an extreme distrust of the self. At her best, as "In Distrust of Merits," or in "Voracities and Verities," she achieves a dialogue of one, an ironic crossfire of statement that continually denies and reasserts the possibility of a selfless assertion of the self. Her recurrent images of Armor ("His Shield," "The Pangolin") are linked to the theme of spiritual combat and come ultimately from Paul's letter to the Ephesians; the armor she describes is the modesty whereby the self is made strong to resist itself, but also strong to assert its being against voracious dogmatisms. Her own poetry, too, practices a "mirror-of-steel-uninsistence," forged by consciousness yet rivaling the unself-consciousness of nature. Moore brings poetry a long step forward in its self-liberation from palpable design. Her style does not embody a morality; it is one.

Denise Levertov starts her poems at a point beyond self-consciousness; the first lines set the style of her fancy irrevocably:

> Have you got the moon safe?
> Please, tie those strings a little tighter.
> This loaf, push it down further
> the light is crushing it. . . .
> ("Departure")

She wants to take them with her, the moon, the light, the sea, but they have a way of escaping and must be tied in with staples. Her poems are a subtle and indefatigable complaint that we possess nothing by being merely conscious of it. But this tension, consciousness, between objects and the self, is better than blur or loss, as she is reminded by a long, all-misting rain:

> Wear scarlet! Tear the green lemons
> off the tree! I don't want
> to forget who I am, what has burned in me
> and hang limp and clean, an empty dress—
> ("The Five-Day Rain")

Perhaps art is the proper fixative, giving life firmness and dreams life. She has a fine version of Gautier's *L'Art* (except for an extravagant, Marianne Moore-ish middle):

> Incise, invent, file to poignance;
> make your elusive dream
>   seal itself
> in the resistant mass of crude substance.

"Crude" is excessive; it shows that she is nearer Lorca than Gautier, and wants to *elide* everything except imagination, even the matter and the art that fixes it. Hence her method of ellipsis, one might almost say of silence, which the words only displace. It needs more respect than I can give here, though it occasionally recalls too blatantly Pound's ar-

tificial haiku; and while she can write an original persona poem—
e.g., "The Wife"—she may also, perhaps intentionally, parody Pound,
as in "A Letter":

> I know you will come, bringing me
> an opal. Good! I will come
> to meet you. . . .

Her danger is in the facile persona; escaping the formalists, she falls
into the hands of the ritualists with their Classical mock, their worship
of the ordered or precise will. But at best, as in "To the Snake," her
Classicism rings true, and also (except for the last line) in her address
to the Great Dahlia:

> Burn, burn the day. The wind
> is trying to enter and praise you.
> Silence seems something you have chosen,
> withholding your bronze voice.
> We bow before your pride.

Ruth Stone knows what she sees and sees what she knows; the eye,
the rational eye, is her strongest sense. She specializes in snapshots of
atrophy:

> The doubtful pleasures of atrophy,
> Squeezed minds licking themselves
> Beside the gold carp sluggish under the waterfall.
> ("Collage")

Yet though her poetry is a "cruel glass," its directness is almost a form
of compassion, as in this view "From the Window":

> This lady who wintered poorly had thin hair
> And sat in the sun under the cascades
> Of forsythia; with a towel and a mirror,
> In black sateen pajamas. I do not think

[113]

In all of Hades there are such desperate shades
As thin-haired ladies.

The temptation to rhyme *shades* and *Hades* and *ladies* returns the worst
to laughter, and I wouldn't say whether a cold or compassionate kind.
But this is her only, if pregnant, ambiguity; there is nothing vague or
wavery in Ruth Stone as in Levertov. She is firm all the way through.
From "The Burned Bridge," which describes how reality suddenly gives
way in the child to a sense of unreality (a Wordsworthian "blank mis-
giving"), we know that she and nature abhor a vacuum equally. This
vacuum is, to some extent, her own imagination, which she fears because it is too familiar with death-in-life: in "Speculation" she has a
corpse tell us how it feels to grow slowly into loss of feeling, and the
gesture she makes in "Private Pantomime" explains something of the
superb tightness of her poems:

Blood and the sight
Of such weak eyes waiting, puts my humor about;
And I thrust both my hands into a pair of gloves, tight.

She too, therefore, through her poem's strong eyes, transcends the merely
introspective, the narcissistic mazes of self-consciousness. Narcissism is,
perhaps, her main subject, and it, not sexuality, takes the place of original sin in her world, and leads to minds and bodies wasted, licking
their wounds in self-multiplied mirrors. Her longest poem, "One Reel
Tragedy," is the myth of Narcissus modernized, and interprets the traditional props of pool or mirror in terms of American camera morality.
Mr. Blink, the pornographic photographer-cum-salesman of this mock
pastoral, woos the innocent Chloris, and his rape of her looks, given
the rhymed sharpness of Stone's couplets, produces a most Popean
work:

And now the simple plot begins in June
When black and red roses prick the bank of noon.
Twirling his Leica, lightly up the walk
He coaxes old Dingee in hunting talk.

[114]

>   Chloris afloat, all plumage, girlish toss,
>   Assails the glass, redresses former loss.
>   His perfect lens reflects her nascent joy. . . .

Ruth Stone never puts the burden of selection on the reader: each poem is truly anthologized, a culled word. The same cannot be said of Jean Garrigue, who throws herself somewhat too willingly on the mercy of the court. Single lines, sudden perfect phrasings, real poetic breath— should one not be content with this? In the abstract there is more in Garrigue than in many contemporary poets, yet it remains abstract and fragmentary, a playing of scales rather than a virtuoso incantation:

>   Your name wearing water in cloud and flame
>   The world bearing flowers out of your name
>   Or in the dim sleep nothing borne
>   But the sound of waters racing your blood
>   And the running of waters and the dim
>   Bemused confession of waters foretelling your coming.

She takes too much after her paradigm of water; one is never sure of the vessel, the total form of the poem. Yet the gathering up of the last verse's movement through the interposition of a second adjective ("Bemused"), and the syncopation of *waters* (sixth and seventh syllables) with *waters* (seventh and eighth syllables) shows her ability to make us forget meaning in favor of movement, though this may create meanings of its own:

>   Bells and their tongues wait
>   Birds in the bell of the bush their small songs halt.

The birds are suddenly seen as the *tongues* of the bush. A whole poem may be spun out of her sense for movement—"Night talk" is the cadenza of an exceptionally airy imagination, which trusts itself to the air as her poem on the fountains of the Villa d'Este to water. Her finest effects come while forging a rhythm which slows time, which goes against nature's will for change present even on the calmest day:

These days, so calm and perfect, haunt my blood,
Palms surging, fine blades in the wind,
Palms surging, fountains blowing, hurt my blood
By worn stone seats, by grassy obelisk,
Or by those walls where stand anonymous gods,
Broken of hand or of the living parts. . . .

But she cannot sustain the moment, and does not have Keats' mythology to explore its dialectic.

Two poems, in fact, the "Discourse from Firenze" and "Soliloquy in the Cemetery of Père Lachaise," deplore the loss of the ancient gods and the freedom of the Renaissance or Keatsian artist, who took from the heaven of man's imagination whatever he wanted, Christian or Pagan or mingled forms. She calls on the cemetery ornaments of Père Lachaise to come alive, not for the sake of the buried but for the sake of poetry. Yet she knows (although she does not always accept her own conclusions) that the modern poet must walk naked. "The passion is to keep the ignorance up," she remarks in her most finished poem ("The land we did not know"). Reduced to the moments and figures of her own mind, she runs the same dangers as Denise Levertov. Her psychological songs (e.g., "I sought from love") are not successful in replacing the Allegory of Love with modern and subtler dramatizations. When she does not frankly strow "The flower of the moment upon the river / Our only libation," she skirts the mock-Classical, as in "A garland of trumpets." But the latter is saved by its meditative rhythm, the slow-motion effects most organic in her:

Held, beheld all in a dream,
The fishermen dark as the sea,
Foam-dappled, wading the shallows
Clear to transparency,
Lightly driving their boats out to sea

The rhythm is more evocative than the words, and Garrigue shows she is familiar with Wallace Stevens' "necessary angel," whose sight gives the earth a second birth in sight. I suppose my disappointments in her volume are the obverse of a real promise, her being so close and yet still so far from "the idea of the real / That more clear than the real gave the real its power" ("A Discourse from Firenze").

For Denise Levertov and Jean Garrigue poetry is largely an attitude of mind, a song gradually finding its words and even its experience. But Anne Sexton, like Ruth Stone, knows her experience, knows it almost too well. Her poetry is, in consequence, less a means of self-knowledge than a form of courage—a means to face self-knowledge. *To Bedlam and Part Way Back* is a remarkable book (the only volume here truly a *book*), in which we feel not only the poet's experience but also something of the morality behind recalling and recording it. There is more here than a case history or a "cruel glass."

The experience itself, though involving a stay in an asylum, is simple, moving, and universal. Sexton describes the loss of a child, or rather the *estrangement* of a mother from her child. Hardly born, it reminds the mother unbearably of her own childhood, and continues to do so after the asylum:

> And you came each
> weekend. But I lie.
> You seldom came. I just pretended
> you, small piglet, butterfly
> girl, with jelly bean cheeks,
> disobedient three, my splendid
>
> stranger. And I had to learn
> why I would rather
> die than love, how your innocence
> would hurt and how I gather
> guilt like a young intern
> his symptoms, his certain evidence.
> ("The Double Image")

It is the womb of self-knowledge the child has opened: named Joyce in order to be nicknamed Joy—"Pretty joy! / Sweet joy but two days old. / Sweet joy I call thee," as Blake writes in "Infant Joy" in the *Songs of Innocence*—she is the fruit of an entanglement in which every birth signifies a death. The estrangement between mother and child is equally present in the previous generation.

With such a theme, developed not paradigmatically in the manner of Yeats, but directly in the manner of Lowell's life studies, did the poet have to exploit the more sensational aspect of her experience? The opening lines of the book,

> You, Doctor Martin, walk
> from breakfast to madness. . . .

may show what I mean. This walker is "metaphysical"; his stride is made to yoke disparate things too obviously. Compare such expressions as "the frozen gates / of dinner" or the self-conscious naiveté of "What large children we are / here [in Bedlam]." Sexton can be so much subtler and gain the same end, as when, also in the opening poem, she rhymes "sins" and "moccasins," "myself" and "shelf," when she uses "hotel" indifferently for asylum and summer refuge, or when in "Ringing the Bells" she adapts a nursery rhyme to describe the "large children." A traditional poem like "Torn Down from Glory Daily," which depicts the tempting down of "king" gulls by crusts of bread, is by its mere obliquity a more powerful picture of the human condition than her efficiently icy vignettes of the asylum. Only in the latter part of the book, and especially its major poem "The Double Image," do I feel the experience on the mad heath properly subsumed in the action of the whole. It is not that the subject is unpalatable, but that in the minor space of a lyric overcondensations are hard to avoid and strike us coldly. The crudities of "The Double Image," on the other hand, are not compelled by the form but by her genius (the poet is talking of her mother):

> On the first of September she looked at me
> and said I gave her cancer.
> They carved her sweet hills out
> and still I couldn't answer.

[118]

The nakedness of the event is intensified by a nakedness of statement which the periphrasis of the next-to-last line only points up, and aptly so if "The Song of Songs" comes to mind, for affected is the entire possibility of love. The obtruding irrelevance of number (present in many poems) adds to the sharpness, evoking as in love songs or magic rhymes ("The first day of Christmas my true love gave to me. . .") the action of fate, its absurd yet demonically just jackpot. I would like to recall also the journey that Yeats' Platonists are forced to suffer against their will:

> Straddling each a dolphin's back
> And steadied by a fin,
> Those Innocents re-live their death,
> Their wounds open again. . . .
>   ("News for the Delphic Oracle")

Anne Sexton undertakes this journey for a greater purpose even than to know herself and realize the Delphic (or Dolphin) imperative. She is to face a Mode of Being fatally estranged from her. She can revive it but not relive it; there can hardly be a deeper spiritual wound. And if she is so intent on turning wounds into words, is it not because many of them were originally inflicted by words, or their impossibility? This is the homeopathic magic of her verse, its true morality.

Schopenhauer, quoted by Sexton in the epigraph to her book, tells Goethe that "most of us carry in our hearts the Jocasta who begs Oedipus for God's sake not to inquire further." The poets considered here have rooted Jocasta out of their hearts. They are in pursuit of the truth, and the truth for them is psychological. But poetry must also cut loose from the psychological at some point. A great poem, like a great myth, enables a person to step out as well as into herself. For the Romantics, poetry was the form of personality most opposed to selfhood, and Shelley openly compares it to love. Yet the post-Romantics (which we are) want "impersonality." The poet hands off various selves as poems. These selves are personae, broken parts masquerading as the whole. Poetry, the most personal of all acts of mind, is also alienated from us by a workshop culture.

For Gwendolyn Brooks, however, the truth is social. Her Jocasta is simply the middle class. If her poetry cuts itself off in principle from purely psychological inquiry, does she escape this view of a poem as a self-alienated part of herself? It appears at first that she does. Having, like Faulkner, her own country, her poems are dedicated to people who live a supremely local, "Bronzeville" life. All are caught between impossibly small choices:

> Mrs. Small went to the kitchen for her pocketbook
> And came back to the living room with a peculiar look
> And the coffee pot.
> Pocketbook. Pot.
> Pot. Pocketbook.

Or they are caught between impossibly big choices, between black and white, man and woman, death and life, fear of life and life. The big and small dilemmas cross in "A Bronzeville Mother Loiters in Mississippi. Meanwhile, a Mississippi Mother Burns Bacon." In this, Brooks' best poem, a white woman tries to fit her husband's crime, the killing for her sake of a black boy, to the ballad heroism on which she was raised. She fails in her attempt, yet cannot break with family demands accumulating while she thinks. If there is something like a slapstick tragedy, this poem comes close to it: superbly dramatic, it depicts with the exaggeration and exuberance of great art the corrupt core of a society, its violence against itself and deadening of the free imagination. Yet sometimes Brooks' verve is curiously reckless: if it can produce such fine ballad ad-libbing as

> Rudolph Reed was oaken.
> His wife was oaken too.
> And his two good girls and his good little man
> Oakened as they grew

[120]

it may also lead to a runaway sophisticated-and-folksy style, to poem purgatives for the oppressed imagination. The latter end of her song on the tough old oaken black man is a case in point. With her ballads and dramatic pieces she is, in fact, more of a workshop poet than the others. The principle of impersonality takes over again, this time in the form of the sophisticated folk poem. The poet at her best rivals the high impromptus of jazz, a raging song too cold for rage.

Representation Now

MILTON, in the opening lines of his ambitious epic, asks to be instructed by a "spirit" that prefers "Before all temples the upright heart and pure." For the thoughtful reader "upright" is a displacement from temple architecture; "pure," however, denotes an inwardness so general or transcendent that metaphorical residues are almost effaced. "Pure," perhaps, of all desire for such structures as temples, such images of magnificence and pomp. Pure, then, of all vain, sensual, earthly thoughts—yet Milton is about to fashion a work exemplary for future generations, the very image or fetish of poetic achievement.

In the 1960s a Renaissance art historian, trying to understand modern developments—Kandinsky, De Kooning, Duchamp, the Dadaists, Pollock, the action painters and the nonfigurative painters, the pop artists, and the Bauhaus constructivists—is forced to confirm a similar paradox. These movements, iconoclastic in appearance or program, yield, through their great if ironic inventions, the elements of a future art. Over and again they signal the end not simply of the image in its presentational or sensuous aspect but the end of art as monumental *oeuvre*. Duchamp's mustachioed Mona Lisa inscribed LHOOQ or Delaunay's iterated ragging of the Eiffel Tower conveys a frustrated yet fertile message. Robert Klein formulates it in his essay "The Eclipse of the Work of Art," when he concludes with these questions: "Can one imagine a state of affairs in which art could do without works? Or can one imagine works which are not embodiments of values and solidifications of experiences?"

But is this not the old Puritan question? The upright heart and pure is grander than all space shuttles, than all such laborious erections. There is the chance of grace without works, or to repeat Robert Klein: "a state of affairs in which art could do without works." Another historian, with a base in the Renaissance, will formulate the notion of the "self-consuming artifact" (Stanley Fish).

At this point in history we are not likely to underestimate the iconoclastic or image-breaking impulse. Its apparent asceticism, Nietzsche showed, conceals a will to power as blatant today as it was when Daniel interpreted Nebuchadnezzar's dream. "Thou, O king, sawest, and beheld a great image. This image, which was mighty, and whose brightness was surpassing, stood before thee; and the appearance thereof was terrible. As for that image, its head was of fine gold, its breast and its arms of silver, its belly and its thighs of brass, its legs of iron, its feet part of iron, and part of clay. Thou sawest till that a stone was cut without hands, which smote the image upon its feet that were of iron and clay, the brass, the silver and the gold, broken in pieces together, and became like the chaff of the summer threshing floors; and the wind carried them away, so that no place was found for them; and the stone that smote the image became a great mountain and filled the whole earth" (2:31–36). I now turn the clock forward once more to a writer of the exapocalyptic 1960s, a deliberate collagist and quotationist before "intertextuality" had become a doctrine or Derrida had invaded these shores. Consider the following from a chapter entitled "Nothing":

> Get the nothingness back into words. . . . To look not at the text but through it; to see between the lines; to language as lace, black on white; or white on black as the sky at night, or in the space on which our dreams are traced. . . . Against gravity; against the gravity of literalism, which keeps our feet on the ground. Against weighty words, the baggage of traditional meaning and the burden of the law; travel light.

By recycling the oracular and aphoristic words of others, Norman O. Brown produces in such books as *Love's Body* a compilation that converts metalanguage, or the language of learning, into the language of love. Scholarship and lyricism meet. But this is only one of the new forms miscegenated from the old. So iconoclasm keeps creating new genres, images, even monuments. Is all art, then, this sort of bricolage?

The "vast Abyss" Milton evokes, on which spirit sits "Dove-like . . . brooding," this "tohu-va-bohu" or "unformed void" keeps getting pregnant. Yet there is a peculiarly modern aspect to the fertile breaking of images and undoing of representations. Walter Lippmann catches it when in *A Preface to Morals* (1929) he defines modern man as "an emigrant who lives in a revolutionary society and inherits a protestant tradition," who can find no fixed point outside his conscience, and does not "really believe there is such a point, because he has moved about too fast to fix any point long enough in his mind." He is deprived, in short, of any sense of authority established by "deep familiarity and indurated association" rather than by ratiocination. This loss of organic surroundings is described by Lippmann in a way that would remind us of Wordsworth and Yeats, were it not so abbreviated. "The ancient authorities," he writes, "were blended with the ancient landmarks, with fields and vineyards and patriarchal trees, with ancient houses and chests full of heirlooms, with churchyards near at hand and their ancestral graves. . . ." I prefer the full nostalgia of Yeats' "A Prayer for my Daughter," his lament for the loss of ceremoniousness; or, obversely, Wallace Stevens' sense of the omnipresence of the fictive, his beautifully elaborated doubt that such a landscape ever existed:

> This is not landscape, full of the somnambulations
> of poetry
>
> And of the sea. This is my father or, maybe,
> It is as he was,
>
> A likeness. . . .

Leslie Brisman, schooled by Milton, rightly remarks that "as" and "or" are liberating words in this passage, breaking up the identity statement "This is my father" into analogy and surmise. The patriarchal trees are no sounder, no closer to substance, than the father-patriarch is. The perfection of technique, the art that no longer hides itself, creates a *mise en abîme* that dislocates persons from their dream of being consubstantial with nature, with an organic environment. More radically still, they may separate the poet from his poetry, the maker (god or man) from his work. This sublime depersonalization is described by Derrida as a "dissemination" disclosed by the very existence of language: words displace whatever may have been "In the Beginning"; they disclose that which cannot return to the father. The concepts of nature and natural language are jeopardized by the very being of language. The proliferation of analogy, ratio, congruence, or symmetry can only be encouraged, not controlled, by poetry or by a scrupling philosophy. Therefore a multiplication of those little and intricately evasive words: "like," "as," "or," "e.g."

I am aware that in the 1920s and 1930s a theory of art existed that revived the Thomistic emphasis on analogy and understood the presence of the word as a word of presence. In Maritain and Beguin, as today in Ong and McLuhan, representation is an aspect of presence, not its questioning: a reinforcement, not an undoing. And even when theorists set representation against presence, as in Malraux's account of both archaic and modern forms of stylization, we are moved by the lucidity of their antagonism rather than by the absoluteness of their argument. We savor the clear shadows flung on the cave of our minds by these word adepts. What is common to both schools—reps and anti-reps—is a recognition that the mind presses against its own ability to fashion simulacra. That ability has augmented fantastically since the Renaissance and its invention of picture space. However quaint Spenser is, he already teaches us how much can be achieved by dwelling in a land of similitude, a region of mere likeness that delights to deceive without actually deceiving.

For Spenser theological terms would have come into play. The relation between natural light and supernatural illumination—between nature and grace—is a crucial and tricky matter. Natural light cannot be trusted; at the same time, it cannot be neglected. What conceptual apparatus, however, can question, in our time, the face value of representations? Or what can undo the media illusion of direct reportage? Can we, to look at it from the negative side, believe *anything* communicated by the mass media? Do seeing and reading still have face value? The present debate over the New Journalism, a genre that blurs the boundary between reportage and fictive interpolation—passed off as reportage—helps to focus the issue. John Hersey, commenting on Norman Mailer and others, has called himself a "worried grandpa" of this trend, and he insists that his *Hiroshima* is journalism uncontaminated by fiction. Yet Mailer is not unaware of the problem. He adds a final section to *The Armies of the Night* that moves from a short chapter entitled "A Novel Metaphor" to a last chapter entitled "The Metaphor Delivered." He does not want to write a novel yet feels driven to it by the supermedia effect that haloes every publicized event. "The mass media," he writes, "which surrounded the March on the Pentagon created a forest of inaccuracy which would blind the efforts of an historian; our novel has provided us with the possibility, no, even the instruments, to view our facts and conceivably study in that field of light which a labor of lens-grinding has produced." "Dark with excessive bright thy skirts appear," Milton writes of God enthroned. The correlative, secular darkness that besets the modern reporter is a powerfully expectant emptiness, created by sheer technique: a dazzling "field of light" which awaits or creates the star-hero that should fill the scene, but also produces a doom of confusion through overexposure, and blinding, trivial details that disintegrate every starry focus.

So absurd and magnetic is this confusion that a John Hinckley and a Jody Foster, who have no connection, gravitate into the same field of light. Things falling apart induce a crazy causality, as in detective novels. The detective novel, in fact, is one of those new fictions emerging to grasp the pseudo-event or eschatological center that cannot hold. As in Nathanael West, as in Pynchon, as in Mailer, the metaphor for this center—America—is never "delivered" but remains an Andromeda writhing in the male novelist's imagination.

Have you ever looked into Michel Butor's *Mobile*, subtitled *"Etude pour une représentation des Etats-Unis,"* and dedicated to the memory of Jackson Pollock? In this sort of writing there is no "milieu": there is a repetitious plurality of place names or personal names disclosed by the black spotlight of print as it moves from stage to stage in an orgy of telecommunications. You can break images but you can't break this square eye that penetrates like a blind focus the privacy of every place and sets up an insatiable claim for up-to-date relevance. "Only connect" then becomes the inhuman injunction of media mentality: if Derrida is prevented from being offered a chair at Nanterre, and Althusser kills his wife, and MacCabe is denied upgrading at Cambridge, the international desk of a famous weekly sniffs out the truffle of a conspiracy and suddenly professes an interest in the hitherto supposedly cloistered academic life. A stringer appears at Yale to tie it all up.

No wonder representation becomes unreal, and must change or purge life constantly in a kind of permanent revolution. Our reality hunger seeks bigger and better modes of fast-breaking news—until art regains its authenticity through sheer force of askesis. Two directions, then, of representational practice can be identified: the *wasting* of older forms of realism, since they turn out to be, in retrospect, strongly encoded forms of fantasy; and the *salvaging* or *purification* of some of the same forms, as if they were restorative archetypes.

Let me—very briefly—illustrate these two tendencies. In the same year as Butor's *Mobile*, Philip K. Dick publishes *The Man in the High Castle*, usually classified as science fiction. It is by no means the author's best work, and it may not be science fiction: it has no space or time machines. But it is about an alternate version of reality, being set in a postwar world where Germany and Japan as victors have divided the globe between them.

To read *The Man in the High Castle* is a curious experience. By any standard it is bad as art and uninteresting as history. Yet the themes of art and history are all-pervasive. Art and history are made to lose their monumental, fixed, authentic character: they dilapidate into a horribly stylized prose (post-Hemingway, telegraphic, pseudo-elliptical Japanese) that fascinates only conceptually. Two quotations will suffice. Their context is the possibility of an "American" type of art in a world where Americans have lost the war and are thought incapable of creating anything of value. The only *objets* appreciated by the occupying

[127]

Japanese are prewar antiques: old firearms, Mickey Mouse watches, and so forth.

Getting up, he hurried into his study, returned at once with two cigarette lighters which he set down on the coffee table. "Look at these. Look the same, don't they? Well, listen. One has historicity in it." He grinned at her. "Pick them up. Go ahead. One's worth, oh, maybe forty or fifty thousand dollars on the collector's market."

The girl gingerly picked up the two lighters and examined them. "Don't you feel it?" he kidded her. "The historicity?" She said, "What is 'historicity'?"

"When a thing has history in it. Listen. One of those two Zippo lighters was in Franklin D. Roosevelt's pocket when he was assassinated. And one wasn't. One has historicity, a hell of a lot of it. As much as any object ever had. And one has nothing. Can you feel it?" He nudged her. "You can't. You can't tell which is which. There's no 'mystical plasmic presence,' no 'aura' around it."

"The hands of the artificer," Paul said, "had *wu*, and allowed that *wu* to flow into this piece. Possibly he himself knows only that this piece satisfies. It is complete, Robert. By contemplating it, we gain more *wu* ourselves. We experience the tranquility associated not with art but with holy things. I recall a shrine in Hiroshima wherein a shinbone of some medieval saint could be examined. However, this is an artifact and that was a relic. This is alive in the now, whereas that merely *remained*. By this meditation, conducted by myself at great length since you were last here, I have come to identify the value which this has in opposition to historicity. . . . To have no historicity, and also no artistic, esthetic worth, and yet to partake of some ethereal value—that is a marvel. Just precisely because this is a miserable, small, worthless-looking blob; that, Robert, contributes to its possessing *wu*. For it is a fact that *wu* is customarily found in least imposing places, as in the Christian aphorism, 'stones rejected by the builder.' One experiences awareness of *wu* in such trash as an old stick, or a rusty beer can by the side of the road. However, in those cases, the *wu* is within the viewer. It is religious experience. Here, an artificer has put *wu* in the object, rather than merely witnesses the *wu* inherent in it. . . . In other words, an entire new world is pointed to, by this. The name for it is neither art, for it has no form, nor religion. What is it? I have pondered this pin unceasingly, yet cannot fathom it. We evidently lack the word for an object like this. So you are right, Robert. It is authentically a new thing on the face of the world."

[128]

Walter Benjamin's concept of a type of presence he too calls "aura" and which is lost in the Era of Mechanical Reproduction raises a similar issue. But the context, in Dick, is peculiarly American. Is there an American vulgate? Or are we simply in the degenerate presence of the vulgar? Henry James posed exactly the same question almost a century ago and created a compensatory elegance. Dick feels himself to be as vulgar as Henry James; he doubts America as a milieu in which art might flourish. The reader is led to an analogy between Dick's novel and the handicrafts or fakes so important to its theme. The style it offers is crafted from a mixture of precious and trashy materials (from *I Ching*, or *Book of Changes*, and from detective fiction, from the good and the bad in Poe, from Nathanael West, etc.) by a shady artisan in abject surroundings. Dick's novel, at the same time, wants to make a strong and specially American statement. It depicts a period in which art, however contemporary, is doomed to be valued only as already a collectible, as the relic of a material culture. These modern antiques are basically what they always were, that is, commodities, but now their fetishistic character is clarified. The second excerpt is even more revealing than the first in its iconoclasm: "wu" is exactly like art or grace—without works. It has passed into an arbitrary body and emanates a dubious charm. It functions like the oracle game that dominates this pseudo-Japanese, quasi-American culture with its elliptical sayings: fortune-cookie formulas derived from the *Book of Changes* via Hammett, Chandler, and the tough tale.

How are we to understand Dick's vulgar but effective attack on our best idols, those of (1) historicity, and (2) realistic representation? There is certainly, as in all science fiction, a release from gravity, celebrated in another context by Norman O. Brown. Yet the mind released from the "aura" of things uniquely attached to place and time feels a threat of disembodiment. Becoming too light, it projects a total loss of presence—the terror of *losing face*, here interpreted by Tagomi, the main Japanese character, as *losing place*. This terror foresees a displacement without remedy, without any cure of the ground. We approach the point—a kind of vanishing point—where representation has lost all face value.

Realism in art—especially the doctrinaire realism of the great novel from Balzac through Proust and Mann—may already be fetishistic, or an aesthetic movement of Restoration. Flaubert's importance, certainly, is that he extroverted the link between realism and its vanishing point—between a fascination with local color and lived reality as the ground of all face value, and the speciousness of every such value. The *book*, therefore, is but a solid vertigo, expressive of an epileptic rather than epic kind of world. "I would like to write a book about nothing, a book without external links, which would be held together by the internal force of its style . . . just as the earth without being suspended moves in the air, a book which would have almost no subject-matter, or at least whose subject would be almost invisible, if that is possible." Sartre links this to the "internal hemorrhage of being" in Flaubert; and Fredric Jameson to the derealizing effect of a *société du spectacle*. "Abolishing the real world, grasping the world as little more than a text or sign-system—this is notoriously the very logic of our consumer society, the society of the image or the media event."

Let me turn now from the wasting to the salvaging of representational form. The obverse of science fiction—its strange jazz-like vortex into which every image of woe and wonder descends—is the askesis of ballet. What is more solid than a Degas painting of those fugacities? Is the surprising later growth of ballet in the midst of media superfetation merely the product of a bourgeois nostalgia, the re-creation of a lost innocence at highbrow level? Is Ballanchine's Candyland another Disneyland, or what Doctorow, in *The Book of Daniel*, names "Autopia"?

Ballet was never merely pastoral. It is, as it was, a strict competitive genre. Despite its spectacular stage dazzle, the courtliness of this form simplifies complex and sloppy bodies, even the body of desire itself, until light—Mailer's "field of light"—mingles with pathos to produce a rigorous and self-purgative art. The abstractness of ballet, like that of silhouettes, combines gravity and levity in an orchestrated world that, though full of puppets, dolls, and courtiers, seems animated by the purest kind of mimicry when compared to that other stage world of relentlessly roving and chattering cameras. Ballet is nonfigurative art sustained by the trot of a simple story line.

This counterpoise of ballet's musical automatism to the compulsive and climactic newsworld is not the sole reason, of course, for its appeal. But it is just possible that ballet has become the ascetic and semiotic art we are seeking: one that restores to abstract signification its representational base. For in ballet legs as well as arms become pointers, they write as well as represent the score being performed. This signing or writing by rearticulated limbs suggests a perpetual enjambment, a poem composed for some multiple-membered god of the East. That pen and penis may have a relation through the finer rigidity of ballet, that this physical writing mutes composed bodies without too strong an aura of mutilation but rather of compensation, is a barely conscious factor, though a factor nevertheless.

Schopenhauer talked of "the primal servitude of willing," and opposed representation, or the sheer pleasure in phenomenal perception—when we drink "A pure organic pleasure from the lines / Of curling mist, or from the level plain / Of waters colour'd by the steady clouds" (Wordsworth's *Prelude*, Book I)—to the obstinate base *(basso ostinato)* of the will. Now whether that will is the will to knowledge itself, or a sublimate of the desire for carnal knowledge, is less important than the fragility of any pure representation enjoyed or constructed by us. Even in the Wordsworth passage quoted above, the lines of curling mist may recall lines of writing, and both images, curling mist and cloud-colored waters, may point to something reflected or reflective, behind or within something else. There is motion and displacement.

Thus representation, however pure or descriptive, tends to transcend itself, as if (to quote Stevens again) "This is not landscape. . . ." What is it then? What foreign thought fills it, or empties it, so that it becomes a place both familiar and unfamiliar, our own and not our own? Is there a primal scene that is being clouded and then unclouded?

Perhaps reading always goes against the grain of representation. It rediscovers the text as will. Nothing can be read at sight. So Roland Barthes, in *The Pleasure of the Text*, describes two systems of reading, both of which abrade the illusion of a single surface. "What I enjoy in

[131]

a narrative," he writes, "is not directly its content or even its structure, but rather the abrasions I impose upon the fine surface: I read on, I skip, I look up, I dip in again." In the second type of reading, where nothing is skipped but every point is weighed, there is again a sort of abrasion: "the excitement," he claims, now "comes not from a processive haste" (as in the first kind of reading) "but from a kind of vertical din," that is, the reader's awareness of multiple codes, polysemy, and intertextuality.

This second system of reading, according to Barthes, is more suited to the modern text, which paradoxically insists on restoring, at that level, the aristocratic or readerly surface of an older literature. The modern text compels us "not to devour, to gobble, but to graze, to browse scrupulously, to rediscover . . . the leisure of bygone readings." "On évite le récit," Mallarmé said; instead of suspense, that vulgar goggling and gobbling, we find a suspension of narrative curiosity. We read by means of a vertical browsing that yields a pleasure which is not an element *in* the work nor a naive residual sensation but "a drift, something both revolutionary and asocial, and it cannot be taken over by any collectivity, any mentality, any idiolect."

Barthes is here revaluing pleasure as a more than hedonistic and conservative quality when it comes to the appreciation of art. Like Stevens he combines the precepts of It must be Abstract, It must Change, It must give Pleasure, into a poetics that resists social or political appropriation. He formulates an alternative to muscular and demystifying ideologies that are highly reductive—as reductive as philosophy when it conceives its task to be a thinking against images.

Barthes hovers between the refraction and the destruction of the surface text. The emphasis, in any case, is shifted to reading and away from representation. Yet even less sophisticated theories, that discover a representation within the representation, are iconoclastic. The primal scene, for instance, as the demystified center of a work of art, may be interpreted in sexual terms, and possibly rightly so, because, on the whole, sexuality is more perplexing than anything else in its mixture of delight and pain. We think against it, as against the imminence of death. And that "troping against death," which is Harold Bloom's un-

[132]

derstanding of the vivifying lie of literature, is the other major fixed idea that sets representation against representation. I learn at 11 o'-clock one night that a friend has died, and whether the death was expected or not, the fact itself, in its finality, haunts and chills my consciousness of time, the ease with which I ordinarily walk and breathe. The sexual fixation also obsesses, but—to distinguish it—has no finality really, rather the strength and defect of repetitiousness, the assertion and defeat of variety, impossibility of closure rather than certainty thereof. The finality of rigor mortis or of statuary, and the jealous non-finality or repetitiousness of the erotic life, are, separately or commingled, the subversive representations to which other representations tend.

Does the entire concept of representation, therefore, collapse? Must we posit representational illusions on the one side and interpretive dismantlings on the other? And is this dualism exacerbated in the contemporary era, insofar as representations lose their face value?

Barthes' solution, which involves a distinction between newer and older, or writerly and readerly kinds of literature, is symptomatic rather than decisive. I suspect that a conflict between representation and reading has always existed. Lamb's famous essay, which argues that Shakespeare is better read than seen, suggests that the trouble is *stage* representation, its overdefinite or potentially sullying exposure. The spectacle-dominated character of contemporary life merely intensifies the scruples we may have concerning stage representation, since politics can now use the reality effect of the media to negate that freedom of mind (Lamb terms it "free conceptions" not "crampt and pressed down to the measure of strait-lacing actuality") which Barthes so desperately hangs onto with his revalued concept of pleasure.

Instead of Barthes' pseudo-historical differentiation between two types of texts, I see a continuum in which even the influence of the media must eventually diminish by diffusing into a new sense of unreality. The provisional conclusion I come to is that art when "strong" or "significant"—value words that show a certain impotence in me to analyze the situation further—art always limits the falling back of representation into will or fixed truth or what Stevens calls "the first idea." Art's ethereal show deepens into a reflection; yet this reflection is like the surface of a calm lake, or an atmosphere of thoughtfulness that rejects absolute positions. Representation or perceptibility, even of ideas, remains more important than those ideas. Should perceptibility itself be what is desired, then we understand why it marks the limit of desire and cannot be reduced further—to covert libido, idea, or will. Seeing is sought, and not merely as a medium for something else. Even philosophy's insistence on clear and distinct ideas may express this "ineluctable modality" of the perceptible that makes what we call representation the unexcludable middle between phenomenal reality and mind, between thinking in images and thinking by means of texts against them.

The Interpreter's Freud

FREUD ALONE proves Emerson's observation that a significant institution is the shadow of a great thinker. We cannot understand Freud without understanding the peculiar quality of his greatness: that quality which made him, which still makes him, a scandal, a shadow we negotiate with. He has imposed on us with the force of a religion. "One must have a very strong and keen and persistent criticism," Wittgenstein remarked about Freud, "to see through the mythology that is offered or imposed on one. There is an inducement to say, 'Yes, of course, it must be like that!' A powerful mythology."

Freud, however, wished to found a science of mind and not a mythology. His first major book on *The Interpretation of Dreams* planted the banner of rational and methodical inquiry in the very swamp of unreason, where few had ventured and, of those, very few had come back, their sanity intact. Yet these rationalist aspirations of psychoanalysis by no means disprove its redemptive and communitarian nature. Though psychoanalysis is not a religion, it still exhibits many features of past religions, including reasoning about unreason, about the irrational forces we live with and cannot entirely control.

Where is language in this field of forces? Especially the language of the interpreter as it takes for its subject other language constructs, presenting themselves as textual, like literary artifacts, or presenting themselves as a mysterious code belonging also to another medium, like hysterical symptoms or dream images. It is not necessary to overem-

Given as the 1984 Freud Lecture at Yale, an annual event sponsored by the Kanzer Seminar for Psychoanalysis in the Humanities, the Western New England Psychoanalytic Society, and the Whitney Humanities Center.

[137]

phasize what we have learned about language since Freud and again since Lacan. The discourse of the analyst remains within the affective sphere of the discourse it interprets; it is as much a supplement as a clarification; and instead of an asceptic and methodological purism, which isolates the interpreter's language from the so-called object-language, creating in effect two monologues, we have to risk a dialogue in which our own often unconscious assumptions are challenged. "The analysand's discourse," André Green has written, "is a stream of words that . . . the analyst cannot shut up in a box. The analyst runs after the analysand's words."

In psychoanalysis especially, because it involves transference and countertransference, because it puts the interpreter, not only the text or person interpreted, at risk, this exchange of words does not always lead to an urbane dialogue. The word *dialogue*, in fact, is deceptive, for there may be, in this situation, more imposition and resistance, more "crisscross" or crazy connections than when Dostoyevsky or, for that matter, Hitchcock, gets strangers together on a train. The Romance of the Railroad penetrates the interpreter's discourse, which hurtles toward its uncertain destination along a branching track of words with exotic expectations, mysterious switches, and—hopefully—good brakes.

To understand Freud's power as an interpreter (whether or not we agree with his findings or their claim to be scientific) it is necessary to read him with an attention solicited by his own immense culture, in which a sensitivity to language stimulated by literature played its part. I begin, therefore, by taking a sample from *The Interpretation of Dreams* to give it a close, literary reading. It is equally important, however, to gauge the transferability of Freud's interpretative method. The second half of my essay, then, will take up a nonanalytic text, a poem of Wordsworth's, and do two things: see it in a Freudian context, but also see Freud in its context.

It is a striking truth that literary analysis, like Freud's dream analysis, does no more and no less than disclose a life in images or words that has its own momentum. Ambiguities, overdetermined meanings, and strange linkages are more obvious than the coherent design they seem to flee from. "My thoughts crowd each other to death," Coleridge wrote. He finds himself in the grip of what he named "the streamy nature of association"; in his Notebooks, especially, not only the dreams he puts down but also his speculative etymologies and related word chains accelerate into a futile "science of the grotesque" (a phrase I take from Kenneth Burke's fine essay on Freud, in *The Philosophy of Literary Form*). But many writers acknowledge explicitly an experience similar to that of "racing thoughts." "I often felt the onset of madness," Flaubert confesses. "There was a whirl of ideas and images in my poor mind, and my consciousness, my ego, seemed to be foundering like a ship in a storm. . . . I played with fantasy and madness, as Mithridates did with his poisons." Or Keats, in a lighthearted vein: "I must be quaint and free of Tropes and figures—I must play my draughts as I please. . . . Have you not seen a Gull, an orc, a Sea Mew, or any thing to bring this Line to a proper length, and also fill up this clear part; that like the Gull I may *dip*—I hope, not out of sight—and also, like a Gull I hope to be lucky in a good sized fish—This crossing a letter is not without its associations—for chequer work leads us naturally to a Milkmaid, a Milkmaid to Hogarth Hogarth to Shakespeare Shakespeare to Hazlitt—Hazlitt to Shakespeare and thus by merely pulling an apron string we set a pretty peal of Chimes at work."

"A pretty peal of Chimes. . . ." Keats' insouciance puts us at an equal distance from the purely formal character of rhyme, as it suggests a flirtatious harmony, and the tongue-tying phenomenon of clang associations. When Freud encouraged "free" association in himself and his patients, he simply took the burden of self-judgment away, so that this inner speech, to which Flaubert and Keats allude, might be fully disclosed. *The Interpretation of Dreams* remains a disconcerting work because of this: Freud's interpretive method is not as separate as one might expect from the dream which is its object. Both dream and dream analysis are streamy, associative structures. The only difference between reported dream and analytic commentary is that the dream is more elliptical in the way it passes from sentence to sentence or image to image. Freud's interpretation fills up these ellipses or "absences" in

[139]

the dream; as Keats too is aware of having to fill in spaces by moving figures across a chequer board without being checked.

Quite often too, like Keats, Freud introduces explanatory material that branches off with a digressive life of its own—especially when that material is a name. An example will be helpful here. In trying to understand a dream about three women, one of them making dumplings *(Knödel)*, Freud recalls the ending of the first novel he had ever read, in which the hero goes mad and keeps calling out the names of the three women who had brought him the greatest happiness—and sorrow. One was called *Pélagie;* and by a path at least as eccentric as that of Keats, the three women become the three Fates; *Pélagie* becomes a bridge to the word "plagiarize," which then also throws light on *Knödel* as a name (the name of a person) rather than a common noun. Suddenly everything alliterates or "chimes." Here is a portion of Freud's analysis from the section on "Infantile Material as a Source of Dreams" in chapter 5.

> In connection with the three women I thought of the Fates who spin the destiny of man, and I knew that one of the three women—the inn-hostess in the dream—was the mother who gives life, and furthermore (as in my own case) gives the living creature its first nourishment. Love and hunger, I reflected, meet at a woman's breast. . . . So they really were Fates that I found in the kitchen when I went into it—as I had so often done in my childhood when I was hungry, while my mother, standing by the fire, had admonished me that I must wait till dinner was ready.—And now for the dumplings—the *Knödel!* One at least of my teachers at the University—and precisely the one to whom I owe my historical knowledge . . . would infallibly be reminded by *Knödel* of a person against whom he had been obliged to take legal action for *plagiarizing* his writing. The idea of plagiarizing . . . clearly led me to the second part of the dream, in which I was treated as though I were the thief who had for some time carried on his business of stealing overcoats in the lecture-rooms. I had written down the word 'plagiarizing' without thinking about it, because it just occured to me; but now I noticed that it could form a bridge *[Brücke]* between different pieces of the dream's manifest content. A chain of associations *(Pélagie—plagiarizing—plagiostomes* or sharks . . .—a *fish's swimming-bladder),* connected the old novel with the case of *Knödel* and with the overcoats, which clearly referred to implements used in sexual technique.

[140]

This is not the end: a further train of thoughts immediately takes off from the "honored name of Brücke," leading ("as though the need to set up forced connections regarded *nothing* as sacred") to the memory of Fleischl (*Fleisch:* meat), a second respected teacher, linked to Freud's experiments with cocaine in what he calls the *Latin Kitchen* (the dispensary or pharmacy).

In literary studies we often ask what the genre of a work may be. It is a question raised when the reader confronts a new or puzzling form; and it certainly arises when we read *The Interpretation of Dreams*. It is hard to call the book a work of science, and leave it at that. Often the fugual connections and especially the word chains are not furnished by the manifest content of the dream: though they may belong to the dream thoughts they do so only by virture of an analysis which is interpolative and like an elaborate joke. One is reminded of Freud's own aphorism: "The realm of jokes knows no limits." What, then, is the genre of this book?

My quotation from the Knödel dream suggests that Freud finds a strange and original way to write a *Confession*. I mean an autobiography that lays bare whatever it may be—certainly sexual wishes, guilt feelings, and social envy, as well as the infantile emotions that spur the quest for scientific fame. *The Double Helix* is nothing compared to Freud in disclosing the *libido* of science. "Freud's frankness," Kenneth Burke wrote, "is no less remarkable by reason of the fact that he had perfected a method for being frank. . . . what for him could fall within the benign category of observation could for [others] fall only within its malign counterpart, spying."

It is the reversal of malign into benign *and vice versa*, which risked, as Burke saw, a "drastic self-ostracizing act—the charting of the relations between ecclesia and cloaca." Freud's *Confession*, entitled *The Interpretation of Dreams*, even transcends Augustine's and Rousseau's, because in addition to a very moving if oblique narrative of self-justification, it launches an extraordinary mode of reading, one that is both wilder and more daring in its very rage for order than either rabbinic exegesis or the figural and typological method of the Church Fathers. Freud's way of interpreting dreams becomes a powerful hermeneutics, rivaling that of the great Western religions. Though his dreambook is an unlikely candidate for a Scripture—being, I have suggested, more like a Confession—it fashions a secular key out of phenomena that this same civilization had repressed by calling them sacred, then irrational, then trivial. Freud not only redeems this excluded mass from insignificance, he also introduces strange new *texts* for our considerations: texts neither literary nor Scriptural but whose discovery throws doubt on the transcription of all previous inner experience. Freud reveals much more than a code for the decipherment of dreams: he invents a new textuality by transcribing dreams in his own way. It is not just the dream which is important, but also the dream text. After Freud we all have Freudian dreams; that is, we report them that way—except for those chosen few who are Jungians.

Psychoanalysis, then, creates new texts as well as transforming our understanding of those already received. Yet because the religious systems of the past also disseminated methods of interpretation that were radically revisionary, it is important to emphasize two features that distinguish psychoanalytic interpretation from these influential modes.

The first difference concerns the transactive relation of text and commentary. The dream text is not an object with Scriptural fixity. Scripture itself, of course, or the many books *(biblia)* we now call the Bible, had to be edited and fixed by a succession of interpretive communities. But Freud allows us to see the commentary entering the text, incorporating itself with the dream: what he called his self-analysis, working on dreams he had, so invests and supplements an original version that it becomes less of an object and more of a series of linguistic relays that could lead anywhere—depending on the system of rails and who is doing the switching. The dream is like a sentence that cannot find closure. Freud keeps coming up with fragments of something already recounted, as well as adding meaning to meaning. This extreme indeterminacy, even if it was there in what we now call Scripture, is no longer available to us, despite suggestive residues of freedom in the early rabbis whose midrashim exposed every inconsistency or gap in the sacred text, or who elicited new interpretations by changing speculatively the received voweling, the *nekudoth*.

A second feature that distinguishes psychoanalytic interpretation is its *kakangelic* rather than *evangelic* nature. I admit to coining this discordant word. The New Testament claims to bring good news, and reinterprets the Old Testament—that is, the Hebrew Bible—in the light of its faith. If the Gospels emphasize mankind's guilt, they also counter it by the possibility of salvation. But Freud brings bad *(kaka)* news about the psyche, and offers no cure except through the very activity—analysis—which reveals this news. "A single Screw of Flesh / Is all that pins the Soul" Emily Dickinson wrote; and her homely metaphor keeps the hope open that on the other side of the "Vail" or "Gauze" of the body, her soul could enter into its freedom and see God or the loved one in full presence. Yet in Freud the "Screw of Flesh" or *la chose genitale* (Charcot) cannot be totally sublimated, not even through the noncarnal conversation which psychoanalysis institutes. For it is precisely through this conversation that the patient becomes more aware of the "mailed [maled] Nerve" as something—pin, penis, pen—without which there is no soul, no signification, good or bad.

The dream analysis I have previously cited reflects this *kakangelic* vision, this "inverse Freudian piety toward the sinister" (to quote Philip Rieff). Knödl, Fleischl, and Brücke do not appear as proper names in the dream, yet Freud's interpolative commentary dwells on the dream's misuse of such names. He calls it "a kind of childish naughtiness" and an act of retribution for witticisms made about his own name. He also mentions a mock-heroic verse written by Herder about Goethe. "Der du von Göttern abstammst, von Gothen oder vom Kote" ("Thou who art the descendant of Gods or Goths or dung"), and he answers it in the name of Goethe by quoting from the latter's *Iphigenia:* "So you too, divine figures, have turned to dust!" That Freud takes it on himself to answer Herder's quibble with a line of such pathos (it alludes to the death of many heroes during the siege of Troy) indicates something more than a regressive sensitivity about one's name. The dialogue of those two verses makes a little drama whose subject is the ambivalence that surrounds great men who have become ego ideals; and the ease with which their names can be profaned, dragged in the dust, causes Freud to balance Herder's childish punning with a compensatory impersonation. In *Totem and Taboo* the avoidance of the name of the dead in primitive societies, though more elaborately explained, still hinges on the same kind of envy or ambivalence. Freud has realized, in short, the profaning power of dreams; yet not of dreams only, but of language as it allows that chiming to mock and madden anything sacred. He has to decide whether *Goethe* or *Kot,* ecclesia or cloaca, evangelism or kakangelism is to be the dominant trend of his commentary. It happens that two members of that strange trinity, Knödl, Fleischl, and Brücke, are sacred to Freud; yet the dream degrades them from proper to ordinary nouns. As ordinary nouns, however, they can become quiet conduits for the dream work; though the plot thickens when we ask what the dream work is seeking to reveal.

For the teaching of two of these men nourished Freud's scientific ambitions: they were among his male Fates. We do not learn particulars of what they taught him, since the dream is after something more universal. If we suppose that the dream conspires with Freud's wish that dream analysis be recognized as a science, then a hieratic form of discourse must appear, analogous to the hieroglyphs the dream itself presents. Yet the dream's mode of expression remains distinctly vernacular rather than hieratic—that is, without terms from the *Latin Kitchen.* While the language of the dream, then, forged in the real kitchen of women and dumplings, reaches for a mysterious vernacular, or mother tongue, the chain of associations characterizing the language of the interpreter fails to transform the dream text into the "purer" discourse or sacred instrument of the scientist: his white overcoat or sublime condom.

Freud is brought back to his childlike if ambivalent veneration for Brücke, Fleischl, etc. He also experiences a related anxiety, that he may be a plagiarist like Knödl and so must clear his name. The dream discloses what infantile jealousies still prop the scientific project; but part of that project—not analyzed by Freud—is the ideal of a flawless discourse, a Latin of the intellect, a dream-redeeming sacred commentary. *Not the dream is holy but the power of the interpretation as it methodizes and universalizes itself.*

"Behold, the dreamer cometh." That is said mockingly of Joseph in the Pentateuch; yet Joseph gains fame not as a dreamer but as a dream interpreter. We glimpse in Freud the dreamer rising to fame not through vainglorious dreams but through the art or science of dream interpretation, which he called "the royal road."

The name "Sigmund Freud" is indeed a misnomer. For in wrestling with the angel of the unconscious, with the evasive dream thoughts, Freud strips away so many layers of idealization, so many euphemistic formulas, that only wounded names are left. But through his unconsciousness-raising we learn what we are up against: profanation, defamation, self-slander, equivocation, distortion, ambivalence, displacement, repression, censorship. Freud neither curses nor blesses that hardwon knowledge; and so his greatness, finally, may be his moral style, that he neither palliates nor inculpates human nature.

From Freud I turn to Wordsworth, respecting his own statement that "The poets were there before me." My text is from the Lucy poems, a group of short lyrics on the death of a young girl, which is a motif that goes back to the Greek Anthology and evokes three highly charged themes: incompleteness, mourning, and memory.

> A slumber did my spirit seal;
>   I had no human fears:
> She seemed a thing that could not feel
>   The touch of earthly years.
>
> No motion has she now, no force;
>   She neither hears nor sees;
> Rolled round in earth's diurnal course,
>   With rocks, and stones, and trees.

"A slumber did myself spirit seal." After that line one would expect a dream vision. The formula is, I fell asleep, and behold! Yet there is no vision, or not in the expected sense. The boundary between slumber and vision is elided. That the poet had no human fears, that he experienced a curious anesthesia vis-à-vis the girl's mortality or his own, may be what he names a slumber. As out of Adam's first sleep an Eve arose, so out of this sealed but not unconscious spirit a womanly image arises with the same idolatrous charm. Wordsworth's image seems to come from within; it is a delusive daydream, yet still a revision of that original vision.

There is, however, no sense of an eruption from the unconscious: brevity and condensation do not lead, as they do in dreams, to remarkable puns, striking figures, or deviant forms of speech. Nor is it necessary to be psychoanalytic to recognize that the trance is linked to an overidealization of the loved person. The second stanza, which reports that she has died, should, in that case, express disillusionment. Yet remarkably this does not occur: the poet does not exclaim or cry out. Both transitions, the passage from slumber to dream, and the breaking of the dream, are described without surprise or shock.

Is there nothing which betrays how deeply disturbing the fantasy may have been? Perhaps, if the emotion was strong, it is natural enough that the words should seek to understate and to seal the impression. There is, however, an uncanny *displacement* on the structural level that is consonant with what Freud calls the omnipotence of thoughts and a general overestimation of psychical acts attributed by him to primitive cultures and, in contemporary civilization, to art.

This displacement is, rhetorically speaking, also a transference: in the initial stanza, the poet is sealed in slumber; in the second that slumber has passed over, as if intensified, to the girl. She falls asleep forever; and her death is specifically portrayed as a quasi-immortality not unlike what his imagination has prematurely projected onto her. "Rolled round in earth's diurnal course," she indeed cannot "feel / The touch of earthly years." This subtle transfer, this metaphor as extended structure rather than punctual figure of speech, is anticipated by at least one local condensation. "Human" in "I had no human fears" (line 2) is a transferred epithet. The line should read: "I had no such fears as would have come to me had I considered her a human—that is, mortal—being." We do not know which way the transfer goes: from the girl to the poet or vice versa. And yet we *do* know: surely the illusion took rise in the poet and is an error of the imagination. Yet Wordsworth leaves that illusion its moment of truth as if it were natural, and not in any way out of the ordinary. He does not take pains to demystify it. Nature has its own supernatural gleam, however evanescent it is.

The supernatural illusion preserves the girl from a certain kind of touch, "of earthly years" in the first stanza, but in the second she is totally distanced. Coleridge surmised that the lyric was an imaginary epitaph for Wordsworth's sister, and F. W. Bateson seized on this to claim that "A slumber" (and the Lucy poems as a whole) arose from incestuous emotions and expressed a death wish by the brother against the sister. The poem removes an object of love by moving it beyond touch. In all but one important respect it confirms Freud's analysis about the way neurotics evade reality. Freud shows how the whole world is eventually embargoed, put beyond touch or contact by a widening fear of contagion. The only difference is that in Wordsworth the whole world enters in the second stanza as an image with resonances that are more positive than sinister.

Wordsworth's poem, moreover, practically offers itself for inclusion in a section of the dreambook that contains Freud's most famous literary interpretation. In "Dreams of the Death of Persons of whom the Dreamer is fond" (chapter 5) he discusses the story of Oedipus. We readily respond to the death of Oedipus, says Freud, "because it might have been ours—because the oracle laid the same curse upon us before our birth as upon him." That curse is understood to be an unconsciously fulfilled wish, a pattern we also suspect is present in "A slumber." But the question for literary criticism, even as it engages with psychoanalysis, is why such a wish, at once idealizing and deadly, and as if fulfilled in the second stanza, does not disturb the poet's language more. Even if the death did not occur except in idea, one might expect the spirit to awake, and to wonder what kind of deception it had practiced on itself. Yet though the poem can be said to approach muteness—if we interpret the blank between the stanzas as another elision, a *lesion* in fact—Wordsworth keeps speech going without a trace of guilty knowledge. The eyes of the spirit may be open, but the diction remains unperturbed.

I want to suggest that Wordsworth's curious yet powerful complacency is related to euphemism: not of the artificial kind, the substitution of a good word for a bad one, or the strewing of flowers on a corpse, but an earthy euphemism, as it were, a balm deriving from common speech, from its unconscious obliquity and inbuilt commitment to avoid silence. To call it euphemism may be inadequate, but the quality I point to resists overconsciousness and demystification.

It is generally the task of the critic to uncover euphemism in any sphere: literary, psychological, political. When Freud tells a patient the meaning of one of her flowery dreams, "she quite lost her liking for it." A kakangelic unmasking may be necessary, although not many would go as far as Kenneth Burke, who praised Freud's method as "an interpretive sculpting in excrement" and put praise in action by suggesting we read Keats' "Beauty is Truth, Truth Beauty" as "Body is Turd, Turd Body." What makes Wordsworth's poetry so difficult to psychoanalyze is its underlying and resistant euphemism, coterminous with ordinary language, and distinguished from the courtly and affected diction of the time.

Consider the word "slumber" as such a euphemism. Then consider the entire second stanza as a paraphrase for "she is dead." The negative aspect of these phrases can be heightened. The "slumber" may remind us of bewitchment or fascination, even of hypnosis. It could be a hypnoid state in which one hears voices without knowing it, or performs actions on the basis of these voices. In another Lucy poem, "Strange fits of passion," such automatism is strongly suggested, and a voice does intrude at the end in the form of an incomplete sentence that expresses, in context, a premonition, but in itself is more ambiguous: "If Lucy should be dead!"

That we may be in the domain of voices is made more probable by the word "passion" in "Strange fits of passion": it meant an outcry under the impact of strong emotions. Yet to pursue this analysis would mean to go from the issue of euphemism to how language is a synthesis not only of sounds but of speech acts, and especially—if we look to infancy—of threats, promises, admonitions, yesses and nos that come to the child as ideas of reference in vocal form, even if (or because) not every word is understood. Such an analysis would also oblige us to explore the text of poetry as an undoing of that synthesis, or a partial recovery of the elements behind the deceptive neutrality of language. Ordinary speech, from this perspective, is a form of sleep-walking, the replication of internalized phrases or commands without conscious affect; poetic speech is an exposure of that condition, a return to a sense of language as virtually alive—in any case with enough feeling to delay our passage from words to things. Speech re-enters an original zone of stress and inhibition and becomes precarious.

That precariousness is both acknowledged and limited by Wordsworth's euphemism. The second stanza of "A slumber," unlike the end of "Strange fits," does not cry out: as a periphrasis for "she is dead" it amplifies and even embellishes that reluctant phrase. It is hard to think of the lyric as a stark epitaph skirting aphasia. And though the traumatic or mortifying event may occasion the euphemism, it cannot be its cause. We must find a "feeding source" (to use one of the poet's own metaphors) elsewhere; and we can find it only in the other threat to speech: the near-ecstasy depicted in the previous stanza. A common source of inarticulate or mute behavior, such ecstasy, whatever its nature, carries over into the second stanza's euphemia.

Epitaphs, of course, are conventionally associated with consoling and pleasant words. Here, however, not all the words are consoling. They approach a negative that could foreclose the poem: "No . . . No . . . Neither . . . Nor. . . ." Others even show Wordsworth's language penetrated by an inappropriate subliminal punning. So "diurnal" (line 7) divides into "die" and "urn," and "course" may recall the older pronunciation of "corpse." Yet these condensations are troublesome rather than expressive; the power of the second stanza resides predominantly in the euphemistic displacement of the word *grave* by an image of *gravitation* ("Rolled round in earth's diurnal course"). And though there is no agreement on the tone of this stanza, it is clear that a subvocal word is uttered without being written out. It is a word that rhymes with "fears" and "years" and "hears," but which is closed off by the very last syllable of the poem: "trees." Read "tears," and the animating, cosmic metaphor comes alive, the poet's lament echoes through nature as in pastoral elegy. "Tears," however, must give way to what is written, to a dull yet definitive sound, the anagram "trees."

Pastoral elegy, in which rocks, woods, and streams are called upon to mourn the death of a person, or to echo the complaint of a lover, seems too extravagant a genre for this chastely fashioned inscription. Yet the muted presence of the form reminds us what it means to be a nature poet. From childhood on, as the autobiographical *Prelude* tells us, Wordsworth was aware of "unknown modes of being" and of strange sympathies emanating from nature. He was haunted by an animistic universe that seemed to stimulate, share, and call upon his imagination. The Lucy poems evoked a nature spirit in human form, perhaps modeled after his sister, and the forerunner of Cathy Linton in *Wuthering Heights*. It makes no sense to suppose a death wish unless we link it to the ecstatic feelings in this poetry. Yet where do these feelings come from? Wordsworth does not actually say he projected his starry emotions upon the girl. It is, rather, *our* habit of giving priority to the psychological state of the writer, *our* inability to consider his euphoria as a contagious identification with the girl, that makes us assume it is a dream and a delusion. For to think otherwise would return us to the world of pastoral elegy or even to a magical universe, with currents of sympathy running along esoteric channels—the very world described as primitive in *Totem and Taboo*.

Reading Freud through Wordsworth now brings us closer to a critique of Freud. The discovery of the role played in mental illness by large-scale wishful thinking, by omnipotence of thought, is a proven achievement. Yet Freud's description of the thought process of primitives and their licensed contemporary relic, the artist, is for once not reflective or dialectical enough. Freud wants so badly to place psychotherapy on a firm, scientific foundation that he exempts himself from an overestimation of psychical acts. At the same time he has made it hard for *us* to value interpretations not based on the priority of a psychological factor. Animism is accepted as a functional belief only in fiction—in Jensen's *Gradiva* or Wordsworth's poems or *Wuthering Heights*—but is considered dysfunctional in terms of mental health unless demystified by psychoanalysis. Perhaps the decisive matter here is not a compulsion to demystify (to be kakangelic) but a failure to draw a certain type of experience into that special dialogue established by psychoanalysis. For the problem with art as with nonclassical anthropological data is that interpretation cannot find enough associations for them. Psychoanalysis distrusts, with good reason, the appearance of autonomy in such artifacts even while recognizing their force, which is then labeled "primitive."

Yet Freud could acknowledge, in passing, that his persistent, even obsessive, mode of interpretation might share the delusional character of superstitions it sought to analyze and dispel. He himself may have suffered from a fear of contagion that placed, as Jacques Lacan and others have claimed, too many protective barriers between his hermeneutics and religious hermeneutics. Those barriers are coming down, or do not seem as impenetrable as they once were. Indeed, in the first part of my talk, I suggested some analogies that made religion and psychoanalysis enemy brothers. But I can be somewhat more specific, in conclusion, about what Freud saw yet tried to close out.

He was always distrustful and demystifying towards eudemonic feelings, the kind that Wordsworth expressed in "A slumber." He considered them a "thalassal regression" (to use Ferenczi's phrase), an attempt to regain an inertial state, the nirvana of preoedipal or undifferentiated being. Wordsworth's attitude was very different. In all his most interesting work he describes a developmental impasse centering on eudemonic sensations experienced in early childhood and associated with nature. Whether beautiful or frightening, they sustain and nourish him as intimations of immortality; and though Wordsworth can be called the first ego psychologist, the first careful observer of the growth of a mind, he shows the strength and usurpation of those ecstatic memories as they threaten the maturing poet who must respect their drive. If there is a death wish in the Lucy poems, it is insinuated

[151]

by nature itself and asks lover or growing child not to give up earlier yearnings—to die rather than become an ordinary mortal.

This developmental impasse is quite clear in the present poem. Divided into two parts, separated formally by a blank and existentially by a death, the epitaph does not record a disenchantment. The mythic girl dies, but that word seems to wrong her. Her star-like quality is maintained despite her death, for the poet's sense of her immutability deepens by reversal into an image of *participation mystique* with the planet earth. There is loss, but there is also a calculus of gain and loss which those two stanzas weigh like two sides of a balance. Their balancing point is the impasse I have mentioned: such a death could seem better than dying into the light of common day. Yet to think only *that* is to make immutability of such value that human life is eclipsed by it. Ideas of pre-existence or afterlife arise. My analysis has tried to capture a complex state of affairs that may resemble religious experiences or pathological states but which Wordsworth sees as an imaginative constant, ordinary and incurable. For those who need more closure in interpretation, who wish to know exactly what the poet felt, I can only suggest a phrase from his famous "Ode: Intimations of Immortality from Recollections of Early Childhood." The meanest flower, he writes, can give him "thoughts that do often lie too deep for tears." The girl has become such a thought.

Yet even here we meet a euphemism once more. Naming something "a thought too deep for tears": is that not a remarkable periphrasis for the inability to grieve? This inability seems to be a strength rather than a weakness if we take the figure literally. "Too deep for tears" suggests a place—a mental place—beyond fits of passion or feelings, as if Wordsworth desired that grave immunity. Yet to call the words euphemistic is to acknowledge at the same time that they are so affecting that mourning is not absent but continued in a different mode. The work of writing seems to have replaced the work of mourning. Is there a link, then, between writing and grieving, such that writing can be shown to assist those Herculean psychic labors Freud described for us, whose aim is to detach us from the lost object and reattach us to the world?

[152]

My main concern has been to understand yet delimit Freud's kak-angelic mode of interpretation. Wordsworth enabled me to do this by showing that euphemism can be an ordinary rather than artificial as-pect of language, especially when the work of mourning is taking place, which is pretty much all the time. I have argued that this euphemism cannot be demystified because it is not simply a figure of speech cov-ering up naked truth. Looking closely at a poem by Wordsworth re-veals a far more complicated situation. The strongest euphemisms in Wordsworth are also the most naturalized; they seem to belong to lan-guage rather than being imposed on it. They are not in the service of evading reality or putting the best face on things. They have an energy, a force of their own, one which counters a double threat to speech: expectedly, that which comes from loss; but unexpectedly, that which comes from ecstasy, even if it is a remembered ecstasy, and so touched by loss. I have sometimes talked of euphemia rather than euphemism, both because we are dealing with a feature basic to language, and not simply to one poet's use of language; and also because the aphasia it circumscribes remains perceptible. Wordsworth's euphemia, in short, is nourished by sources in language or the psyche we have not ade-quately understood. They bring us back to an awareness of how much sustaining power language has, even if our individual will to speak and write is assaulted daily by the most trivial as well as traumatic events.

This sustaining power of language is not easily placed, however, on the side of goodness or love (eros) rather than death. Writing has an impersonal, even impersonating quality which brings the poet close to the dead "whose names are in our lips," to quote Keats. *Personare* meant, originally, to "speak through" another, usually by way of an ancestral mask, which made the speaker a medium or an actor in a drama in which the dead renewed their contact with the living.

It is not surprising, therefore, that there should be a hint of the in-voluntary or mechanical in stanza 2 of "A slumber": a hint of the indifference to which the girl's difference is reduced, and which, how-ever tragic it may be, obeys a law that supports the stability a survi-vor's speech requires. "O blessed machine of language," Coleridge once

[153]

exclaimed; this very phrase is symptomatic of the euphemia without which speech would soon cease to be, or turn into its feared opposite, an eruptive cursing or sputtering as in Tourette's syndrome. Coleridge has to bless the machine *as* a machine; yet his blessing is doubly euphemistic, for he knew too well what the machine could do in its unblessed aspect, as an uncontrollable stream of associations which coursed through him by day and especially by night.

It is here we link up once more with Freud, who created a new hermeneutics by charting compulsive and forced connections which "regarded *nothing* as sacred." Someone said of a typical lecture by Emerson that "it had no connection, save in God." Freud's kakangelic method removes all vestiges of that final clause. The recovered dream thoughts have no connections save in the negative fact that their capacity for profanation is without limit. All other connections are the result of a secondary process extending from the dream work's disguises and displacements to more conscious revisions. At times, therefore, the manifest dream content may appear saner than an interpretation that reverses the dream's relatively euphemistic bearing or disintegrates its discursive structure. Instead of completing dream texts, or by extension literary texts (or, like Jung, encouraging their synthesis), Freud makes them less complete, less fulfilling. The more interpretation, it seems, the less closure.

But did Freud himself regard nothing as sacred? I have already suggested that if the dream is unholy, and is shown to be so by the interpretation, the power of that interpretation as it methodizes and universalizes itself is something very near to holy. One wonders how else Freud could have continued his work without falling mute, without being overcome by the bad news he brought. The dream peculiar to Freud, as interpreter and scientist, a dream which survives all self-analysis, is of a purified language that remains uncontaminated by its materials, that neither fulfills nor represses an all-too-human truth. I hope Freud's shade will understand this parting remark as a blessing on the only scientist I have ever been able to read.

The Weight of What Happened

THERE IS A speculation by the well-known mythographer Mircea Eliade that major religious holidays are not only commemorative (celebrating a past event), but also soothers of a burdened memory. They cancel a debt by a sort of solemn orgy; they undo, especially in the Judeo-Christian tradition, a past that weighs on those who take history seriously, who cannot see it as merely contingent, as a meaningless and catastrophic accumulation. As Nietzsche said in *The Use and Abuse of History:* "Life is absolutely impossible without forgetfulness." The modern historical sense, he added, may prevent that forgetfulness and may injure our ability to live by enforcing a state of perpetual wakefulness.

The Jewish Day of Atonement could be taken to corroborate this insight. We remember all our debts toward God, all sins of commission and omission, but only in order to be purged of them, in order for a New Year to begin also within the individual. This paradoxical disburdenment of memory through ritual rememoration was also cryptically expressed in the Baal Shem Tov's famous "Memory is Redemption," now inscribed on Yad Vashem, a house that testifies to the most ruinous episode in the history of the Jews. Yad Vashem, the museum in Jerusalem, documents the Holocaust in the light of a phrase that is basic to every attempt to make sense of a catastrophe which threatens to turn us all into Nietzsche's insomniac philosopher.

The present essay was occasioned by the publication of two books: Yosef Hayim Yerushalmi's *Zakhor: Jewish History and Jewish Memory* (Seattle: University of Washington Press, 1982); and *From a Ruined Garden: The Memorial Books of Polish Jewry,* edited and translated by Jack Kugelmass and Jonathan Boyarin (New York: Schocken, 1982).

[155]

To "understand" the Holocaust, we are using for the first time all the resources of modern historiography. What in previous eras of pogroms, massacres, expulsions, was remembered mainly by being absorbed into a repetition or extension of existing prayers—into that kind of collective mourning—is now much harder to treat ritually: first, because of the enormity of the event, many find no true analogy; then, because by a reversal of traditional procedures, the call to remember *(zakhor)* is no longer satisfied by Days of Remembrance alone, but aspires to a writing so fearfully detailed that it may never be erased from the conscience of the nations.

This modern turn to historiography may have significant consequences. Yosef Hayim Yerushalmi has argued that it is causing the first real rupture between Jewish memory and Jewish history. For to document something faithfully and endlessly cannot give the relief that comes from ritual observance, which stresses "not the historicity of the past, but its eternal contemporaneity." The collective memory, working through ritual and recital within the confines of Bible, Talmud, and similar texts, remains redemptive or integrative. Yet many today cannot choose "myth" over "history"—a possibility still open even after the expulsion of the Jews from Spain, which saw some history writing in the modern sense, but mainly a spreading mysticism. Nor does Zionism help settle the balance between ritual memory and historiography: it weakens Jewish memory by its revolt against Diaspora continuities, and also weakens historiography by vacating historical time between Masada and the founding of the state of Israel.

Yerushalmi fears that the historical sense, which modern Jewish writers themselves cultivate with luminous persistence, will hasten the decline of Jewish memory. The historian's task, therefore, "can no longer be limited to finding continuities in Jewish history, not even 'dialectical' ones. Perhaps the time has come to look more closely at ruptures, breaches, breaks, to identify them more precisely, to see how Jews endured them. . . ." Yet he does not guarantee this venture success: he refuses to substitute for myths of history a myth of the historian. To be a "physician of memory" is indeed the right vocation. But since among the Jews memory did not depend on historians in the first place (the "collective memories of the Jewish people," he writes, "were a function of the shared faith, cohesiveness, and will of the group itself, transmitting and re-creating its past through an entire complex of interlocking social and religious institutions that functioned organically to achieve this"), the historian, as he puts it sadly, seems at best a pathologist rather than a physician.

The collective memory is not easy to define. In principle, it should be possible to understand what is Jewish (or any other persistent group identity) from an embodied knowledge, a set of practices and symbols which have attracted a variety of explanations, some in the form of stories. To such questions as "What mean these stones?" or "What mean ye by these ceremonies?" there are various kinds of answers, not all convergent, not all official. Jewish tradition for a long time did not codify them. It preserved and kept probing; it expected scholars to memorize everything and find their own way among the authorities. Every scholar was immersed in this labor of reading, transmitting, and sorting the past; it was not left to someone called a historian.

This is clearly less true today, and in that sense it is correct to talk of a decline of the collective memory. Story and history separate. Yet this also liberates story, makes it stand in its own light, reveal its own character. We have learned that stories cannot be abbreviated by an intellectual method, or foreclosed by spiritual hindsight. Christian typology, which turns the Hebrew Bible into an "Old" Testament prefiguring a "New" Truth that completes it, suffers imaginatively from such a foreclosure, though Christian story generates, of course, parables of its own, episodes that are enigmatic enough to haunt as well as guide the reader. From Judah Halevi's twelfth-century theological work, *Kuzari*, advocating story-telling over philosophical argument, to Walter Benjamin's essay in our time on how storytelling is becoming a lost art because we insert too much explanatory material, there is an awareness, however easily trivialized ("Pepperidge Farm remembers," spoken in a great-grandpa voice), that something like a collective memory exists. Unlike Halevi, of course, Benjamin knew that the collective memory, as an uninterrupted or self-reparative process of handing down wisdom from generation to generation, seemed now in jeop-

[157]

ardy, and that contemporary ideologies like Nazism were leaping into the breach by professing a politics of repristination, a violent return to an aboriginal state of purity that, in effect, elided both story and history.

It is not oral transmission as such which is crucial, rather the fact that ritual and recital combine effectively to make memorable stories which survive when other channels of communication fail. Whether or not we fully understand how this collective memory works, we know that in Jewish tradition learning and legend have reinforced rather than subverted each other. We also know that historicism in its earliest phase recovered the oral traditions of other peoples and that the major effort of nineteenth-century philology was to analyze ballad, Bible, and epic as the expression of a communal spirit. Even as individualism asserted itself, communal forms were retrieved. Often, however, a virulent nationalism took hold of that research and politicized it, so that the concept of a "people" or "folk," and of collective rather than individual expression, was used to censor and suppress nonconformist tendencies.

Any talk about the "collective memory" must be approached, then, with circumspection. The imputed character of such a memory may itself be the outcome of historical anxieties. It is premature to assume that a collective memory once existed that is now endangered by modern developments. The only certain thing is that the contemporary historian has a self-image of his discipline which sets up an opposition: "a Jewish historiography divorced from Jewish collective memory and, in crucial respects, thoroughly at odds with it."

Must we accept Yerushalmi's stark contrast between these two sources of knowledge and identity? It is certainly important to insist on a difference not sufficiently studied; yet there is a tendency, which one finds equally in literary studies (Yerushalmi admits that his distinction reflects an "evergrowing modern dichotomy"), to exaggerate the organic, or ideal and unitary character of a previous kind of memory, as if unconscious adhesion to a way of life were more genuine than a broken or born-again pattern. The breaches and breaks Yerushalmi wishes to identify more precisely, and the endurance that helped the

[158]

Jews to overcome them, may have always existed. But now there are fears, more prophetic than realistic, that the rise of the historical sense will doom altogether a collective memory associated too easily with continuity and authoritative transmission.

This is a time, then, when we should ask what middle terms or significant links can be found between Jewish historiography and Jewish memory—links that might be strengthened once more. That such intermediate forms exist is suggested by Yerushalmi himself in certain of his comments on the Holocaust. He remarks that though it has engendered more historical research than any single event in Jewish history, "I have no doubt whatsoever that its image is being shaped, not at the historian's anvil, but in the novelist's crucible." The novel, he suggests, shows that Jews, while not rejecting the burden of history out of hand, expect to be relieved from it by a new metahistorical myth, like those Sephardi Jews who chose mysticism over history to explain the cataclysm of the Spanish expulsion.

I am less sure that fiction can play the role attributed to it by this distinguished historian, who speaks urbanely yet in bitterness of heart. He feels the need to acknowledge the rise of something (fiction) that is inherently profane and perhaps profaning, yet which in previous eras was kept within the boundaries of ritual and recital. Fiction is, no doubt, an image maker today, and open to popular misuse, especially in the form of televised simplification. But that is why, first of all, we have such an increasingly complex literary criticism, a hygiene of reading with iconoclastic overtones. Like the historian, the literary critic looks "more closely at ruptures, breaches, breaks," not to defeat tradition even more, but to show the heteronomic rather than hegemonic structure of every significant mode of discourse, sacred or secular. But equally important are "memorial" genres that perpetuate, even today, the collective memory in a nonfictional yet highly imaginative form.

Among these genres are the video memoirs incorporated, for example, in YIVO's film about Jewish life in Poland before the war, *Image Before My Eyes,* or the tapes being made by Yale's Video Archive for

Holocaust Testimonies. This new oral history has not yet found its place: it looks suspicious to the positivist historian, yet it should not be left by default to the literary critic's tendency to turn everything into narratology. A second link to the collective memory is represented by another YIVO-inspired work, *From a Ruined Garden*, a selection from the "memorial books" of Polish Jewry indispensable to historians interested in the survivors of the Holocaust as well as the Holocaust itself.

As the editors tell us in their fine introduction, most memorial books, or *yizker-bikher*, are written in Yiddish, and they describe salient aspects of the life of both small and very large Jewish communities in Poland. At least six hundred such books exist for Eastern European Jewry alone. Some are in Hebrew or English or whatever language the survivors speak. Compiled on shoestring budgets, they are an unusual example of collective authorship, commonplace books that bring together whatever documents the survivors could save. They contain the records, known in each community as its *pinkes*, historical narratives based on all kinds of sources, from encyclopedia articles to eyewitness accounts. But they are interspersed with personal sketches and reflections, vivid characterizations of both eccentric and leading personalities, and learned summaries of folklore and linguistic habits. Some contain maps and photographs. The first modern books of this kind emerge after World War I and the Ukrainian pogroms. Most *yizker* books, however, were compiled in response to the Holocaust. They are the equivalent in words to communal tombstones erected by *landsmannschaften* (fraternal societies of emigrés and survivors) in their home cemeteries. "No graves have been left of all those who were slain," we read in such a book. "Beloved and precious martyrs of Koriv, we bring you to burial today! In a *yizker-bukh*, a memorial volume! Today we have set up a tombstone in memory of you!" The recently announced Yad Vashem project to build a "Valley of the Destroyed Communities" extends this work of mourning. It has to embrace not individuals alone, but entire communities in which the Jews were among the oldest settlers. Of three million in Poland, only ten percent survived.

Let me say at once how difficult and disconcerting it is, how moving and necessary, to encounter this collection. Every story or testimony in it is and is not like every other. I wonder whether such a treasury of sorrows has been published before. Who has not seen, in certain Catholic churches of Europe, a wall crowded with notes to the Virgin Mary, hopeful plaques and inscriptions in all sizes and shapes? To me it seemed as if I had come across an endless wall of such tablets, stretched across time, pregnant words snatched from an underworld of private and communal tragedy. The dead cannot speak; here the survivors speak for the dead as well as for themselves; or like Esther-Khaye, the *Zogerin* ("Sayer"), for the illiterate and the grief-stricken unable to talk:

> Just at daybreak before the High Holy Days, this picture is to be seen: a large crowd of women, led by Esther-Khaye bearing her book of supplications, set off for the cemetery. The way to the graveyard is not far from town, and as Esther-Khaye enters, she feels at home, among people she knows. "Good morning, God," she begins in a tragic melody, "Your servant Esther-Khaye has come. . . ." And approaching the grave, she looks over at the woman on whose behalf she is supplicating, and words begin to pour from her mouth, as if from a spring.
>
> First she calls out the name of the deceased and strikes the gravestone three times with her hand, speaking as if to a living person: "Good morning to you, Rive-Mindl the daughter of Hankev-Tsvi, your daughter Sore-Rivke has come, for she wants to see you and pour out her bitter heart before you. Look, Rive-Mindl, at what has become of your daughter, if you were to arise now and see what has become of your daughter, you would return to the grave. Request, Rive-Mindl, a good year for your daughter, a kosher year, that she may know no ill, exert yourself for her sake, why are you silent? Why do you not supplicate the Lord of the Universe?"

Taken from the Zabludow *yizker* book, published in Buenos Aires in 1961, this story, like many others, has no direct relation to the Holocaust. Yet it is recalled, together with grim and graphic accounts of the destruction, because these volumes memorialize a vanished life in its vigor. One finds depictions of the market, of special festivals, of a girl's schoolroom, of anarchist and other political demonstrations and deaths, of local quarrels, of Jewish fighters in the Spanish Civil War. There are reminiscences from the real Chelm (known in legend for its naive

[161]

townsfolk), sayings attributed to the Dubner Magid, and a grotesque *fait divers* from the camps: "How I read Yiddish Literature to an S.S. Captain." The sections dealing specifically with the Holocaust and its aftermath take up only a third of the volume. Emphasis falls on the variegated, often joyful, culture of the Polish Jews, on what existed before the garden was ruined.

The task of anthologizing must have been trying. The editors, anthropologists by profession, chose what they found most compelling: humorous or tragic stories illustrating everyday life and its underlying tensions. Even if what they left out is important, at least the quarry of these sources has begun. A scholarly "Bibliography of Eastern European Memorial Books" is appended. There are also German-Jewish memorial books to be explored, though they tend more to the learned monograph. They can be found in the Leo Baeck Institute.

Can we reflect on the art revealed by this collection? The vignette presenting Esther-Khaye has the intimacy of Yiddish, and we cannot call such provincial stories "great" or "heroic," accustomed as we are to Western literature. Yet the intimate detail builds up typical characters or scenes, and evokes an acute sense of the difference made by speech—from lighthearted joking to bearing witness—in a universe of death. Esther-Khaye, seen in retrospect, stands for the difficulty of mourning, and for the increased strain of that effort after the Holocaust, when there is not enough voice to go around. Even the familiar prayers barely save themselves. Yet if the effect here is anything but heroic, there is a category of the memorable which is "above heroic," and which lies at the heart of all imaginative writing as it reanimates the colors and figures of a culture that should not be allowed to die a second time by becoming a nostalgic and frozen memory. What is delightful about Esther-Khaye is precisely her spontaneous, creative use of a traditional ceremony and its formulas. Everything is familiar, yet nothing is rigid.

From a Ruined Garden is an indispensable sourcebook that shows Jewish memory interacting with history. It renews a genre going back at least to the fourteenth century. Yerushalmi points to the famous *Memorbuch* of Nuremburg which summarizes persecutions in Germany and France from the First Crusade of 1096 to the Black Death of 1349. Without these books in modern form we would have only the records of the perpetrators: orders of the day, intake lists, lives reduced to itemized effects, names and numbers in endless series. By the poetic justice of the *yizker-bikher*, there is a *gilgul*, or a transmigration, of names—belonging to places, persons, and customs—extended as in a Mourner's Kaddish, though here by means of story and testimony.

Is it the literary scholar in me that responds so strongly to these names saved from obliteration, as if they were revenants who are offered the life from which they were cut off, if only in the body of these memoirs? Despite Yerushalmi's caution that "although *Memorbücher* may contain important historical information, they cannot be regarded as historiography," I regard them as a type of history with its own form and reason, a popular and restitutive genre. That genre is historical rather than historiographical: penetrated by contingency, by the fact that these survived and these did not, but also by an insurgent memorial tradition that gathered in and recorded, in a spontaneous and composite, rather than ritual and integrated form, the fullness of these names. On the one hand, the unutterably sacred name of God, called *haShem*, "The Name"; on the other, motley syllables often more like nicknames, sometimes short (Yosl, Schloyme Healer), sometimes evocative of rabbinic grandeur (Rabbi Reb Yoshuah Yankev).

As the *Sefer Kalushin*, the memorial book of the town of Kalushin, writes of a tragedy in the last century, when a synagogue was burnt: "The place stood empty; only the terror and the legends remained." That remains true here too. The names return; fragments of ordinary life are recovered; the *landsmannschaften* piece together emblems and synecdoches of their former existence. Yet nothing fills up. Some of the terror is given shape and purged. But one cannot say that these memories bring relief, even if they take the place of tears. Nor do they drift toward a new myth. Relief comes only, perhaps, in glimpsing a life that is still familar to us, that has not been estranged. It is not fantasy we view, but reality—a reality which knows how to make use of fantasy "year in, year out, every time with the same familiar pattern" as is written of Esther-Khaye's performance.

But there is not yet such "tranquility" as Yehuda Amichai's poem on Jerusalem offers, moving rhythmically from the task of remembering to a natural forgetting:

> Everything here is busy with the task of remembering:
> the ruin remembers, the garden remembers
> the cistern remembers its water and the memorial grove
> remembers on a marble plaque a distant holocaust. . . .
>
> But names are not important in these hills,
> like at the cinema, when the credits on screen
> before the film are not yet interesting and at the end of the film
> are no longer so. The lights come up, the letters fade,
> the rippling curtain comes down, doors are open and outside is
>   the night.

Social Science and the Humanities

A FAMOUS PASSAGE in Friedrich Schiller's *Letters on Aesthetic Education* (1795) describes the "wound" which culture, through specialization or the division of social and intellectual labor, inflicts on the spirit of man—and of woman too:

> It was culture itself which inflicted this wound upon modern man. Once the increase of empirical knowledge, and more exact modes of thought, made sharper divisions between the sciences inevitable, and once the increasingly complex machinery of State necessitated a more rigorous separation of ranks and occupations, then the inner bond of human nature tore apart, and a disastrous conflict set its harmonious powers at variance.[1]

I cite this passage without any claim that what Schiller names aesthetic education could bind up this wound, or reverse the fall into division. His myth of corruption presupposes a Greek or Classicist harmony that may never have existed. Neither Hegel nor Marx nor Nietzsche managed to demystify totally this illusion of an earlier state in which man was more than the image of his function. Even today the concept of culture includes that of aesthetic education, so that we paradoxically

1. Friedrich Schiller, *On the Aesthetic Education of Man*, Elizabeth Wilkinson and L. A. Willoughby, eds. and trs. (Oxford: Clarendon Press, 1967), p. 33. I have revised the translation somewhat.

The present essay was first delivered at a Conference on Humanities and the Social Sciences, sponsored by the Rockefeller Institute in New York, January 31, 1975. The ending is slightly revised.

[165]

turn to culture (the arts) in order to heal the wounds of culture (civilization). The problem dramatized in Schiller by a historicizing myth also motivates conferences like ours which seek to bring the sciences into one fold with the humanities.

Another way of stating the problem is as follows: while we suspect that the divisional or departmental approach to knowledge is irreversible, a distinction can still be made between curriculum and curriculum vitae. The "major," which, as etymology suggests, helps to mature the student, does not make him necessarily into Wallace Stevens' "Major man." Nor does anyone expect it to do so. Still, all education aims to raise the student to this majority, to give him "mündigkeit" or a right to his own voice. The question of education, then, as it affects both the humanities and social sciences, is how correspondent, how reciprocal, curriculum and curriculum vitae can be.

The solution of the 1960s—to hypostatize that decade once more—was to try to make curriculum and curriculum vitae immediately, totally reciprocal, by bringing the academy into the street and the street into the academy. A kind of street classroom was established within the university; the privacy of teaching as well as of intellectual inquiry in general was challenged; and in a secular version of the apocalypse, all the doors were to be opened. In this context, one became almost too aware of Goffman's "the self as performed character," for suddenly this performing self, this protean personality, was all around, provoking new experiences and opening more doors than could be entered with one body or one mind.

What was learned during those years is too deep or utopian or simply too frustrating to be talked about casually: my reason for mentioning the immediate past is that its desire to make the intellectual curriculum coincide with the life curriculum reminds us of the fact that the turmoil of those years has not yet produced as authoritative a philosophical document as Schiller's *Aesthetic Education* (though Marcuse tried) or as mature a poem as Wordsworth's *Prelude*. For Wordsworth's autobiography may be the first poem to be "mündig" and utter "words

[166]

which speak of nothing more than what we are." The human rather than hieratic voice of "Tintern Abbey" and *The Prelude* modifies Wordsworth's pastoral vision into an anguished sense of what maturity means. Wordsworth is major man speaking in a human voice.

Maimonides said that institutions can never be fully justified in rational terms. One always comes up against a divine or authoritarian origin. But structures must be justified, and the way we do that is by endlessly defining them. Curricula in the modern university are more in the nature of structures rather than institutions. Each year we are asked to justify or rationalize them anew, and the result is a kind of perpetual, low-grade administrative *angst*. We are always uneasy, always defensive, about curriculum arrangements. And this not after a single decade but after half a century of revision and experimentation. Should we return to an era of benign neglect of teaching arrangements, though not of teachers? Have we become too client-oriented or youth-student-oriented? Is it merely regression and nostalgia on my part that makes me respond so sympathetically to C. S. Peirce's praise of Johns Hopkins of a hundred years ago?

> One university in our country, the Johns Hopkins University at Baltimore, has been carried on upon the principles directly contrary to those which have governed the other colleges. That is to say, it has here alone been recognized that the function of a university is the production of knowledge, and that teaching is only a necessary means to that end. In short, instructors and pupils here compose a company who are all occupied in studying together, some under leading strings and some not. From this small institution with half a dozen professors and a hundred and fifty students, I am unable to tell you how much valuable work has emanated in the four years of its existence in philology and biology.[2]

The "production of knowledge" has, of course, a strangely contemporary sound. It evokes the opposite of a "qualitative" approach to

2. C. S. Peirce, *Values in a Universe of Chance*, Philip Wiener, ed. (Garden City, N.Y.: Doubleday-Anchor, 1958), pp. 334–35.

[167]

education. The ethic behind it, capitalist or materialist, only strengthened a liberal arts ideal which aimed at education rather than production, at increasing quality of mind rather than quantity of learning. Yet no one would claim that the liberal arts ideal is, today, alive and healthy and performing its liberal function in Schiller's sense of releasing us from antithetical yet equally pressing slaveries of natural instinct and external authority. We have seen, in fact, a distinct decline of Socratic in favor of advocacy teaching, a development abetted rather than hindered by our tendency to fragment the curriculum in the name of liberalization, innovation, modernization, experimentation, etc. How hard we play! How each teacher tries to justify what he is doing, burdening himself and the university with a secular theology! The new *homo ludens*, as Robert Lifton has described him, is subject to quasi-religious conversions: which would be o.k. if he did not try converting others, or insisting that all structures fit his fits.

Further visionary tinkering with the curriculum could well be preceded by more reflection on past curricula. This reflection should itself be part and parcel of the curriculum, though not formalized as yet another course. We should know more about the university as an historical institution; we should know about trivium or tripos as a societal as well as university function; we should know about alternative ways of socialization and career choice; we should be fully informed about the patron saints or representatives of the professions we might be choosing. When I started to think about "Humanities" and "Social Science" as words, I realized I knew next to nothing about either phrase: I was using them as meaning self-evidently what they must always have meant. It did not occur to me that "Humanity" was once distinguished from "Divinity" as a branch of knowledge, then specialized to refer to the study of the Classics because they were the consecrated core of a nondivine—that is, non-Christian or secular—type of humane learning. As to Social Science it probably became current at the time of Auguste Comte and implied a distinctive ideology which linked science to a vision of social progress.

Why couldn't we talk about the "Human Sciences" instead of the "Humanities," as they tend to do in France? Something like this happened in England around the time the phrase Social Science began to circulate. In 1851, Cambridge, always scientifically minded, founded a "Moral Science" tripos, and it is not insignificant that both Bertrand Russell and I. A. Richards "read"—as the expression goes—Moral Science. Richards is especially interesting for us, because he exemplifies a fruitful combination of humanities and social science. When he went to Cambridge in 1911 there was no English tripos, so he felt he had to choose History. But he soon wanted out. One morning he went to his supervisor in a grim mood and said (in his own words): "I didn't think History ought to have happened."[3] This antihistorical bias is, of course, revealing: it is part of the general ideology of science and ultimately allies Richards with Bentham rather than with Coleridge. In any case, Richards was introduced to C. K. Ogden and read Moral Science. So much for History and English, our two most populous humanities departments.

Yet old structures revived, like new ones, will not of themselves effect a more genuine contact between the humanities and social science. To say that we should consider reinstituting a Division of the Moral Sciences is simply to undertake a kind of historical hygiene[4] and become aware of the wounded and even cankerous—the more vulnerable the more fertile—nature of modern curricula. Our present pattern of courses is a patchwork of special interests, which optimists disguise as a progressive, modular system. In reality each course or unit is a parapolitical entity, a fiefdom ruled by a teacher (or group of teachers); and however easy to enter, it exacts a weighty tax at the exit point. This punitive tax, called a term paper or exam, supposedly guarantees

3. See his interview with Reuben Brower in *I. A. Richards: Essays in His Honor* (New York: Oxford University Press, 1973), p. 19.

4. An exemplary if somewhat monumental act of this kind is Hans-Georg Gadamer's *Truth and Method* (1960). There are also books more focused on the university as such; see for example E. M. W. Tillyard's *The Muse Unchained* on the development of the English School at Cambridge. Gadamer points out that the influential German term "Geisteswissenschaften" was introduced in 1863 via a translation of John Stuart Mill's *Logic* (1843), the sixth book of which is entitled "The Logic of the Moral Sciences." If only the adjective *Moral* had managed to sustain its symbiotic relation with the noun *Science!*

the integrity of the course by showing that the student has learned something, or that his plan of study was rational. Unfortunately, the subject examined is too restricted by the time allowed or the intellectual range. The student who gets really interested must short-circuit his interest, or take a forfeit on his grade in another course.

It should be clear that the English system of *reading* is better than the American one of *studying*—but only in one respect: there is more leisure, and the boundaries imposed on student-reader are less exigent because they are those of books or tutorials rather than unit courses. There is the crunch at the end, it is true; the grand, climactic examination; but that fosters character as well as intellect, although it may have the undesirable social effect of determining too much the subsequent career of the student. The American system allows many small chances, many second chances; but while it leads to acculturation, I don't think it leads to independent thought and genuine erudition. Yet what holds me back from endorsing the English, especially the Oxbridge, system, is that its defensiveness vis-à-vis American graduate education (still comparatively Hopkinsian in spirit), as well as its own retrenchment into enclosed fiefs like "English" and "French," has so influenced the present atmosphere that the English undergraduate, however well read, is even more unfit for larger views than our o-brave-new-graduate-school B.A.

Should we, then, disestablish History, English, French, and all such fields? And in their stead contrive a structure to restore the bond between the humanities and the social sciences? I am afraid that the most to be hoped for is an historical awareness of the problem, and so a skepticism about structures—or a rebalancing of values in favor of person over structure, so that the magic is taken out of the machine and put back into the person (however much of a machine, deeply and organically speaking, the person might be). We are in a postinstitutional society when it comes to education, just as we are in a post-Classical culture when it comes to literature. The "canon" of sacred or Classical writings appears more and more as a world within a larger world, within a "verbal universe": one which keeps reorganizing itself by sheer proliferation. Likewise, we seem to have entered an era of structures, and they cannot be justified but only rationalized—rationalization being, really, a perpetual doctoring to change or save some educational scheme. We plan in order to keep planning, just as on the level of literature we write to keep writing. Or is the opportunity for curricular change our one chance to act in community? The committee as *Gemeinschaft*. Change as disease and cure at once.

The great fear up to now has been that the world or nature would grow old, but I foresee a grimmer decadence: we shall grow, and have no aim but growth. "He didn't think History ought to have happened," Richards thought; for what does history lead to but the consciousness that instead of harmony, balance, development, ultimate purpose, there is simply growth and nothing but growth? Hegel disagreed, and saw the long odyssey of the human spirit rewarded by a more perfect ability to think concretely; but Hegel is to us what the Greeks were to Schiller. Richards struggled hard to transform the Greek or Pastoral mystique of harmony into a progressive model reconciling stimulus and response, impulse and act, the individual and his environment. He believed in aesthetic education even if it became for him part of a technique of successful communication. But the price of believing in communication—that is, of making it a perfectible "science"—is already clear. Our newest unifying discourse, embracing both the humanities and the social sciences, is semiotics; and the unity offered by semiotics involves an intellectual imperialism which degrades every phenomenon into a sign, until we live in a new infinity, the universe of signs. Perhaps each scientific revolution merely discovers another infinity, and a corresponding aporia. Late in life Paul Valéry wrote a pastoral dialogue in imitation of Virgil. Called *Dialogue of a Tree*, it suggests something of the ecstasy and bathos of sheer growth through its fable of the God-Tree:

> It was the greatest and most beautiful being under the sky, when, divining perhaps that its tree life was only tied up with its growth and that it only lived because it grew larger, there came upon it a sort of overweening and arborescent madness. . . .

[171]

The Humanities, Literacy, and Communication

IN HIS *Origins of Knowledge and Imagination* (1978) Jacob Bronowski describes the difference between communication in animals and in human beings and restates with new force certain simple facts. One is that

> the human response to another human signal is rather slow, compared to most animal responses. Unlike the bees that run off to fetch nectar [the reference is to Karl von Frisch's famous work on the dance language of bees], we do not answer at once. Indeed, we have a rather long delay period. This is certainly something physiological that happened quite early in human evolution, this delay time in the circuit between input through the ear and output through the mouth.

Whether or not we go along with this evolutionary view of human speech, it is clear that reading and writing constitute an intensification of "delay time" and that the whole issue of human response in the context of signals has complicated itself.

In reading or writing, the signaling and responding functions are taken out of their immediate, their urgent or physiological context. They are reflective rather than reflex acts. Even when the context remains practical, when we read or write in pursuit of a well-defined aim, we sense no absolute closure. What we write has a future, and though the text may try to close off the future, there is a future nevertheless; and with that future, as in law, there are unpredictable contexts. In human communication, every signaling and responding "circuit" is experimental: the circuit, by its "delay time," makes the function visible, allows us to see it in action as well as to enact it.

But the notion of "delay time" also strikes us because it suggests a pattern close to "delayed gratification." Within Bronowski's prose lurk other ideas that carry us along, that motivate our interest unexplicitly. Language is like that. "Delay" is close to "relay," so we may glimpse, through Bronowski, a vision of the continuity of life from primeval times to the words I am now putting together.

I return later to the allusive, or "words within words," character of writing and to the "context" of communication, a context that is not totally predictable or controllable. The human—that is, actively receiving—mind is always motivated by its own felt need; not selfish, necessarily, but responsive to a situation that includes both itself and what is being perceived. There is a phenomenology of the communicative process. As I write this essay, I am aware of my time and my audience and of some who have tried, before me, cultural criticism.

Allow me, then, my own response, in the context of the fading of the humanities in contemporary society. I am aware, first of all, that the practice of law is proliferating and is affecting language, while the humanities are suffering a recession. Has the study of law separated itself in an unfortunate and divisive way from philosophical and humanistic—distinct from advocacy-oriented—concerns?

Political philosophy, legal philosophy, remain part of the humanities; yet, in general, Plato's *Republic* is studied only in the freshman or sophomore year of college. There was a time when the humanities were the indispensable access route to the profession of law. Now law school is the only access route to law. The reason for this is not only the self-interest and blindness of the legal profession, nor is it the growing complexity of modern institutional life that is more and more involved in litigation. The humanities gave up the study of law when they divided into special fields, and they gave up the study of religious texts under somewhat different pressures. The study of letters fell back on "belles-lettres" or "literature," as if that were more *natural* than these other *positive* disciplines. Yet can humanists claim to know about interpretation without considering the relation of Vico to Roman law or of the Talmudic rabbis to the strictures of the Mosaic Code? or of Philo to the Septuagint? And if that seems too vast for our "practical" curriculum, how can we forget the general truth that for so long a time the interpretive activity developed with a view to or against documents considered binding?

Let me become more basic still. To express something in writing or formulaic speech is already a delaying device: a "writ" is served, even when the juridical aspect of it is only implicit or symbolic. You remember that in Homer strangers are asked certain formulaic questions, equivalent to "Where have you come from?" and "Who are your parents?" Are these questions merely curious, or are they perhaps the beginnings of a law of hospitality that prevents the out-of-hand slaying of the unidentifed person?

"Delay time," it seems to me, is not unrelated to "due process"; but when we are not in clearly defined legal situations, the relation between "signal" and "response" becomes indeterminate, multidimensional. This is the territory we call symbolic, and we move about in it with hesitation. It is full of traps for the practical- or literal-minded thinker. For we tend to be caught up in unfathomable proceedings or to be reminded of languages and customs still to be deciphered. The bulk of our fiction consists of mysteries of this kind, of disorienting adventures in a strange or fancied world.

The late Reuben Brower could introduce a collection of interpretive readings (inspired by a humanities course at Harvard) with an essay entitled "Reading in Slow Motion" (*In Defense of Reading*, Reuben Brower and Richard Poirier, eds., 1963). His essay emphasizes the gulf between activities in which speed is of the essence—in which there must be response to a signal within a reasonable time—and humanistic reading, which takes place in a milieu of signs rather than signals, which needs more decoding or does not call for a single predetermined range of response, and which can affect the entire system through "feedback" and even alter the quality of our consciousness of time and language.

Often we remain at a loss about how to bring reading and practical life together, because our time scale in reading is so different from that in situations demanding a nearly immediate response; reading is, in a curious way, a *cultural* rehearsal of the "unimaginable touch of time"

[174]

introduced by the infinitizing perspective of Bronowski's *natural* science. A split develops not only between the humanities and the world in which speed is encouraged but also between types of interpretive reading within the humanities themselves. There are those who wish to maintain as close a contact as possible with the personal life of authors or of their society and who employ everyday concepts of character and representation to that end, and there are those for whom reading brings in question the entire representational process, delays practical and moral judgments, and leads into perspectives as structurally complex as those of science.

I realize it may be unwise to make so divisive a distinction between practical and theoretical knowledge. Computers are used even in the humanities, and we can use any tool—the computer, newspapers, picturing, song, and story—to communicate or "hand on" what we know. The distinction is not of my making; something like it has always existed, and it is always being reformulated. Let me define it, then, in my own way. The crucial problem, I shall suppose, lies not in the difference between abstract and concrete thought but in the difference between information and its assimilation as experience. How may what is handed on—which, as information, history, or data, is always augmenting—remain a critical and active part of our awareness?

In raising this question every thinker has a debt to Hegel, particularly to the *Phenomenology of Mind* (1807) and its famous preface. I cannot summarize Hegel—who can?—but a single quotation may indicate how deeply he understood the relation between knowledge and experience. Study in antiquity, writes Hegel, was different from study now: then the natural consciousness had to test itself against everything; it had to produce the abstract forms and even its own concept, that of the thinking subject or ego. In modern times, however, the "individual finds the abstract form ready-made: the exertion of grasping it and appropriating it" is the real task. Our work now is less to purify the individual from immediacy and sensuousness than to sublimate fixed, determinate thoughts and so to experience the actuality of

[175]

general or abstract ideas. And, Hegel concludes, "It is far more difficult to make fixed thoughts fluid, than sensuous experience."

Now the humanities, obviously, have some rather powerful ways to save the imagination from abstractness and convert fixed thoughts into fluid ones, or abstract knowledge into experience. They continue in us the capacity for communicating ideas and feelings through storytelling, narratives of all kinds (including histories), and art. Moreover, Hegel's understanding of the "seriousness of the Concept," how it develops or works itself out in time, makes no distinction between science and the humanities. They are both *Wissenschaft*, a *libido sciendi* that "descends into the depth of the subject matter." Science, Hegel says, as the crown or apex of intellectual development, is not complete when the new concept is formulated.

> The beginning of a new spiritual stage is the product of a far-reaching revolution in multitudinous forms of culture and education; it is the prize for an immensely tangled path and an equally immense amount of exertion and toil.

A new concept or aim taken by itself is merely a "naked result," or "the corpse which has left the tendency behind."

Hegel does suggest one way of differentiating science from the humanities. His description of the educative process *(Bildung)* indicates that what we now call the humanities is simply a certain tempo of development that both precedes and follows on the "qualitative leap" of every new concept or spiritual stage, and without which the concept or spiritual stage can neither come into being nor prevail.

The humanities, then, always in "slow motion" compared to the sciences or to the immediate demands of the practical world, are neither more nor less archaic than other communicative modes. They differ only by being more crisis-proof, by responding less obediently to social pressures, by not throwing all their resources into a direction enjoined by an external demand or even by their own internal state. They are archival, memorial, conservative, cyclopedic. The humanities

[176]

calendar, like the religious calendar, though not confined to fixed dates, allows the store of experience to come before us once again, as we incline—fast and forgetful—into the future. Here and there contact is made between these calendars or wheels moving at different speeds; and the meshing that occurs, which can be very powerful indeed, not only at the point of contact but as it provides a design for mutual and coordinated work, is what we call experience.

There has been much interest lately in that meshing, for it is also called creative knowledge, and it can happen in the sciences as well as in the arts. The general aim of any culture is to understand creativity and then to use that understanding to provide an environment in which creativity flourishes even more richly. It is generally acknowledged that creativity cannot be controlled; there is something accidental about it, as there is in wielding the pen and in writing a genial poem. But we do know that the practical life must mesh with the contemplative, and that the humanities sustain the contemplative life in us and prevent it from becoming mere dreaming or withdrawal. They are the slowly moving wheel that allows us to connect with past traditions at different points in our precipitous careers. Each individual thus has some chance for a "renaissance" because of the humanities. Through them we join our lives to a larger life that is neither alien nor mystical—that way lies superstition—but a portion of our own recovered history.

The danger, of course, is indeterminacy. Becoming aware of humanity through the humanities turns us into a being made of many beings; and we move more slowly as this composite. Instead of speeding up thought and smoothing the tongue, a humanistic training may produce a curious stutter in both. For example, we begin to fight with and over language; whether we should speak French or English, or what kind of French or English. In that sense the humanities are dangerous; they impede practical communication; they ask that we do not live in homogeneous time; they inspire a "self-determined indetermination" that can darken every step of thought or language. Yet it is only when we realize the complexity of the mediations in which we live that we live at all. Humanists are the anthropologists of their own culture.

[177]

Humanities, Literacy, and Communication

Moses used Sinai to a great extent in his communications with God.

Unknown freshman, circa 1978

The word "communication" is charged with value and seems to have entered the realm of ultimates. Older words like "understanding" or "belief" now emit a faint glow of obsolescence, a quaint sense of something inward and metaphysical. Communication, by contrast, is the outward and open form of our togetherness, our capacity for community. Under its aegis we imagine ideal networks of being in touch, perfect invasions of each other's privacy, global antennae reaching into every home. We communicate, but what? Well, whatever it may be. The system stands ready, and it must be fed. The medium is the news.

But news is not productive of understanding. It discourages delay time; it violates, as Valéry remarked,

> our inner sense of the interval between desire and possession, which is no other than the sense of duration, that feeling of time which was formerly satisfied by the speed of horses, and now finds that the fastest trains are too slow. . . . If every morning there is no great disaster in the world we feel a certain emptiness: we say, "There is nothing in the papers today." . . . We are all poisoned.

Hence communication may work against understanding. Dreaming, Freud suggests, is absolutely necessary for mental health: it helps to digest the day's residue, the sensory and now also the data overload. The more information we are asked to assimilate, the more a private life or a dreaming room is needed. But what if we enter the state of the violent hero in Burgess' *Clockwork Orange,* who can only be cured by having his eyes held open night and day? Television and the increasing dominance of the media do precisely that. Our eyes and ears are no longer ours. The media give us the means to elide our private existence. They do the dreaming for us. Canned dreams are confirmed by canned applause. The freedom to think, the time to assimilate, is affected. Can we still "experience"?

Walter Benjamin said in the 1930s that newspapers were one of the many evidences of our inability to understand what is communicated.

If it were the intention of the press to have the reader assimilate the information it supplies as part of his own experience, it would not achieve its purpose. But its intention is just the opposite, and is achieved: to isolate what happens from the realm in which it could affect the experience of the reader. The principles of journalistic information—freshness of the news, brevity, immediate comprehensibility, and above all lack of connection between individual news items—contribute as much to this as does the make-up of the pages and the paper's style. ("On Some Motifs in Baudelaire," in *Illuminations*, edited by Hannah Arendt; translated by Harry Zohn)

But the problem was noted as far back as Wordsworth. His preface of 1800 to *Lyrical Ballads* singled out a fatal convergence of industrialization, urbanization, and journalism during the Napoleonic wars.

A multitude of causes unknown to former times are now acting with combined force to blunt the discriminating powers of the mind, and unfitting it for all voluntary exertion to reduce it to a state of almost savage torpor. The most effective of these causes are the great national events which are daily taking place, and the increasing accumulation of men in cities, where the uniformity of their occupations produces a craving for extraordinary incident, which the rapid communication of intelligence hourly gratifies.

Wordsworth attacked, in what he named *lyrical* ballads, the very concept of the newsworthy event, composing lyrics that were anything but sensational. They displaced the avid reader's attention from the unusual or fantastic incident to the sensitive response that an ordinary life might elicit. His almost plotless ballads are our first instance of minimalist art. But they are not yet abstract like that art: they surround familiar thoughts and happenings with an imaginative aura. The strange subtlety of Wordsworth's poems was intended to retain ear, eye, and imagination, to wean them from the age's degrading thirst after "outrageous stimulation."

It is not possible to engage here in a history of the imagination in terms of stimulus and response or of the way the humanities have always intervened to ensure freedom of response, even if doing so meant a damping of the stimulus. Should the stimulus be associated with language, and it is most of the time, then the question of literalism—did the author really mean that?—arises. The relation of literal and figurative meaning is central to literary study, which is always asking, Can we say what we mean? Can we be certain of anyone's meaning? Is language not always other than the particular meanings that try to control and contain it? Consider the etymological play of medieval authors. Despite our condenscension toward it, do we not run after meaning with the same passionate perplexity? Here is how the author of the *Legenda Aurea*, or *Lives of the Saints*, explains the name Saint Eufamia in Caxton's translation:

> Eufamia is said of eu, that is good, and of femme, that is woman, that is to wit a profitable, honest, and delectable, for in this treble manner she is said good. She was profitable to others by conversation, honest by ordinance of manners, and delectable to God. Or Eufamia is said of euphonia as sweetness of sound. Sweet sound is made in three manners. . . .

The drive for meaning, for the direct relation of word and essence (*nomina numina*), is as compulsive as a blood sport. But the humanities follow poets like Valéry and Wordsworth by working within and against that drive, by displacing our attention from the act of possession to the interval, the delight in aesthetic play, the freedom to interpret what is arbitrary yet must be given meaning. The very name "humanities" distinguishes them not so much from science and art as from divinity: from *that* blood sport, its ecstatic and messianic passions. These passions are found wherever the *libido sciendi* seeks to convert oblique signs (*vestigia*) into tokens of manifest truth. Though science, like the humanities, teaches us to let the oblique be the oblique and even to unmask directness as oblique (as requiring sophisticated interpretation), the tendency to undo "delay time" in favor of immediatism has moved more deeply than ever into everyday life. The more we are surrounded by images and sounds that can be summoned at the touch of a button, the more science must join with the humanities to ensure the survival of both the dreaming room and the reading room. Whether the mind will remain imaginative, able to build on the least suggestions, or whether it will become torpid, stupid, blunt, requiring ever greater stimulants, depends on whether the arts of reading and writing remain the base of all further construction.

Understanding is not a rogering activity except in highly predetermined and structured contexts. In this sentence "roger" is a metaphor taken from space flights, star wars, and technological talk. The word would not be understandable to those who have not seen telecommunications or pictures of space flights. Even there, to say "roger" is not enough; usually one must repeat the message, both to impress it on the memory and to signal its correct reception. There is no context-free communication, because the context of communication includes the complexity of a speaking and receiving mind.

In less predetermined situations or in situations where the context has still to be defined—where, for instance, you are not strapped to a machine or where, to fly at all, you must ascend, like Blake, in a visionary chariot having wheels within wheels (or words within words)—that is, in writing or reading anything at all complex—there is double jeopardy: you are carried by a machine whose intricacy none can master, and you alone are responsible for its guidance. Modern politics tries, through an apparatus of advisers and public relations personnel, to *manage* communications nevertheless: the apparatus connects with the incredible panoply of space-flight technology when the President of the United States puts in his call to the returned astronauts. Meanwhile, in the classroom . . .

Crosscutting from space-flight communication to the classroom produces a fantasy effect. We realize that only one common denominator exists between those worlds: a remarkable support system that makes contexts available and intelligible. The support system, or machine womb, of space flights is a triumph of managerial society that celebrates itself in the ease of that phone call between president and astronaut. How simple and context-free communication has become. "Thank you, Mr. President." The context, that is, the immense support system, is invisible for that moment. Time and space do not interfere. The moment of contact itself, its actualized possibility, is the thrill: the machine works. A supreme roger takes place.

For educational institutions, the support system is indeterminately vast, elastic, and—increasingly—unmanageable, by both the political machine and the internal administrators. In the university, the student often feels processed rather than educated. And because we are dealing with youthful, questioning, rebellious energies, and because our authority in dealing with such energies is limited—by our own energies as well as by our attitudes toward authority—the context keeps interfering and becoming visible, so that the support system itself moves to the foreground of the learning activity. The academy continually demystifies itself as part of its relentless examining of social systems or the suppositional structure of whatever calls itself a science. Moreover, since education rather than ecstasy is the end, no supreme roger—at most a eureka—is the expected cry.

And none of us can forget that the pre-twentieth-century school, with fewer masters or professors and fewer teaching aids, educated a small yet remarkable number of individuals. We retain this residual protestant or iconoclastic sense concerning the importance of a different kind of roger: of being put in touch with oneself and of distrusting the machine in spiritual or intellectual development. Education, especially in the humanities, cannot be rogerized.

You may think me too gloomy and may consider my brief only one more yelp at the powerlessness of the individual in the machine age. I don't mind yelping if it helps. But let me turn back once more to the prescribed question: What can the humanities, and literary study in particular, contribute to a society in which "communication" is the operative ideal?

My answer would have to be, "mainly doubt and delay, but a methodical doubt (like that of Descartes) and a testing kind of delay." John Keats coined the term "negative capability," meaning by it the opposite of a nervous jumping to conclusions or a vampiristic assumption of intimacy with the thoughts and feelings of others. The study of literature is a help in avoiding such abuses because words, as the most intimate and ready means of communication we have, are most likely

[182]

to be abused by impatience and vampirism. When we realize that words are never simple promissory notes, that they are never straightforwardly referential, that they are mediating rather than immediate and therefore cannot be evaluated without a constant awareness of their verbal and situational contexts, then we marvel that they signify at all and that the "delay time" required for their proper understanding does not extend into infinity.

How far we can get with a "contextual theory of meaning" was shown by I. A. Richards. He put the issue on the map for literary studies in England and America, though I have elsewhere accused him of reinforcing rather than purifying the "dream of communication" in us (see *The Fate of Reading and Other Essays*, pp. 22–30). Richards insisted that the "one and only goal of all critical endeavors, of all interpretation, exhortation, praise or abuse, is improvement in communication." In his *Practical Criticism* (1929), which announces this conclusion and which continues to be enormously influential, Richards goes on: "The whole apparatus of critical rules and principles is a means to the attainment of finer, more precise, more discriminating communication."

I am not going to argue with that. I quote it for its bias. Seven years later Richards' emphasis changes, however subtly. In *The Philosophy of Rhetoric* (1936), he urges an inquiry into communication that should be

> philosophic, or—if you hesitate with that word, I do myself—it must take charge of the criticism of its own assumptions and not accept them, more than it can help, ready-made from other studies. How words mean, is not a question to which we can safely accept an answer either as an inheritance from common sense, that curious growth, or as something vouched for by another science, by psychology, say— since other sciences use words themselves and not least delusively when they address themselves to these questions. The result is that a revived Rhetoric, or study of verbal understanding and misunderstanding, must itself undertake its own inquiry into the modes of meaning. . . .

The end of the inquiry is the same, a study of misunderstanding and how to use it to improve communication. But the means to this end

[183]

are less assured: psychology, singled out in the prior book as "the indispensable instrument for this inquiry," may be delusive in its own use of words. Moreover, by introducing the word "philosophy," Richards suggests that the practical or empirical side needs an assist: that no one field of inquiry can suffice as a master context; indeed, that "meaning" is itself a matter of context or of the interinanimation of contexts.

Richards, whose authority is his honesty, his practice of never saying more than he can—and of sometimes saying less—comes then to the point where he must admit that our ability to learn through the handling, recognizing, and, most important, abridging of contexts is still inexplicable. Here is how he puts it, and I promise it will be my last quotation:

> One item—typically a word—takes over the duties of parts which can then be omitted from the recurrence. There is thus an abridgement of the context only shown in the behavior of living things, and most extensively and drastically shown by man. When this abridgement happens, what the sign or word—the item with these delegated powers—means is the missing parts of the context.
>
> If we ask how this abridgement happens, how a sign comes to stand for an absent cause and conditions, we come up against the limits of knowledge at once. No one knows. Physiological speculation has made very little progress towards explaining *that*, though enormous strides have been made this century in analysing the complexities of the conditioned reflex. The shift, the handing over, is left still as inexplicable. Probably this "learning problem" goes down as deep as the nature of life itself.

Back to Bronowski, then! The only thing we have learned is the strange idea that what a sign or word means is the missing part of the context. It links up with the psychological fact that we like to be reminded rather than informed, and here too a linguistic theory of meaning touches on a literary theory of meaning via the allusive or intertextual (word within word) character of literary diction. Richards' next chapter analyzes and illustrates the "interinanimation" of words in such masterly uses of language as Shakespeare's.

[184]

Can we identify in a theoretical and accurate way the "missing part" that seems essential to the economy of meaning or symbolic process? You probably know the range of speculations on this question, as exhilarating as hypotheses on the origin of the universe. Post-Saussurian semiotics, Lacanian psychoanalysis, philosophical theories of naming, Bronowski's theory of inference: they each have their own way of circumscribing the relation of meaning to the "missing part." Yet my subject is not theories of meaning: it is the relation of the humanities to society and how language as a communicative process fits into that relation. Having problematized the idea of communication, having gone to the wire in suggesting that meaning itself is the "missing part" of language, I must add something more positive about the teaching of English and of literature generally.

The positive part of my essay, then, is the following. *We are the only profession that asks people to do their own writing—and reading.* It is not our function to build a class of clerks who do the writing and reading for the other professions: to edit, revise, and secretary for them.

Too many in our society try to graduate from the work of writing (not to speak of reading): just as it is a status symbol to have a chauffeur, so it is becoming a status symbol to have a writer. Ghostwriting and ghost reading are all about us; they obviously weaken the sense of what it means to write, and they make the appreciation of literary study harder.

In the eyes of government or business or those who make essential decisions, we are often a specialized service. Our function is to help *others* write or to provide writing skills on call. They would like our motto to be, "Let us clean up your prose." Or "Leave the writing to us." This attitude dehumanizes thinking by separating thinking from writing. Thinking becomes "executive thinking." Only those who do their own writing know how problematic "communication" is, what unexpected thoughts and issues may arise, what a struggle it is to sift and winnow ideas, to find one's way back, or to find a new way.

In fact, writing teaches, paradoxically, that someone else seems to write for us: that there is a ghostwriter in every hand. Serious writing is an uncanny thing. A society built on ghostwriting hires a ghost to get rid of the ghost who takes over your hand as you write, who makes your clichés unhappy or reminds you that even your ambition to write comes from deep down or expresses something not quite as objective or unpersonal as you think.

There is nothing harder than to face a blank page, to *start*—when you can't rely on a joke or have someone else do a first draft that you edit. That blankness of starting is essential, and in a scrupulous writer it recurs; it compels the one who writes to relive not only the first panic at going public but also the queasy feeling that the definitive statement one is about to make is subject to interfering thoughts that seem to come from nowhere—and often subject to words rather than thoughts, words that turn you this way or that. The very instant of writing, Pascal's fly buzzing, the book your eye chances to light on, a telephone call, the hangover of a dream, a literary echo—these are the stuff guiding the pen that claims authority. We notice, and are amused by, a slip of the tongue, and we have learned to study such parapraxes: but who can tell a slip of the pen that is always slipping on the pathless page?

I will go further: the compositional skills we learn are indeed important, but they deal primarily with the task of subordinating, with a judgment about what is to be excluded, or what has priority, or in what order and with what emphasis things are to be put. These skills defend the writer against what Durkheim, the sociologist, called anomie, which writing more than any other activity makes us feel as a matter of course. Durkheim used the term "anomie" to characterize a state of mind in which the rule or norm seemed lost, to the point where the mind despaired of finding it. Today, I think, the word "surnomie" is equally appropriate: there are so many principles of order, so many directives, such a tangle of laws and advices. Each year we discover a new formula for teaching reading and writing. It would be better to admit at the outset that these activities are anarchic in the sense that either too many rules guide them, as in a bureaucratic context, or no sure rule at all, as in creative reading and writing.

The genuine writer knows that practice never ceases: you don't graduate from writing any more than you do from thinking. Writing is an activity that takes place in time and cannot leave time. The conclusion to be drawn from what I have alleged is twofold. First, the literary humanities cannot be reduced to a school for a specific skill. Composition may be a skill, editing may be a skill, but writing is something more. We can teach composition, and we can give courses—bigger and better—in expository prose: but it all remains a come-on to introduce the student to the discipline of writing by making it habitual.

Too great an emphasis on skill may actually limit the ability to write for oneself. It suggests, as I have said, a secretariat that might put thoughts—executive thinking—into the proper form. This depersonalization of writing, this subtle and gradual proliferation of a class of ghostwriters, is the one really dangerous development in contemporary intellectual life. It leads to the point where the decision makers delegate the writing—and therefore, whether they know it or not, the thinking—to others.

Second, the literary humanities not only make writing available to each person but maintain the essential link between reading and writing. Again, reading is more than a skill, especially when it reaches the level of philosophic or legal or cultural interpretation. It is almost a mode of life, something you cannot shake off, something that follows and pursues you. Reading is fate: we are like characters in a certain kind of mystery story, who are drawn unwillingly into a plot that we alone, rather than the official investigator, can unriddle. Leaving writing and reading to specialists is like leaving interpretation to the police department.

Imagine a world in which you cannot think except by reading and writing. That is our world.

Wild, Fierce Yale

THERE ARE NO departments of Literary Criticism; and even proposals to have a Criticism question in official examinations can cause turbulence in academic circles. What is at stake? By now, of course, a political element has entered, and many suspect that under the name of "criticism" all kinds of illegal goods may be smuggled in. Customs is instructed to make a proper search. Is "criticism" a hidden agenda for Marxism, Lacanianism, structuralist antihumanism, etc.?

Originally, the resistance to allowing criticism the curricular dignity of, say, the Age of Pope came from a simpler source. It was argued that criticism had no existence apart from the works it scrutinized and that, on the whole, critical texts did not form a special tradition: nothing that could or should be institutionalized. Though René Wellek's *History of Modern Criticism* tried to show that Saintbury's attitude of connoisseurship was inadequate, and that critics used something more than rationalized notions of taste—they also borrowed or converted ideas that might be said to constitute an unacknowledged philosophy—there was a reluctance to extend self-consciousness in that direction. Criticism, it was thought, should remain auxilliary. If it intended to raise the question of its universal or principled bases, it might apply to philosophy, not to literature, for its academic entrée.

It is certainly unusual to read essays about literature that oblige us to think about *them* rather than primarily about their object or occasion. Not that we don't enjoy some of these essays, especially time-

A review of Christopher Norris' *Deconstruction: Theory and Practice* (London: Methuen, 1982).

[188]

honored ones: Charles Lamb on Shakespeare's plays in relation to their stage representation is as delicious as it is dated. Yet unlike Lamb's piece, the contemporary critical essay often demands a knowledge that is highly specialized, and uses a vocabulary drawn from various theories. One can feel terrorized rather than instructed—let alone delighted.

Specialization is not the only problem. There need be no objection to the linguistic analysis of a literary work, if it is clearly conducted as such. But essays that mix linguistics with psychoanalysis or social remedies seem basically uncritical, in the sense that even the educated reader cannot tell, faced by such "motley in the brain," what is scientific or scholarly, and what is not so. There is a deeper problem, caused by our very hope that criticism could save us from specialization, or fragmentation: we have identified it as *the* rehumanizing activity, so when it becomes technical or claims a field of its own—when criticism says, "Let us be like other departments of knowledge"—it seems not only to mistake but even to betray its nature.

Criticism, in any case, is no longer what it was; and Christopher Norris' compact book, *Deconstruction: Theory and Practice*, is more useful, in its open-minded descriptive acuity, than other, more complex and defensive, treatments. Occasionally Norris falls into distancing gestures about "going too far" or "rhapsodic philosophizing"; most of the time, however, he clarifies the present situation by defining the intellectual milieu of a controversial array of writers active in America since about 1955, though not achieving full notoriety till the advent of Derrida and his invasion of American academic criticism in the 1970s. Deconstruction in America, he sensibly remarks, "is not a monolithic theory or school of thought but a gathering point for critics who are otherwise divided on many central issues of technique and style." His book has considerable range, therefore, not only in philosophical backgrounds, but in its focus, which goes beyond the "Yale School" to Jakobson, Macherey, Althusser, Barthes, and Foucault on the Continental side and Leavis, Empson, Eagleton, Jameson, Culler, Said, Rorty, and others on the Anglo-American side. Wittgenstein's relation to language and skepticism is too skimpily treated, but at least it is there.

Norris' account centers on the "American Connection," but he does

[189]

not overemphasize it. He corrects the historical equivalent of an optical illusion by showing that the Yale critics had their own practice with roots in the New Criticism, a movement they questioned long before Derrida arrived on the scene. They questioned it by a more rigorous application of its own emphasis on the text rather than on the text's historical frame. But even the text as its own frame is questioned by this group, which did not privilege unity by vesting it in the "achieved" or "coherent" form of a literary work. Their tendency, fed by many sources including Freud, was not so much to radicalize ambiguity and to delay closing the interpretation as to see *through* literary form to the way language or symbolic process makes or breaks meaning. To hold that making and breaking together risked, sometimes, giving the impression of enchanting disenchantment; the word "flower" (to cite Mallarmé) evoked something absent from all bouquets; but the main thrust of this American deconstruction that did not know its name was to create a more dialectical and open view of how literature worked. The rhetoric of "tension," refined by the New Critics as irony, paradox, and controlled ambiguity, seemed too self-enclosing a version of literariness. It was felt that the New Critics promulgated under aesthetic cover a language ontology that made poetic and religious claims converge. So Father Ong could point out that wit and paradox also characterized the language of faith: the New Critics had shown how a transcendent presence could be brought, by analogy at least, into the confines of a secular (literary) construct.

Norris has important remarks on this earlier phase, which struggled to break with incarnationist and imagistic theories of expression. The *practice* of deconstruction was forged in America, even if the *theory* had to await Derrida; moreover, such émigré scholars as Paul de Man began to suggest that the problem did not rest exclusively with literary studies, whose practice was in advance of its theory, but also with philosophy, whose theory tended to avoid reflection on its own linguistic and figural character. Norris' book is therefore a great advance on Frank Lentricchia, whose *After the New Criticism* depicts the Yale critics as camp followers of changing philosophical fashions. Norris describes an independent and difficult search, which is attracted to philosophy not as a saving mechanism but as a lost relation. A critique of philosophy's neglect of its own style leads the American dissidents of the 1960s and 1970s to recognize the importance of Heidegger and Sartre, then Derrida, and to come up with a reading list very different from that of Anglo-American literary studies. It includes Rousseau, Hegel, Nietzsche, Mallarmé, Freud, Saussure, and Lévi-Strauss.

In dealing with deconstruction, one is obliged to take up the polemic swirling around it. Norris, fortunately, does not blame that polemic simply on the obtuseness of the opposition. He knows that vital prejudices are involved, and they go beyond the curriculum and departmental territorial imperatives. I have mentioned the feeling that deconstruction is a philosophy of disenchantment. It has been accused of fostering an extreme linguistic skepticism and of undermining the creative or reconstructive side of language. The fear is often expressed that literary studies so conducted may lose what small hold they have on the practical mind; or that reading will be replaced by premature and corrosive habits of analysis. The Common Reader (if still alive) tends to view criticism, like reviewing, as an extension of civilized conversation; and an urgent, severe, or enthusiastic style creates embarrassment. What motive can there be for making literature more rather than less difficult? The difficult critic is initially the guilty one: he has committed a kind of solecism, which estranges him from his equals, sets up the suspicion of cultic or solipsistic behavior, and is not atoned for except by longevity.

Norris generally avoids vulgar polemics in favor of historical placement and a careful résumé of terms and concepts. This is all to the good, and it has produced an outstanding primer. His book is by no means an apologia, however. Though Norris maintains that deconstructive critics have "provided the impetus for a total revaluation of interpretative theory and practice," he then distinguishes impetus from achievement by dividing these critics into two groups. Both are contained within Derrida, the largest phenomenon on the scene. Yet Derrida, like Humpty Dumpty, falls apart into tendencies that converge without coinciding. One tendency is characterized by an exuberant attempt "to turn the resources of interpretative style against any too rigid

[191]

convention of method and language." The other is "more toughly ar-
gumentative"; its courage is intellectual as well as stylistic.

Norris, clearly, prefers the second to the first, acknowledging the liberating play and iconoclasm of the first group, but seeing more impetus
than achievement in it. For him the rigor of Paul de Man is central,
because it allows no conceptual bypass in the way challenges are put,
and a drastic shift in reading habits is demanded. De Man does not
play about: his sentences are succinct to the point of being ascetic.
Texts are read for symptoms of blindness that limit and constitute them.
"Blindness and Insight" (the title of de Man's first collection of essays,
written in the 1950s and 1960s, but published in 1971) go together in
ways that no method can resolve. Critical texts must therefore be read
"with the same awareness of ambivalence that is brought to the study
of non-critical texts." De Man, Norris concludes, is "the fiercest of Yale
deconstructors, with a rigor not easily explained unless in ethical terms."
Harold Bloom, too, is admired, because of a related if antithetical
fierceness: he "sets up as the opponent from within, meeting the deconstructors point for point on rhetorical ground of their own choosing." Bloom does this to limit their "serene linguistic nihilism" and
their Pascalian dislike for terms that acknowledge the pathos of self or
subject.

It would be dishonest not to mention that my own work (together
with that of Hillis Miller) is placed "on the wild side." It has vigor but
not rigor. Norris sees it as playful and skirmishing, a kind of sacrificial
scouting action. Its style matters, but what matter is that? Norris is
half-grateful to find someone without "deconstructive violence" or
"tactics of double reading automatically generated," and at least he
does not dismiss the playful aspect as "a kind of textual fiddling while
Rome burns." Yet there is, in Norris, something very Roman or Latin-
severe, which restricts issues to "the age-old quarrel between literature' and 'philosophy.' " Reduced to that ground, he demonstrates the
philosophical rigor of deconstruction and objects to the rhetorical virtuoso. But if the virtuoso may be faulted for substituting an ideal of
brilliance for the lost ideal of certainty, can we be sure that rigorous
deconstruction aims for certain knowledge rather than being a *docta*

ignorantia in secular guise—an uncompromising antifoundationalist kind of thinking? And if that is the case, how do we judge between rigor and serious play?

Norris' expository talent is marked by a certain reticence. He does not analyze his own, pressured situation. Perhaps the genre of the handbook is to blame; or he admires, despite himself, the "great virtue of the English," which is, according to Basil de Selincourt, "their unconsciousness." One can only guess at another factor: the problem, with so much disinformation around, of presenting deconstruction as a movement necessary for the survival of literary studies.

In England, as in America, literary studies are being absorbed by cultural studies and advocacy teaching. It is unlikely that the conservative curriculum and the inertial force of traditional criticism can do anything about this. A fortress, however redoubtable, is still a retreat. That American deconstruction is often accused of being a new formalism suggests it may indeed be a "third force": one that refuses to shut literature in on itself *or* to abandon it for an ideological, text-transcendent position.

It is, I hope, this recuperative and truly conservative strength of deconstruction that appeals to the younger generation, rather than its esoteric and sophisticated mechanics. By situating deconstruction historically, Norris helps to disclose some features that make it an important form of *literary* commentary. Some even claim there is no theory of deconstruction, only a highly volatile mixture of philosophical analysis and literary analysis. Norris himself makes a similar point when he characterizes it as post-structuralist: opposed, that is, to "a mode of analysis" whose "insights are set on nothing less than a total explanation of human thought and culture." Deconstruction remains "closely tied to the text it interrogates" and does not "set up independently as a self-enclosed system of operative concepts."

The Frankfurt School (not mentioned by Norris), though prior to both structuralism and deconstruction, also opposed totalizing explanations. It reinforced deconstructive thought and sometimes provided a political alternative. The influence of the Frankfurt group, however—Adorno, Marcuse, Benjamin, Loewenthal, among others—did not break out of social and into literary thought until recently. Norris in any case sees that deconstruction has made an impact on literary studies precisely because, unlike structuralism, it does not seek to be a "science of literature," and rejects all projects for a metalanguage or master code.

When Barthes, therefore, in his post-structuralist phase, proposes a "theory of the text," it is not an attempt to overcome the text by an arrogant movement of thought. The roles of letter and spirit are reversed: the letter of the text lives on and undoes idealizations that seek to get rid of the letter. Derrida's essay on "White Mythology" makes the same point by extracting from Western metaphors of luminosity (such as the "light of reason") their bias toward unmediated vision. There is no transparence of thing to thought. The meaning cannot displace the medium. A text, precisely when authentic, will not do away with itself: we never reach the luminous limit where words disappear into their objects like shadows at noon.

There is no necessary relation, then, between theory and arrogance. Reading Norris on deconstruction dispels that defaming prejudice. But the moral question raised is really an intellectual one. What positive force is there in abstract thought; and does that kind of thought have a place in literary studies?

The fear of abstraction is a fear that the thinker will be abstracted from realities. So Yeats declared that Chaucer's poetry was vital for him: it saved his imagination from abstraction. The worried social thinker also turns to the humanities to prevent imagination from going abstract, from losing itself to pseudo-science or vicarious fantasy. This worry makes strange bedfellows: it is common to the Leavis tradition and to certain Marxist groups. Both link an abstracted (distracted) imagination to the consumer values of a dominant culture in which the diffusion of mental or material goods may lead to their dilution. When Jean Baudrillard, in France, develops a *critical* semiology which views the "sign" as an abstraction of image from product brought about by commodification, and sharply differentiates it from the more organic "symbol" of premodern societies, we are reminded of T. S. Eliot's thesis (taken up by Leavis) that there was a dissociation of sensibility from thought during the seventeenth century. Leavis seeks to prevent

[194]

further cultural decay by drawing a firm line between literary language as a medium of "lived" experience and philosophy's concern with explanation and abstract methodology. "Criticism on Leavis's terms," Norris writes, "is a matter of communicating deep-laid intuitive responses, which analysis can point to and persuasively *enact*, but which it can by no means *explain* or *theorize* about."

Leavis pushed to the limit a markedly English distrust of abstraction. In the modern period, moreover, that distrust is exacerbated by the survival of visionary poetry. Milton's *Paradise Lost* is a scandal: a monument to dead ideas, a petrification of the English tongue. Wordsworth, great reformer that he was, saw that mythology, like science, was the source of "mighty abstractions," and struggled to refuse them. Yet mythology, as the science of the divine, continued to produce powerful science fiction as late as Blake and Shelley. Yeats needed Chaucer, precisely because he was drawn to Blake's Star War epics with their Giant Forms expanding and contracting in mysterious space. Blake thought he had bounded abstraction; we are less sure. Yeats flirted not only with the fantasy world of the Celtic twilight but also with "Babylonian starlight": the spirit of geometry haunting the gyres and diagrams of *A Vision*.

Modern visionary poetry is itself, then, a symptom of the drift to abstraction. More exactly, it seems both to embody and oppose that drift. A crucial problem for modern criticism is how to value modern visionariness. In England the problem was often evaded by the strange historical simplification which saved Dante's kind of vision, but not Milton's or Blake's, by positing a fall from grace (the "unified sensibility") into an Era of Abstraction.

Before deconstruction hit, critics in America, from Northrop Frye to Harold Bloom and Paul de Man, had already questioned that myth of history. (Its more sporadic critique in England is summarized by F. W. Bateson in the first volume of *Essays in Criticism*.) Here again what seemed to be a humanistic matter concealed a religious sanction, for the myth was clearly intended to limit "abstract" (unauthorized) vision as well as abstract or rationalist thought. The "abstract" or belated visionariness of the Romantics projected them into the foreground of

[195]

literary polemics and induced a hermeneutic perplexity which even today is not resolved. For to reject Blake (or Shelley or Milton) is to admit that they cannot be read according to humanistic criteria: that they lack worldly and anthropomorphic grounding. It is to accord them "unreadable" or pseudo-scriptural status. Yet to accept them is to show that their "mighty abstractions" are not abstract at all: that they have redeeming social value. It is tantamount to demythologizing them and replacing their abstractions with clear, referential meanings.

What deconstructive thought has done is to generalize this perplexity: to see it as endemic to all literature, not only visionary literature. Our philosophy of reading, in short, is inadequate. By dichotomizing art and abstract thought we have developed a method of reading too exclusively phenomenalist in character. To read was to realize: to stress the imagistic or presentational power in words, to put creative language totally on the side of embodiment and vividness. Even if it was understood that some sort of abstract or generalizing effect inhered in figures of speech, the assumption that linked quality of life to qualitative language also favored interpreting that quality as sensuous and organic.

Derrida points out that the entire history of ideas, insofar as it is based on the notion of the idea as a faint image, capable of being restored to some of its original luster by the artistic thinker—that this entire history may be built on a reduction of the ideas it seeks to honor. Using Hegel's "Thinking is a verbal matter," Derrida promotes the link between word and concept rather than between word and image, and criticizes as "logocentric" those who claim to think in words while thinking of words as images—as verbal icons that reflect, however faintly, the Johannine logos or incarnate Word.

Most theories of art must therefore be "deconstructed" to disclose the way they substitute thinking in images for thinking in words, and overvalue the representational function of art. Consider the following exposition of Bergson's aesthetics by Hulme: "Artists attain the original mood and induce us to make the same effort ourselves by rhythmical arrangements of words, which, thus organized and animated with a life of their own, tell us, or rather suggest, things that speech is not calculated to express."

[196]

For Derrida as for Valéry—both reacting to this kind of theory—speech *is* calculation: a very potent form of abstract thought which can use mimesis for its own ends but is not limited to mimesis. Norris does not go back far enough to spot the lingering presence of Bergson. He tries to fit deconstruction into the tradition of language skepticism, which is a mistake, since the defects of language are far more important to Hulme than to Derrida. "It is only the defects of language," Hulme writes, "that make originality necessary. . . . You could define art, then, as a passionate desire for accuracy, and the essentially aesthetic emotion as the excitement which is generated by direct communication." To read or write is not—for Derrida—to enhance a faded image or direct referent, and so attach an abstraction (the conceptual word) to its worldly source. Such grounding is just as reductive as the opposite move, the *relève* of scientific thought. Think of "primal scene" interpretations of fiction: they may humanize a figurative passage, but can they explain its peculiar verbal energy?

My point here is not to denounce humanistic modes of grounding or relevancing: it is rather to focus on the incurably conceptual force of verbal thinking, and to identify that, even in literature, as a force rather than a failing. One might argue, in fact, that humanistic kinds of relevance, which make a text understandable in worldly terms, lead to their own *relève* (the English word "relief" would also be appropriate), because such an understanding is a reductive and potentially vulgar simplification. Hence a second kind of relevance appears on the scene, no more abstract than the first, but which maintains fiction in its strange and abstruse—because insistently linguistic rather than iconic—aspect. But since there *is* a picturing power in words, it would be fairer to say that the relevant image is always deferred. Writing, as a system, keeps differentiating itself, aiming to be descriptive, aiming to be image as well as idea or, to quote a minor poet, "to be the thing it sings." Without a "logocentric" ambition, always undone by a movement Derrida has named *différance*, there would be no play in language, and the variety of tongues would be even more mysterious than it is.

What is truly offensive in deconstruction is not, then, the dread *aporia*, the doubleheaded *chiasmus*, the treacherous if trivial *mise en abysme*, and other guild mysteries. Nor does the offense lie, despite much rumpus, in opening the curriculum to include critical texts as primary, or refusing sharp distinctions between critical and creative. The stumbling stone remains close to the issue of skepticism—not about language, but about grounding the conceptual force of words in a referential system, especially one dominated by idea, icon, or unified image. In philosophical circles this problem manifests itself as "undecidability" (of intention as the basis of meaning). In literary circles it is the notion of "unreadability" which causes most trouble. "Unreadability," however, like "misreading," may give the wrong impression: for rarely has reading been taken so seriously.

Recently the ontological difficulty of defining what is literary and what is not has revived the role of the reader and of interpretive communities. Reader reception theories abound. Yet deconstruction does not take that particular tack. It is absolute rather than relativizing when it describes reading the unreadable as an "allegorical" process. Allegory, in fact, once despised as bloodless and abstract (compared with image or symbol), makes its comeback as a structure governing both writing and interpreting. Allegory has always had a riddling side, so that its connection with "unreadability" is almost commonplace. But what is the logic of a figure so obvious in form and devious in meaning? It is tempting to take evasive action at this point by alluding to Walter Benjamin's work. I won't do so except to quote his famous aphorism: "Allegory always leaves empty-handed."

You cannot, in short, fill the figure (allegory is not allegoresis, and even the latter, practiced by the great medieval interpreters, does not guarantee fullness of meaning); and this suggests once more the unreadability of major texts, or a residual and powerful abstractness disclosed in works that have resisted reading time after time, and so produced a more than provisional conflict of interpretations. The classic work of art becomes a classic, i.e. secular, by sustaining itself within and against readerly appropriation. As Wallace Stevens declared in "Notes towards a Supreme Fiction": *It must be Abstract.*

[198]

Reconnoitering Chaos: A Statement on Contemporary Criticism

The imagination, like certain wild animals,
will not breed in captivity.
> —*George Orwell*

ITERARY CRITICISM, a kind of awareness we carry with us, not only the articulated thing put down on paper and published, but a spirited readiness to discuss, evaluate, and quarrel about whatever is happening in the world of literature—literary criticism as this at once combative and contemplative mix is bound to be in touch with more than literature. Every cultural event butts in and casts its shadow; and the borders once so snobbishly guarded between high art and everything else—journalism, detective fiction, science fiction, soap operas, film, letters—are crossed easily, though they do not cease to exist but haunt the scrupulous critic in subtler, sometimes internalized form. The line between all genres or "orders of discourse" becomes precarious, a fine line; and the very possibility of trespass fades. Is transgressiveness still possible when deviation is the norm? The survival of the fittest invades the realm of taboos, but no taboo seems fit to survive very long.

We can all cite some instances of experiments that blur or transgress boundaries. Robert Lowell's "imitations" efface the distinction between the original text and his translation of it; Truman Capote writes his "nonfiction novel" and Norman Mailer his "truelife novel"; and E.

L. Doctorow places real persons and invented characters into the same time frame. Going further back we come on John Hersey's *Hiroshima* and André Malraux's novelistic reportage of the Spanish Civil War in *Man's Hope*. Even biographies are no longer the stodgy things they once were but lively accounts that blend unreserved speculation with stupefying doses of factual detail. Everything tends to be swallowed up, for good or bad, in the "New Journalism," or in the "Maybe" of Lillian Hellman, where memory and wishfulness mingle.

When I read John Leonard's typical description of Milan Kundera's *Book of Laughter and Forgetting*, that "calls itself a novel, although it is part fairy tale, part literary criticism, part political tract, part musicology and part autobiography," I feel both encouraged and discouraged. Encouraged, because Leonard recognizes that the issue is not the death of the novel but the freeing up of all kinds of prose. Discouraged, because an amorphous and voracious superprose is emerging, as full of routines and exploits as a circus, and therefore prone to flatten everything into equivalence.

The American novel has scarcely recovered from Nathanael West, when there's Thomas Pynchon with an appetite for comic routines as magical as Moses' rod that devours all others. Under the influence of the media, moreover—described as a "black hole" by certain French sociologists—as push comes to shove, so blur becomes mash. We can still call Al Saperstein's *Mother Kills Self and Kids* a novel, yet it is also an overflow sociological tract (somewhat like Doctorow's *The Book of Daniel*) on the persistence in America of Miss Lonelyhearts; and it is certainly an Anatomy of Melancholy. Saperstein depicts a culture that does everything to inspire a belief in privacy or inwardness, but only the better to rape you. It turns into a grim folk tale about a mirror-oriented, self-consuming, necrophiliac society.

Let me continue in this vein, still talking about fiction rather than criticism: about the environment in which criticism presently tries to stay alive. The prose of our best novelists is as fast, embracing, and abrasive as John Donne's *Sermons*. It is polyphonic despite or within its monologue, its confessional stream of words. (There are "sinews in thy milk," Donne remarked of God's style in Scripture.) The interlace of faction and fiction, of some primary source—Scripture or newspaper account or social document—and derived text, that is, novel or artifact, yields the same dimensionality, if not the same authority, as in Donne. In terms of authority, there is only a prophetic sort of clowning or shadowboxing.

Think of Mailer, who always puts himself on the line, sparring, taunting, as macho as Hemingway but deliberately renouncing taciturnity. Mailer places himself too near events, as science fiction or other forms of romance place themselves too far. He is always in the bullring, whether it is the six inches of no-man's land between the U.S. Army and the demonstrators in *The Armies of the Night,* or the same six inches between men and women in the orgiastic novels. He is right, though, in remarking that fiction must penetrate the historical account, for events tend to be either too far or too near. "The history is interior . . . ," he says. "No document can give sufficient intimation: the novel must replace history at precisely that point where experience is sufficiently emotional, spiritual, physical, moral, existential or supernatural to expose the fact that the historian in pursuing the experience would be obliged to quit the clearly demarcated limits of historical inquiry."

John Hersey has protested this quitting of clearly demarcated limits: he calls himself the "worried grandpa" of the New Journalism and insists that his *Hiroshima* is a documentary reportage and not, in any way, a work of fiction. If we quit the old genre rules, or similar demarcations, how can we escape the situation of those Pulitzer Prize judges taken in by a reporter's fraudulent exposé of "Jimmy," the eight-year-old drug addict? How can we tell reality from reality-fiction? But if Hersey's *Hiroshima* to contemporary sensibilities in a post-Hemingway and journalistic era has the force of fiction as well as the ring of truth, how can we be sure, except through external testimony, such as bringing the interviewees back, or through the proven probity of the writer (his *ethos* in distinction from his *pathos,* the older rhetoricians would say), how can we be sure the events are not, to a degree, fictionalized?

The dilemma becomes more acute when we reflect that the media themselves—photography, film, television—have taught us much about *trucage*. Their realism, like Renaissance picture space, is an acquired technique. They mean to deceive; and this power of deception is part of the meaning, as it was in the days of Romance. Seeing is only seeing; and the more *see* there is in films, the more color and visual realism, the more conflicted our response. The sophisticated viewer knows too much about technique and *trucage;* while the unsophisticated viewer may experience a similar feeling of unreality coming from the very fact that film must blunt, by its daily iteration, the terrible things it depicts. We sup full of horror when we want; and through countless programs of Action News, even when we do not want. The gulf between seeing and believing has never been wider.[1]

This, then, is our environment, the environment also of the critic; and its confusions are not improved by a conservative reaction that we sense everywhere in and outside the academy. Instead of facing the problem of what criticism can do under these conditions, the conservative reaction makes of literary criticism the last refuge of Neo-Classical admonitions against mixed genres, against quitting the demarcation between criticism and art or criticism and anything else—philosophy, religion, the social sciences.

One quotation typical of this mindless conservatism must suffice. In a recent issue of *Novel,* Julian Moynahan calls Northrop Frye and by implication the Yale critics "pod-people . . . many of them dropouts from technical philosophy, or linguistics, or the half-science of sociology," and he wonders how to get us out of "the fair fields of Anglo-American literary study."

Now even I half-sympathize with the man—how nice if criticism were neoclassically separate and pure: fiction here and criticism there, and so forth. But this separatism was never more than partial, even in

1. See Jean Baudrillard on the dominance of simulacra in "Consumer Society," and concerning the media, "Requiem for the Media" in *For a Critique of the Political Economy of the Sign* (St. Louis: Telos Press, 1980). The most terrifying account of the attrition of concreteness and practical life because of the advertising or consumerist character of mass culture is found in the unpublished continuation of the chapter on the Culture Industry in *Dialectics of the Enlightenment* by Horkheimer and Adorno. This continuation, "Das Schema der Massenkultur," is printed for the first time in Adorno's *Gesammelte Schriften* (Frankfurt/Main: Suhrkamp Verlag, 1981), 3:299–335.

[202]

the so-called Neo-Classical period; and it will prove to be, at most, an episode in the history of art, spurred by a naïve view of realism and scientific objectivity. For not only does literary criticism have its own boundary problems today, not only are interesting new kinds of commentary emerging, but the line between original text and critical commentary may always have been precarious, at least not as distinct as the conservative scholar holds it to be. The rabbis and church fathers, as well as the later kabbalists, even when they thought they were honoring the literal sense of Scripture, were producing inventive interpretations, ingenious adjustments to received and authoritative truth under the pressure of daily events that could not easily be reconciled with that truth. They stuck to the text: it was part of their sacred marriage. Gershom Scholem's work has taught us how Jewish mysticism, at least, was an extraordinary "exegetical" response to history, to the harsh contemporary reality that had to be harmonized with the promise in the Bible. Sainte-Beuve puts it most succinctly when he remarks of Ballanche's prose epic, *Orpheus,* based on Vico's reanimation of the dry bones of Roman Law: "The commentary has entered the text."

I am not trying to explain away the offense of modern commentary, of Jacques Derrida in *Glas* or Roland Barthes in *S/Z* (his study of Balzac), of Ihab Hassan's paracriticism or Maurice Blanchot's self-reflective critical narratives, or Heidegger's ruminations or Harold Bloom's "misreadings" or—to add novels that unfold a synthetic poem—Nabokov's *Pale Fire* and D. M. Thomas' *The White Hotel*. These works of scholarship, or fiction based on scholarship, have recognized their affinity with an older tradition of exegesis: they too are crossing the line and merging the expressive force of interpretive commentary with the inspiring, sometimes disruptive, force of the work of art that is the object of the commentary. Whatever distinctions of value and character we wish to make between these writers, they all challenge T. S. Eliot's magisterial pronouncement that there can be no creative criticism.

In *Criticism in the Wilderness* and *Saving the Text* I try to define the symbiosis or tangled relations of literature and literary commentary. I present an argument and tell a story. The argument, to start with that,

[203]

distinguishes two chief tendencies in criticism. One is comparable to the philosophical method Sartre characterized as a "purifying reflection" and Paul Ricoeur as a hermeneutics of suspicion. This brings to every sacred or received text, to its diction or thought, a scrutiny motivated by the wish to expunge divinity from it, to make literature completely *litterae humaniores*—perhaps because only as such is it ours and subject to criticism. The other brings to texts a dangerous enthusiasm, one that allows the possibility of a sympathetic or redemptive contagion between book and reader, to the point where the interest shifts, at least in part, to a new creation: the text about the text, the one produced by critic or commentator.

The story I then tell may be called the historical part of the argument. It shows how the English critical tradition, after the Puritan revolution of the seventeenth century, and by a complex reinforcement that included Jacobinical fears, Popery fears, the impact of French universalism and then of the French Revolution, consolidated itself as a *via media* institution. English critics refused *enthusiasm,* and even smelled it out by a kind of fee-fo-fum directed against the non-Englishman: against the esoteric, technical, exhibitionistic, overly earnest—whatever disrupted good conversation. Out of the rigor of that impulse some of the most remarkable British (not only French) literature comes: what is Jane Austen but the flowering of a perpetual reflection on the humane wit of conversation compared to any other form of human display: the dance, duets, cutting a figure, theatricals, the hunt, even reading (in excess)?

There were great energies, there still may be such, in that tradition; but there was also a drift toward gentility; and this gentility, today, so my argument continues, is fee-fo-fumming against Hermann the German. I mean the hermeneutic or philosophical criticism that arises in Germany around 1790 and which so greatly tempted Coleridge: that of Schlegel, Hegel, Schiller, Schelling, Schleiermacher.

Nothing divides the two cultures of criticism—Continental and Anglo-American—so much as their attitudes toward "the abominable Hegel."[2] The English tradition, especially, characterizes Hegel as a vam-

2. The phrase, adopted by William Pritchard, was coined by William James.

pire or bogeyman who sucks facts dry by a "dialectical" method that creates fantastic historical generalizations from a minimum of concrete or researched knowledge. Critics after T. S. Eliot try to save the English mind from such contaminating habits of speculation or "abstraction," as Yeats called it. But Yeats still regarded philosophies as severe or unconscious poems. Our more academic critics, however, evince a disabling fear of ideas, so that one recent authority actually claims that "most English great poems have little or nothing to say."

As part of my story, I simplify the history of criticism after Arnold by postulating a sequence: first an Arnoldian concordat, which declares that criticism is not inimical to the creative spirit but rather the herald of a new literature of imaginative reason; then a New Critical reduction of Arnold's position, which agrees that the significant work of art is indeed powerfully and insidiously intelligent but denies the obverse, that there could be a "creative criticism." The critical spirit, Eliot stated, had to be carefully watched lest it usurp upon the creative. Lastly, I claim that we are now in the midst of a reversal that stands the New Critical reduction on its head by demonstrating that there is such a thing as creative criticism, or a creative element in criticism.

I have to accept the fact, perhaps as a liability, that the concept of a "creative criticism" was circulated in Eliot's time by J. E. Spingarn, who wrote in a well-known essay of 1910 called "The New Criticism" (republished in his *Creative Criticism* of 1917): "Criticism at last can free itself of its age-long self-contempt, now that it may realize that esthetic judgment and artistic creation are instinct with the same vital life. This identity does not sum up the whole life of the complex and difficult art of Criticism; but it is this identity which has been lost sight of and needs most emphasis. . . ." Eliot's testy denial of this "identity" (ultimately derived from Croce's theory of expression) may have been an overreaction. Let me quote from Mencken's essay of 1919 entitled "Criticism of Criticism." Mencken was for Spingarn, but he glimpsed the truth that creative criticism was hardly a novel concept—it went back at least to the German Romantics. "A professor must have a theory," he begins, "as a dog must have fleas." And he continues, "What [Spingarn] offers is a doctrine borrowed from the Italian, Benedetto Croce, and by Croce filched from Goethe—a doctrine anything but new in the world, even in Goethe's time, but nevertheless buried in forgetfulness."

Given the swirling polemics of this earlier period, in which Eliot began his critical career, we have to be cautious and not fall into a propagandistic rather than productive use of what remains a good slogan. Eliot's own criticism, certainly, is larger than his doctrine. Let me clarify, then, without a complex regression to the German Romantics, what is meant by such phrases as "the creative element in criticism."

It is my view that criticism cannot be judged inferior to creative writing unless you accept responsibility for a hierarchic position, a genre theory like that by which the later eighteenth century considered a still life or a Dutch domestic scene inferior to grand historical portraiture. Lowering criticism as a service function, moreover, to practical or pedagogical aims of the most obvious kind, must eventually demoralize us all—if it has not already done so—by allowing the public world, and administrators in our own university world, to view the humanist as a luxury, or at best as the purveyor of a specific skill, that of reading, and (if possible, and it is not always possible) writing. While the English New Criticism still considered literacy as a complex good, among the highest achievements of culture, and while critics like F. R. Leavis even tended to mystify the Cambridge English School as *the* road to literacy, American New Criticism, with a greater though ambivalent respect for science and an imposed commitment to mass education, was gradually forced into a compact that reduced literacy to a technique and the text to a commodity. If, then, the study of literature turned toward France in the 1970s, it was because it had to. This expatriation did not, as with novelists and poets of the 1920s, include England; it turned the European continent against England and tried by this means to recover from the involuntary decline of the gentleman scholar, as from the creation of a corps of amateur technicians, employees of a society that cared less for criticism and culture than for scientific or fiscal accountability.

The result has not been happy. We face an increasingly polarized situation. The genteel tradition, too defensive, has little to offer except the old charges: that this newest criticism is unintelligible and that it will corrupt the prose manners of the young. Arnold lives; but too many Arnoldian epigones cannot conceive that criticism is a comparative and historically varied activity with its own inner dialectic. They are no doubt the moral majority, but they depress themselves—and us—by insisting on a single kind of "conversational" decorum. Yet those who have turned to Continental thought or the *sciences humaines* have also fallen into reductive habits. A new species of coterie writing has emerged, restricted in its range and terminology. It seems unable to open itself to a past, that is, to the Arnoldian tradition still with us; it remains indulgently fixed on a few reiterated texts. Worst of all, it can be scientistic instead of scientific, or is unable to transmit its findings in a form that may be tested—tested, I mean, by a more than mechanical application, tested on art outside the restricted canon, and by criteria that are not only diagrammatic but also, in the broad sense, ethical. Thus the theory and the practice of criticism, instead of moving closer, instead of interacting, collide in a phobic manner.

Practical criticism never grew up. As the university expanded and disciplines proliferated, the old desire for faith and commitment began to reassert itself against the critical spirit. This reaction was inevitable because criticism was denied any creative potential, and because American society shifted the burden of basic education to the literary humanists, who were expected to find the most economical tools to do the job, and therefore became tools themselves.

Science was largely exempt from this burden or charge; not intrinsically, of course, but insofar as it was recognized that science had to have an advanced theoretical component in addition to the applied or practical dimension. That scholarship or critical commentary should have this advanced component, that one might distinguish properly, in this regard, between an Academy and a School, was never denied by a specific doctrine. Yet this combination—the prestige of science, the economic drift that makes even learning a commodity, and secularization, which removed the Bible and then every canonical text as a shared book in the curriculum, a book, like nature's own, whose secrets might be disclosed only by a higher or "scientific" learning—these converging tendencies became, in their very inchoate, inarticu-

[207]

late specificity, the prison whose corner we occupy. Out of this corner I too write; and what I write remains practical criticism, though I have sought to enlarge it, to insist on a new *praxis* that would not neglect theory or a reflection on the social and institutional context.

Let me now take up in order two objections to this enlarged and more reflective practical criticism. The objections, which often go together, are, first, that it flouts common sense, that its very method of close and rigorous reading dehumanizes; second, that it is a new formalism, avoiding or losing touch with social issues. (A third objection, which impugns the effectiveness and sometimes the good faith of this criticism, charging its practitioners with playing the market rather than truly attacking socioeconomic realities, is a variant of the second. However facile, this charge should be taken up separately, because it entails a longer discussion than I give later about the relation of "high" or university culture to mass culture.)

Common Sense

Most of the hostile critics belong to the Common-Sense School. They know when they order a ham sandwich they are going to get a ham sandwich—and should they be served a pastrami special, they don't attribute it to the complexities or indeterminacies of language but to getting someone else's order mistakenly.

Hence, whatever view they hold about the way literature is written, the Common-Sense School insists that *criticism* should be written as if one were ordering a ham sandwich. They always know what they want, or what literature wants of them. Intentions are clear or should be made as clear as is humanly possible. It is therefore disturbing to this school that critics should claim to be "creative." (Prose standards exist, of course, based roughly on what seems clear to any reasonable person, clear enough to be argued with and eventually reduced to a consensus.) They cannot accept that critics should hunger for something other than ordinary language, that critics should interpose a style of their own and complicate their function, which is to make the work of art accessible.

Instead of thinking about what is being challenged—their conception of a near-absolute separation between literary and literary-critical discourse, or between literature and commentary—the Common-Sense School goes on the attack. Gerald Graff and Frederick Crews accuse contemporary theorists of wishing to write in a style in which the truth cannot be told, or one that evades argument. Essays that make readers work too hard, or that deflect them from getting their money's worth in the form of the literary-critical equivalent of the ham sandwich, are destructive of an enterprise that intends to keep within the bounds of common sense. The stylish critics are merely shielding themselves from being argued with—say those who claim to know what argument is, despite the age-old dispute between *ratio* and *oratio*, or logic and rhetoric.

It does not require a deep look into past history to see that the position of the Common-Sense School is historically naïve. Its partisans overlook the era of structuralism, because structuralism was in part a critique of "reasoning" or "argument" based on culture-bound notions of common sense—notions preeminently French and English and going back to British empiricism of the eighteenth century. They forget that structuralism tried to place the "common nature" of man on a new basis, broader than the prestige attached to Western, "enlightened" cultures.

They also forget that post-structural theory is questioning structuralism's reliance on such "universals" as binary opposition. The attempt to forge a new, nonelitist sense of the "common nature" of man—demonstrating the functional similarity of sophisticated analytic thought and primitive classification—is now felt to be reductive as well as redemptive. For the diagrammatic view of literature encouraged by the structuralist method suggests a totalized form of understanding too much like Hegel's Absolute Knowledge, though purged of Hegel's dialectical and historical gymnastics.

Whether there might still be a total form of understanding—modern

[209]

civilization being fragmentary rather than holistic—is a principal theme in Georg Lukács's *Theory of the Novel* (1920, though written circa 1915). Today the epic, Lukács states, is no longer a viable form insofar as it reflects "Greek" integration. The novel, however, with its large, if unintegrated, scope inherits the epic's strength. Lukács adopts both Hegel's view of the organic, balanced nature of Greek culture and the possibility that our un-Greek, i.e., problematic and unbalanced, world could achieve a holistic perspective at the level of science or philosophical method. "Theory" can have integrity, even if its subject, the novel, cannot achieve cosmic or cultural integration. In *History and Class Consciousness* (1923), totality moves still closer to a crucially utopian perspective: a point of view from which to overcome the fragmentary, fetishistic, and reified nature of capitalist societies. Now totality is clearly a mental need independent of the particular culture, and always retrieving lost unity.[3]

Yet totality as a political scheme—totalitarianism—has made us suspicious of all systematic thought as it rationalizes what is and what is not—I mean as it aspires to the total intelligibility of history or envisions an ultimate order. So Plato and Hegel and every so-called metaphysical thinker comes under attack. In England and America, though, this attack too often plays into the hands of an omnipresent anti-intellectualism. We rarely find, in these countries, that merging of philosophical, philological, and political concerns so powerfully exemplified in Nietzsche, Lukács, and Heidegger. We owe something to Derrida and deconstruction, if only because they have kept the scandal of these writers, and even of metaphysics, before us. The rethinking of

3. A discussion of totality and methodological perspective ("totalization") is found in Frederic Jameson's *The Political Unconscious* (Ithaca: Cornell University Press, 1981), pp. 52ff., 190ff. For a critique of Lukács's theory, see Paul de Man, *Blindness and Insight* (New York: Oxford University Press, 1971), ch. 4. De Man stresses the category of temporality as that which causes the totalizing form to collapse. Cf. also his ch. 2, p. 32: "Understanding can be called complete only when it becomes aware of its own temporal predicament and realizes that the horizon within which the totalization can take place is time itself. The act of understanding is a temporal act that has its own history, but this history forever eludes totalization." A previous critique of Lukács, based on his tendency to premature totalization (and his neglect of historical "mediations") is given by Jean-Paul Sartre in *Search for a Method*, Hazel Barnes, tr. (New York: A. Knopf, 1963).

metaphysics, or what it might mean to make an end of such philosophies, creates tremors that shift the very concept of philosophy toward a denial of the possibility of closure in any sphere of thought. This denial is then exemplified by the method of close reading now known as deconstruction, which keeps metaphysics alive by an interminable reflection on end-terms. Metaphysics, which insists on an end beyond the end, is the joker in any politicophilosophical speculation that wishes to "totalize" thought or history.

Thus the alarmed tone of those who think that post-structural critics are destroying common sense or the possibility of shared and rational discourse may be attributed to their wish to elide history and return to the *status quo ante*—to the empiricism criticized not only by structuralist and Marxist, but by all those who, like Heidegger or Empson, are aware of the complex nature of words. The stones our modern purists cast are those of a reasoning that is supposedly more humane than quasi-philosophical and linguistic wrangling. While no one should object to the preference of the Common-Sense School for one mode of argumentation over another, by exercising this preference blindly, Graff and Crews, and even M. H. Abrams and Wayne Booth, simplify the historical moment in which literary theory emerges manifestly as theory: roughly in the 1920 to 1970 period, when philosophies of language interact with political and scientific currents that ponder the issue of totality.

An aside. I do not claim that common sense cannot be effective. Only that the Common-Sense School is insensitive to its own vulnerability. George Orwell, to choose an exemplary writer, never abandons common sense in his essays, and he uses every possible weapon against the political lie and the ruthless generalization. Yet he knows that authoritarian pressures may cause common sense to give way. Organized lying can come to seem like common sense, and organized lying is not a temporary expedient for a totalitarianism which demands "the continuous alteration of the past." A schizophrenic system of thought is developed, says Orwell, in which common sense holds good in everyday life and some sectors of science but is routinely disregarded by politicians, historians, and sociologists. Prose especially, he adds, cannot survive when the independent writer is attacked for ivory-towerism or exhibitionism or clinging, against history, to unjustified privileges. In the long view, Orwell concludes, it is not the manipulators of the press, or the film magnates, or bureaucrats that are the worst symptom but a "weakening of desire for liberty among the intellectuals" ("The Prevention of Literature," 1946).

Theory and History

While the Common-Sense School denies, often tacitly, the heterogeneity of discourse, the Social School charges literary theorists with impoverishing the concreteness of human and historical reality. Theory, with the possible exception of Marxism, is taken to be essentially antihistorical. Yet theory, in the period we are considering, is actually a critique of historical kinds of reasoning and branches out in two quite different, if related, directions.

Structuralism may indeed be antihistorical, even antihumanistic, insofar as "humanism" and "history" are imbued with privileged Western ideas. The centrality of self or subject may then be challenged—structuralism is no different in this regard from the "Eastern" world view presented, for example, in Malraux's influential *The Temptation of the West* or in Heidegger's focus on Being over beings, his overcoming of Western ontology. Malraux interprets history-writing as the West's apologia for missionary and colonizing activities—part of its *Kulturpolitik*. But Malraux adds the wrinkle that Western self-assertion brings on its own fever of self-transcendence: the relentless interrogation, namely, of every concept and institution, until "God is dead" and even "Man" (or ego-centered Western religion) must eventually suffer that fate. This Western form of ascetic self-purgation, Malraux insists—following Nietzsche's *Genealogy of Morals*—is perhaps even more scarring than that of the East.

Theory, then, suspicious of history-writing, wants no truck with rightist or leftist or Hegelian or Marxist philosophies. It knows that historical reflection succumbs to dogma or becomes, willy-nilly, propaganda. But are we not stuck with history in this form? Can we really pretend to leap clear of a situation that has prevailed so long that it is in our language and continues to shape even the most radical political schemes?

Theory therefore also goes in a different direction, and considers the fact that historical claims (genealogical or messianic) of legitimacy are the way authority is rationalized—that is, talks about itself. Hence the question is no longer, Can we deliver truth from propaganda or from propagandistic sorts of history, but rather, Can anything function as a corrective for this condition? If the language we live with is both words and the Word (by Word I mean the propagandistic or messianic *logos*), then there is no exit toward pure secularism on the one hand, or toward lost and sacred truth on the other. We must continue to live in the sacred jungle of a heterogeneous language.

Out of this impasse, however, a new consciousness arises. Theory, also *in* language, is not so much antihistorical as deconstructive: it lives within what it criticizes and tries to isolate certain antibodies. One of these is art, which seems to have the potential to resist ideologies while being deeply immersed in convention. Art may simply become a counterideology, of course. But there are attempts to make theory, especially the theory of art, anti-ideological in essence. We see this both in Malraux and in the formalists. The latter claim that the specific content of art is mainly a "device" motivating the artist's struggle with a world of forms imposed by society or pastmasters. Malraux talks of the lucidity of art in the face of these various seductions and impositions: both modern art and primitive nonrepresentational art, for example, are a making rather than a matching, an iconoclastic stylization that breaks with the realm of appearance—with the tyranny of nature or convention. Malraux's achievement is to have recognized a link between art's modern and its ancient function. That function is reticence, cunning, resistance—against whatever is perceived to be fate. And, at present, propaganda or propagandistic versions of history are fate.

In this light, too, the vexed question of the artifact's indeterminacy, polysemy, or even "unreadability" begins to make a kind of sense. These are heavy terms and each is ensconced in its own system. Whatever core of truth may lodge in such terms, their motive is again to defend art against easy types of readerly or ideological accommodation. The "intransigence of theory" recommended by Theodor Adorno, the "A poem should not mean / But be" of the New Criticism, Mikhail Bakhtin's "polyphony," or the various concepts—"pleasure," "bliss," "drift"—shored by Roland Barthes against some ultimate jargon, these very different notions link up to affirm "something both revolutionary and asocial which cannot be taken over by any collectivity, any mentality, any ideolect" *(The Pleasure of the Text)*. Each jargon or fiction, Barthes also writes, "fights for hegemony; if power is on its side, it spreads everywhere in the general and daily occurrences of social life, it becomes *doxa*, nature . . . the supposedly apolitical jargon of politicians, of agents of the State, of the Media, of conversation. . . ."[4]

Our experience of modern propaganda methods, their ability to program or brainwash entire nations, is as frightening, in its way, as the modern superweapons. Not accidentally did Malraux and also Walter Benjamin construct a theory that both questioned and asserted art's power to withstand political appropriation. The formalists, encompassed by Soviet ideological pressures, and the New Critics, in the midst of the 1930s turmoil, also tried to save art from ideology without having to fall back on an art for art's sake or aestheticist position. The dictatorship of the propagandists, their manipulation not only of the mass media but also of scholarship, became a reality in Nazi Germany and Stalinist Russia, and is the one historical fact that must not be forgotten in any general consideration of the emergence of literary theory as increasingly anti-ideological.[5]

It was not Malraux, of course, but the Frankfurt School that, in the wake of fascism, alerted us to the basic concepts of art theory in a technological and propagandistic age. (We know Malraux read Benja-

4. There are problems, of course, with theory as a *project* of the sort I have described. It could turn out to be futile or utopian or both. Wishing, for example, to rid language of clichés and slogans, it introduces its own jargon; seeking to be rigorous and purifying, it mimics the "purity" of doctrinaire positions.

5. After writing this I came across Jacobo Timerman's *Prisoner Without a Name, Cell Without a Number* (New York: A. Knopf, 1981). Both the role of "historical" justification and the mechanism of interrogation he describes show once more how the fantasy of thought control operates, nightmarishly, in totalitarian regimes.

min's essay of 1936, "The Work of Art in the Era of Mechanical Reproduction" before writing his *Psychology of Art.*) Often using Hegel against Hegel to evolve a "negative" dialectic, or an unprogressive philosophy of history, these thinkers emphasized the nonconformist character of intellectual and artistic achievement. Art is that which cannot be *gleichgeschaltet* or *aufgehoben*—which cannot have only one dimension. Nor can philosophy, properly understood. The scrupulous sociological analyses developed by Theodor Adorno, Max Horkheimer, and Hannah Arendt did not disconnect the political question: they engaged it at a level where every flat and shallow literalism, every political cliché, was exposed. Political appropriation, they showed, was not forceful in itself; it did not have, to back it up, a special logic, even if "dialectical materialism" came closest: it merely exaggerated the danger of internal conflict and suggested that, at the limit, the only controlling and simplifying force would be . . . War. That leveling tendency, as Barthes suggests, can also assume a deceptively urbane aspect, an insidious intellectual respectability, so that vigilance is required even when no overt political terror is nigh. The tenet of the uniformity of nature, for example, inherited from the Enlightenment, was eventually directed by totalitarian regimes and philosophies to sinister uses—"sinister unifying" is Kenneth Burke's phrase.[6]

The monolingualism that afflicts technologically advanced democracies may also have a sinister effect, especially if it depicts literacy as merely a skill: something teachable without a personal immersion in

6. Kenneth Burke deserves special mention because of his position that the critic is necessarily a "propagandist" who keeps the fact of propaganda before us in order to contribute to "a change in allegiance to the symbols of authority." See, especially, *Attitudes Toward History* (Boston: Beacon Press, 1961), pp. 234ff. Feminist criticism may also be part of the protest against the "uniformity of nature," insofar as this concept denies particularity to woman's experience. Consider, for example, "androgyny" in the light of Lukács's or Hegel's vision of wholeness, and you face the question of the historical suppression and then sidelining of woman's experience. That experience then appears to be as fragmented or unintegrated as the world reflected by the modern novel. It is moving to read in Carolyn Heilbrun's *Reinventing Womanhood* (New York: Norton, 1979) how recent feminist scholars have "wrestled with the angel of reinterpretation, refusing to desist until they had wrested from the angel the blessing from the female past upon the female future" (p. 94).

the literature of the language. Substituting technical or bureaucratic jargon for the imaginative creole that could arise from the jostlings of street language against standard language, or from competing vernaculars learned through their respective traditions—whether oral or written—this skill-oriented approach leads to fatal political simplifications as well as to a disastrous impoverishment of the culture. For all the great cultures we know of have had a mixed linguistic inheritance and a developed literature that is always revising and recasting its body of variant stories. In these stories, in these literatures, there is no overall unity: their structure is that of a stratified, precarious assemblage whose gloss or consistency is often undone by the grain that continues to show through, by the insubordinate play of language against meaning, by an explosive proliferation of legend and commentary that no treaty can entirely stop. To try to stop it by doctrinal means, whether religious, political, or aesthetic, is an act of repression.

The results of such a repression, even if civilized—that is, performed in the name of democratic concepts of order, assimilation, and educability—are clear. In East London, as in some inner cities of America, we find not hunger strikes but language strikes: the young adults there refuse to speak the dominant tongue. They refuse its passwords, however good the latter may be, however socializing and potentially nourishing. The tragedy here is not only that politicizing a language deprives youngsters of an education, of their redemption from inarticulateness in all areas; the tragedy is also that to strike language starves language, making it as instrumentalized as the tyrannous discourse the strikers resist. Nothing is more disheartening to those who know the educative and liberating force of the "school of tongues" we call literature than political types of rhetoric which kill off the possibility not only of agreement but also of vigorously debated forms of speech.

The objections, then, of the Historical School or the Common-Sense School have no cogency. But where there's smoke there's fire; and the real problem of contemporary movements in criticism is that there is too much smoke in the form of a variety of insubordinate concepts, all of which seek to counter, instinctively or methodically, the danger of a dictated language.

What, in closing, can I suggest? Let us recognize that the claims of the Enlightenment, or of humanism, were severely damaged by the two world wars. The gassing, bombing, and desperate trench warfare of the First World War made it clear that the era of individual heroism was in jeopardy, that destiny was passing into the hands of those who held the technological advantage and could use it for purposes of destruction. The rise of totalitarianism, leading to the Second World War and the Holocaust, confirmed our worst fears. "Suddenly it becomes evident," writes Hannah Arendt in *The Origins of Totalitarianism,* "that things which for thousands of years the human imagination had banished to a realm beyond human competence can be manufactured right here on earth, that hell and purgatory, and even a shadow of their perpetual duration, can be established by the most modern methods of destruction and therapy." Mastery over nature extended itself to thought control and to a program of indoctrination so thorough and successful that an entire people was treated not as a part of humanity but as animals—lice, vermin—to be exterminated. Philosophy was powerless before these events, except that social thinkers, fortified by Freud's study of group psychology, saw in fascism the signs of a displaced religious mania. But this only deepened the perplexity, because now, while humanism had failed as a political philosophy, the return to religion was also cut off. We remembered the bloody history of religious politics which was supposed to have been ended by the "sweet science" of humanist philosophies of toleration, and we saw that the messianic passions were merely channeled into political religions or sporadic evangelical cults. Deconstruction, and similar movements of verbal hygiene, would have arisen, I believe, even without a technical basis in linguistics or semiotics: they mark the crater left by the demise of humanism, and they denounce all quasi-religious rhetoric that rushes unthinkingly into that void. Deconstruction is a theory of language rather than a philosophy of life, not because it is "nihilistic" but because it has seen how language can be manipulated and overdetermined. And *that* it can be manipulated, for good or bad, is not avoidable: the so-called arbitrariness of the sign points once again to the free will of the users of language, placing the responsibility for the scrupulous reception and production of words on each person, whatever the odds.

This emphasis too is misleading; for language, especially literary lan-

[217]

guage, has its own life, its own way of surviving mechanical or propagandistic impositions. "Poetry is the fore-knowledge of criticism," Paul de Man has said: what deconstructionists do is to read so closely that a text opens again and reveals both the fearful or joyous energies of language and the tricks closing them off. These tricks may be internal, the artist's own defenses, or external, the premature assimilation of a book by normative commentary. We do not have to be sophisticated theorists to question a text's monologic life, apposing to its pathos irony and distance, seeing through its apparent purity to material or metaphorical residues, countering insidious attempts to homogenize meaning while disclosing, for all to mark, complex resonances, hiatuses, and equivocations.

Our very commitment to literacy and mass education makes it imperative that we respect the labor involved in reading and writing, the stresses and strains of acculturation and of balancing particularity against principles of order. Learning is painful as well as pleasurable; and learning is closely associated with writing and rewriting—with the malaise of never achieving a definitive or more than questioning way of stating things.

If the study of literature remains disputed and problematic, it is precisely because there cannot be an "absolute" but only a "standard" prose, a language of convenience. This language is a substitute Latin, an artificial and ideal diction that masquerades as a vernacular. We need it to purify the dialects around us, to achieve a degree of shared and stable speech, but it has only provisional authority and should never stifle linguistic inventiveness. There must always be a tension between difficult or inventive (including "street") modes of speech, and familiar, conversational ones. This tension between intelligibility and difficulty, as between ordinary and extraordinary language, may be the only *literary* constant in any age. To repress or deny that tension is to impoverish the past, cheat the present, and cheapen the ideal of literacy itself.

INDEX

Index

Index

Index